Vocational A-leve
Leisure and Recreation
Options

Vocational A-level Leisure and Recreation Options

Malcolm Ferguson, Julie Gibson, Malcolm Walton

Longman

An imprint of **Pearson Education**

Harlow, England · London · New York · Reading, Massachusetts · San Francisco
Toronto · Don Mills, Ontario · Sydney · Tokyo · Singapore · Hong Kong · Seoul
Taipei · Cape Town · Madrid · Mexico City · Amsterdam · Munich · Paris · Milan

In this book you will find helpful icons showing which Key Skills the Activities can be used for:

 Communication

 Application of number

 Information technology

 Working with others

 Problem solving

 Improving own learning and performance

Pearson Education Limited
Edinburgh Gate
Harlow
Essex CM20 2JE, England
and Associated Companies throughout the world

ISBN 0 582 43220 0

British Library Cataloguing-in-Publication Data

A catalogue record for this book is available from the British Library.

Set by 35 in Humanist, Rotis Serif, Caslon
Produced by Pearson Education Asia Pte Ltd.,
Printed in Singapore

Contents

Introduction

Vocational A-Level Leisure and Recreation Options has been written specifically for the vocational A-level leisure and recreation courses. It follows exactly the structure of the new Leisure and Recreational option units developed by Edexcel, including all the units that are externally assessed. The book will also be invaluable to students and staff following the vocational A-level leisure and recreation courses offered by AQA and OCR awarding bodies. This book is a companion volume to *Vocational A-Level Leisure and Recreation* (Gibson and Wood, published by Longman in July 2000).

The option units provide an exciting opportunity to study specialist areas of the leisure and recreation industry, building on skills learned from other units and from your own practical experience. Case studies and realistic activities will stimulate individual and group study in line with the philosophy of vocational A-levels. The authors have considerable experience of working in industry and education, ensuring that the contents are current and relevant in terms of preparing for assessment and introducing you to specialist skills which will help you gain employment. Guidance is also provided to identify key skill opportunities.

Simple language is used throughout and links to internet websites provide opportunity for further research. Used wisely, the book will provide sufficient stimulus to produce evidence for your portfolio and prepare you for assessment. Remember though, to earn a high grade requires originality and creativity, evaluation and analysis. The book will provide guidance and direction to support your practical skills and help you achieve this.

Good luck with your course and your future career!

Acknowledgements

The authors are grateful to Ray Youell for providing Units 21 and 23 of this book. These were adapted from Units 18 and 19 of his book *Travel and Tourism Options* (Longman 2001).

All photographs were supplied by David Cave Photography.

Whilst every effort has been made to contact copyright holders of material used in this book we apologise to any whose rights may have been unwittingly overlooked and will be pleased to make the necessary acknowledgement at the first opportunity.

About the authors

Malcolm Ferguson is a chief examiner and principal moderator for leisure and recreation and has been actively involved in the writing of the new specifications, in addition to compiling the external assessments for the AVCE. He is currently a manager in a further education college and an experienced author, lecturer and verifier in a wide range of vocational sport and leisure qualifications. Malcolm is an experienced practitioner in the sport and leisure industry, a former international coach and a senior tutor for many sports coaching awards.

Julie Gibson is a principal examiner for leisure and recreation and is compiling the external assessments for the new award. She has a wealth of experience as an author, deliverer, assessor, and as an internal and external verifier in both leisure and tourism at all levels. She is also currently converting to a standards moderator. She is a local authority principal recreation officer and is involved in the development of many of the current Sport England initiatives.

Malcolm Walton is section leader for leisure, tourism and sport at Tamworth and Lichfield College. He is also a principal examiner for the leisure and recreation external units in marketing and running a leisure facility. In addition he acts as a moderator and reviser across a number of subject areas. He has considerable experience in leisure management, having worked for a number of years in both the public and voluntary sectors, and has been involved in developing the new optional units for the VCE in leisure and recreation.

Exercise physiology

Objectives

- **Describe the structure and function of the skeletal and muscular system**

- **Describe the structure and function of the cardio-respiratory system**

- **Understand the efficiency of the cardio-respiratory systems during exercise**

- **Understand the energy requirements related to different types of exercise**

- **Describe the effects of exercise on the nutritional needs of individuals**

- **Understand how all of the above affect the physiological systems during exercise**

This unit will introduce you to the major structures and systems of the human body and the effects of exercise and diet on the different body systems.

We usually take our bodies for granted; they function automatically and we rarely have to give them a second thought. This balanced state is easily disrupted by illness or injury and it is only then that we tend to pay our bodies the attention they deserve.

In order to develop our fitness programmes and achieve the optimum benefits and performance, we must understand the basic details of human physiology and apply our knowledge of sport to these details to produce a superior programme for performance.

Unit 8 Fitness, testing and training will enable you to apply some of the theory included in this unit. You will also find exercise physiology useful when studying Unit 10 Principles of sports coaching.

The skeletal and muscular systems of the human body

In order to understand the functions of the human body we must look at the structure first; this includes the skeleton, muscles and joints and their relationship to produce movement.

The skeletal system

There are four main functions of the human skeleton:

- ✪ **Protection**
- ✪ **Support**
- ✪ **Movement and attachment**
- ✪ **Blood production**

Protection

The skeleton is designed in such a way that the delicate parts of the body are protected. The delicate parts are the major organs; for example, the rib cage protects the heart and lungs, while the cranium protects the brain.

Support

The skeleton gives the human body structure. It supports the organs and tissues and gives us our form. Without it we would collapse under our own body weight. The bones are also used to suspend the vital organs.

Movement and attachment

The skeleton is jointed to allow movement. A joint is the articulation of two or more connecting bones. The joint provides either stability or mobility depending on its structure. A stable joint provides little movement, whereas an unstable joint provides a wide range of movement. Muscles are attached to bones by tendons.

Blood production

Both red and white blood cells are produced in the bone marrow; the bones also store minerals for other body functions.

There are two main parts of the skeletal system:

The axial skeleton

This consists of the skull, vertebral column, ribs and sternum and its main function is to support the body.

The appendicular skeleton

This consists of the arm and shoulder girdle, the legs and hip girdle, and its main function is to allow movement of the limbs.

Activity 7.1

Take a look at the skeletal system on page 5 where you will see that the major bones and joints of the body are clearly labelled. Identify and label the axial and appendicular skeletons on each body.

Major bones and joints of the skeleton

If you are going to develop a fitness programme for a client or analyse a sports movement or techniques, you must have an understanding of the major bones in the human body and explain how the skeletal system contributes to movement and fitness. Figure 7.1 illustrates the major bones in the body. The joints of the skeleton are explained at the end of the section.

The following sections will explain how the skeletal and muscular systems work together to produce a range of movements and how these systems are affected by exercise.

The muscular system

Microscopic features of the three types of muscle

Muscles are primarily concerned with movement but with over 600 voluntary muscles we do have some control over our form; through muscle building we can develop the muscles to their maximum potential and thus affect our individual shape.

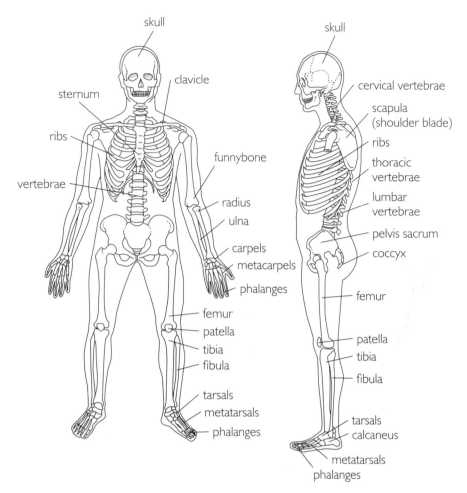

Figure 7.1 *Major bones in the body*

There are three muscle groups:

✪ **Striated muscle**: Striated (also known as striped or skeletal) muscles are voluntary muscles; we call on these muscles by nerve stimuli, for instance when we are simply walking or paying sport. The voluntary muscles make up 40 per cent of our body weight and there are over 150 in our head and neck. The voluntary muscles are identified in Figure 7.2

✪ **Smooth muscle**: These muscles are involuntary, in other words they will contract and relax whether we want them to or not. They are made up of **spindle-shaped cells**. Examples include muscles found in the blood vessels and those that operate the bowel, uterus and bladder

✪ **Cardiac muscle**: The cardiac muscle is highly specialised and is found only in the heart. It is involuntary and is made up of **branched fibres**, giving it a striped appearance. The rate of contraction of the cardiac muscle is part of a complex nervous and chemical system

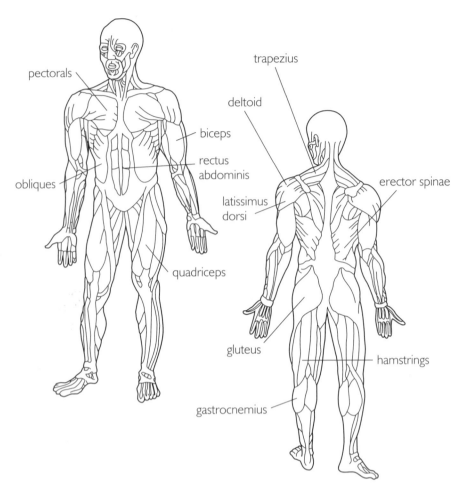

Figure 7.2 *Major voluntary muscles in the body*

Arrangement of the muscle groups and their attachment to bone

Figure 7.2 identifies various muscle groups; they are all striated or voluntary muscles.

Examples are:

- ✪ *Trunk: latissimus dorsi, trapezius, erector spinae*
- ✪ *Abdomen: obliques, rectus abdominus*
- ✪ *Shoulders: deltoids*
- ✪ *Upper arm: biceps, triceps*
- ✪ *Hip: hip flexors*
- ✪ *Thigh: quadriceps, hamstrings*
- ✪ *Lower leg: gastrocnemius, soleus, tibialis anterior*

Muscles are attached to bones by **tendons**; these act as buffers to sharp movement and help prevent injury.

Strong bands of fibre called **ligaments** attach bone to bone; these add stability to the joints.

Question

Why may tendons be important to runners and in what part of the body are healthy tendons vital for these sports people?

Function of muscle groups

Muscle action produces movement; there are various types of muscle action depending on the joints involved. They are (Figure 7.3):

- ✪ **Abduction – movement of the bone away from the body mid-line, either in a horizontal or vertical plane**
- ✪ **Adduction – movement of the bone towards the body mid-line, either in a horizontal or vertical plane**
- ✪ **Extension – the increasing of an angle between bones**
- ✪ **Flexion – the decreasing of an angle between bones**
- ✪ **Rotation – movement of the bone around a central axis, for example the arm rotates at the shoulder**
- ✪ **Circumduction**
- ✪ **Supination**
- ✪ **Pronation**
- ✪ **Eversion**
- ✪ **Inversion**
- ✪ **Dorsiflexion**
- ✪ **Plantarflexion**

Activity 7.2

You will find pictures of the human body on page 8. Identify and label the muscle groups outlined earlier in this section on the body.

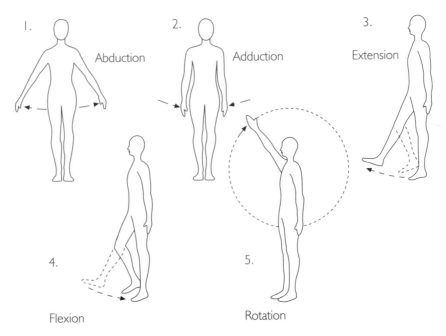

Figure 7.3 *Measurement through muscle action*

The relationship between muscles, joints and bones in movement

The muscle types and groups have now been clearly explained; however, it is the relationship between the joints, the muscle and the bone that produces a specific movement and it is this relationship that allows the human body to be so precise and accurate.

Synovial joints

Accurate and smooth movement relies on one particular type of joint – the synovial joint. All synovial joints have the following characteristics:

- ✪ **The bones are covered with *articular (hyaline) cartilage* which is tough, yet smooth and shiny. This reduces friction between bones**

- ✪ **Within the joint there is a liquid which is yellow and oily. This is called *synovial fluid*, which also reduces friction; it provides a medium between the bones which can absorb any debris and also feeds the hyaline cartilage**

- ✪ **The synovial fluid is produced by the *synovial membrane* which surrounds the joint**

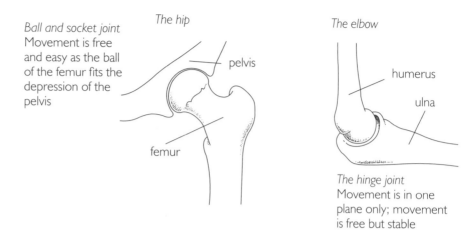

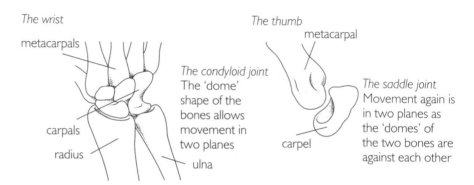

Figure 7.4 *Four types of synovial joints*

✪ **The bones are held together by strong fibrous bands called *ligaments*; these add stability to the joints**

There are four types of synovial joints:

✪ **Ball and socket (e.g. the hip)**
✪ **Hinge (e.g. the knee)**
✪ **Condyloid (e.g. the wrist)**
✪ **Saddle (e.g. the thumb)**

Figure 7.4 provides further information.

Levers

Body movement actually occurs when the **striated muscle** pulls hard enough on the bones. The muscles use the bones as **levers**. Levers are rigid; they comprise a pivot (the point which is hinged) and two points of force, one of which is an object or weight, the other is effort or energy.

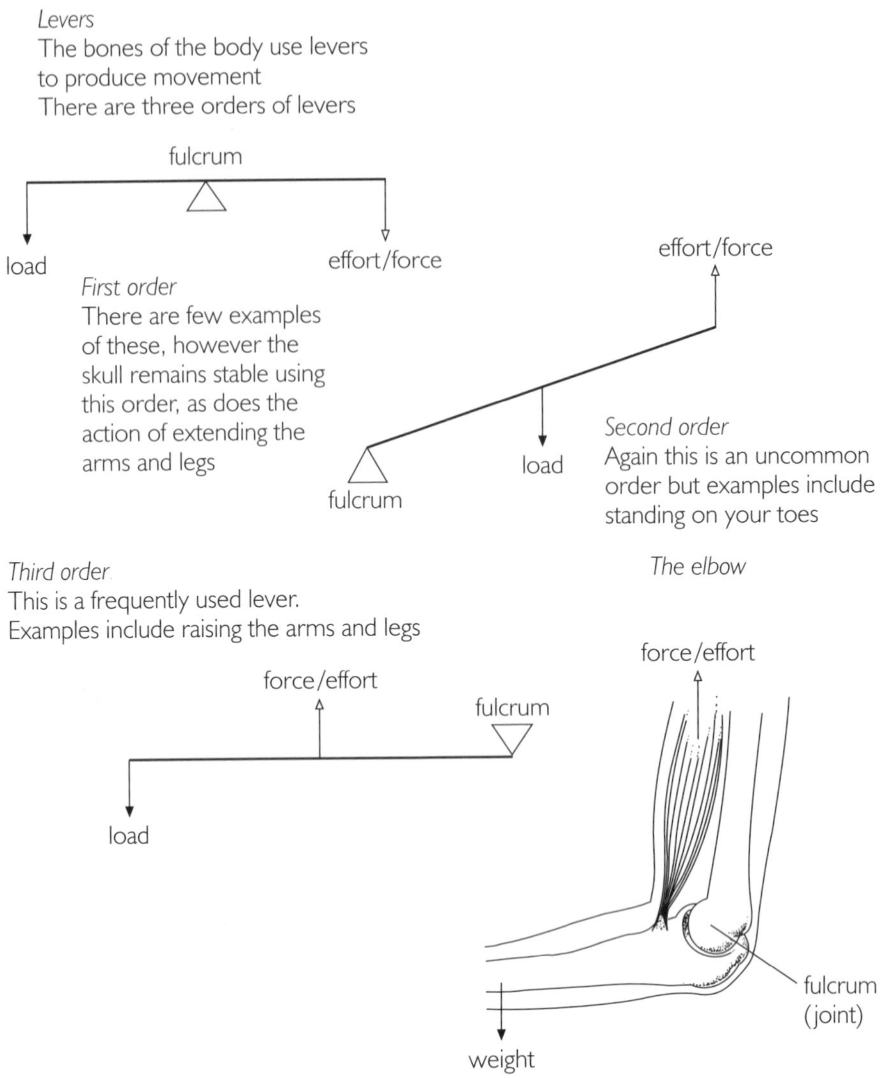

Levers
The bones of the body use levers
to produce movement
There are three orders of levers

fulcrum

load   effort/force

effort/force

First order
There are few examples
of these, however the
skull remains stable using
this order, as does the
action of extending the
arms and legs

fulcrum

load

Second order
Again this is an uncommon
order but examples include
standing on your toes

Third order
This is a frequently used lever.
Examples include raising the arms and legs

The elbow

force/effort

fulcrum

force/effort

load

fulcrum
(joint)

weight

Figure 7.5 *The three types of levers*

There are three different types of levers depending on the positioning of the
pivot, force and effort; the body uses all three (see Figure 7.5).

Pair principle

If a muscle acts across a joint and pulls two bones closer together, another
muscle is needed to pull them apart. Therefore every contracting muscle,
known as an **agonist**, also needs an extending muscle in order to produce
movement. The opposing muscles are called **antagonists**. This is known as
the pair principle.

The main muscles used to produce movement are called **prime movers**; as
these contract the antagonist must relax.

Synergists

Muscles that assist agonists and antagonists are known as **synergists**. These provide stability, as does a **fixator muscle**. For example, during elbow flexion the agonist is the biceps, the antagonist is the triceps, and the synergists are the brachioradialis and the brachialis.

Contraction

When the muscle contracts and shortens (for example the biceps in a biceps curl) this is called **concentric contraction**. When the muscle lengthens (for example during a triceps extension, the biceps lengthen), this is known as **eccentric contraction**.

The human body produces fine, skilled movements as a result of bones, muscles and joints acting in harmony. Every individual and all sports use this relationship but with differing priorities. For example, skiing relies mostly on the lower body, swimming relies mostly on the upper body and aerobics relies on both equally. This element is introductory to allow you to understand the basics of human physiology. Unit 8 Fitness, testing and training enables you to apply this knowledge in your chosen area.

The effect of exercise on the skeletal and muscular system

Muscle fibre

Striated skeletal muscles consist of a mixture of slow twitch and fast twitch muscle fibres. These types of muscle fibres are so called because of the speed of their contraction. The type of muscle fibre will vary amongst individuals; for example, marathon runners may have more slow twitch fibres in their leg muscles whereas sprinters may have more fast twitch fibres.

Exercise can increase the size of the fibres but not the number of fibres within a muscle – this is usually inherited rather than developed. The result of increased muscle size in addition to the number of fibres will result in stronger muscles; this is evident in body-builders who have trained their muscles to achieve maximum strength and power by increasing the size of their muscle fibres by exerting maximum stress from weightlifting.

Muscle soreness

There are a number of factors which can cause muscles to tire as a result of exercise; some of these include:

- ✪ Lack of energy source
- ✪ Lack of water in the body leading to dehydration
- ✪ Increase in body temperature
- ✪ Insufficient blood supply

The muscles may become tired during or after exercise and it is common for those people who are not used to strenuous exercise to feel muscle soreness 24 hours after a period of exercise.

Activity 7.3

It can be difficult to appreciate the effect of exercise on the movement of bones, muscles and joints of the body by reading a book. It may be easier to practise some exercises and apply the theory from this chapter to explain the movements made in these exercises.

Different activities use different parts of the body. Complete the table below to identify for each exercise the following:

- ★ The major muscle group used
- ★ The muscle action used
- ★ The synovial joint used
- ★ Which bones are used as levers
- ★ Is the muscle contraction concentric or eccentric?

Exercise	Muscle group	Action	Synovial joint	Levers	Contraction
Bicep curl	Biceps	Flexion	Elbow	Humerus, radius, ulna	Concentric
Tricep extension					
Hamstring curl					
Leg extension					

The cardiovascular and respiratory systems

Structure and action of the heart and functions of the cardiovascular system

Cardiovascular system

The two main components of the cardiovascular or circulatory system are

- ✪ **The blood**
- ✪ **The heart**

Our bodies require oxygen to be supplied to all our cells in order to survive; this includes the muscles. Oxygen is carried to the muscles by blood. Blood is pumped around the body by the heart and is transported in blood vessels of varying sizes.

Functions of the blood

- ✪ **Delivers food and oxygen to the cells via the digestive system and lungs**
- ✪ **Transports waste products to the lungs and urinary systems**
- ✪ **Transports hormones**
- ✪ **Regulates the body's temperature; heat can be dissipated or conserved by the action of the blood vessels**
- ✪ **Regulates normal pH**
- ✪ **Fights infection as an integral part of the immune system**

Blood vessels

Transportation of blood is via blood vessels; these carry blood from the heart, distribute it and then return the blood to the heart. These can vary in size from 1 cm to 0.001 cm.

- ✪ **Arteries**: Blood vessels that take blood away from the heart are called **arteries**. They lie deep in the body and at the surface. If one is severed it will result in significant blood loss. The largest artery in the body is the **aorta**, which transports oxygenated blood from the heart to the rest of the body. These branch off and divide into smaller vessels called **arterioles** and then even smaller vessels called **capillaries**. The capillaries are microscopic (only one cell thick) and semi-permeable. This allows nutrients to pass through the body tissues and at the same time waste products to be passed back into the blood.

✪ *Veins*: Capillaries, which function in a network, then start the passage back of blood to the heart via **venules** and then larger vessels called **veins**. The largest vein in the body is the **vena cava**, which transports deoxygenated blood from the body to the heart.

The heart

The heart is a hollow muscular organ about the size of a closed fist: it contains four chambers (see Figure 7.6).

The two thin-walled chambers at the top of the heart are called **atria**. The blood flows, in one direction only, into the heart.

Two thick-walled chambers at the bottom of the heart are called **ventricles**. The blood flows out of the heart from the ventricles.

The heart is situated in the thorax between the lungs and the diaphragm. It is a finely tuned organ; it transports blood around the body at a rate of 45 litres per minute when required, such as when exercising. At rest it beats 45–80 beats per minute, rising to 180 beats per minute during exercise.

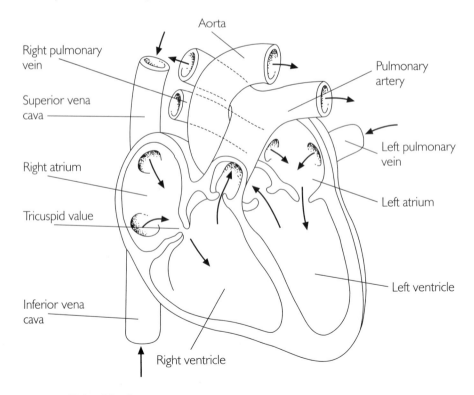

Figure 7.6 *The heart*

Heart rate check

During exercise the heart rate can increase rapidly and it is important that you warm up for at least two minutes before strenuous exercise for two main reasons:

1   **To raise your core body temperature**
2   **To increase the blood flow to your muscles to prepare your body for more vigorous physical activity**

A good warm-up will also ensure that there is sufficient blood flow to the heart and avoid unnecessary pressure on the heart.

It is also important to monitor the heart rate during exercise; the heart rate during training can indicate the optimum level of exercise for a person. If the heart rate is too high then the athlete can decrease the level of activity, if too low then the level of activity can be increased.

The use of equipment to monitor the heart rate has become very popular. A common method uses a belt around the chest which sends a message to a watch worn on the athlete's wrist. The watch displays the athlete's heart rate and can be set to alert the athlete if the heart rate is too low or high.

However, not everyone will have access to such equipment, so you need to understand how to take a heart rate check manually. This is done by taking a measurement of the number of pulse beats over a specified time period.

Taking a pulse

The pulse can be measured through the wrist or neck.

Wrist

1   **Turn your left hand so the palm is facing upwards**
2   **Take your index and middle fingers of your right hand and place them on the thumb side of your wrist**
3   **You should now be able to feel your pulse**
4   **Count the number of beats for 10 seconds**
5   **Multiply the number of beats by 6 to work out the number of beats per minute**

Neck

1   **This pulse is found at the bottom of your neck; this is called the carotid pulse**
2   **Take the first two fingers of your left hand and place them in the groove of your neck near the jaw bone**

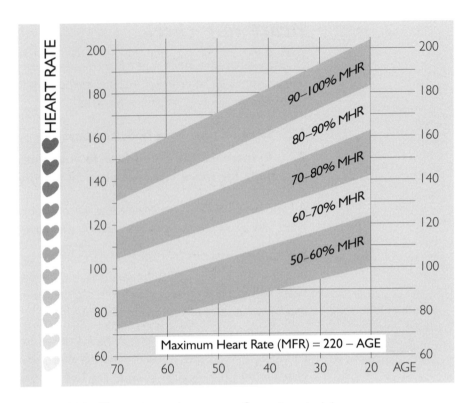

Figure 7.7 *The optimum heart rates for various training ranges*

3 **You should now be able to feel your pulse**

4 **Count the number of beats for 10 seconds**

5 **Multiply the number of beats by 6 to work out the number of beats per minute**

Optimum heart rates

Figure 7.7 highlights the optimum heart rates for various training ranges.

Calculate your own training heart rate

You can work out your own training heart range using the Karvonen Formula. In order to do this you will have to work out your resting heart rate and heart rate reserve.

Step one

Resting Heart Rate (RHR)   = your pulse at rest
Maximum Heart Rate (MHR) = 220 – your age
Heart Rate Reserve (HRR)   = Maximum heart rate – resting heart rate

Example

24-year-old person with a resting heart rate of 65

Maximum heart rate = 220 − 24 = 196
Heart rate reserve = 196 − 65 = 131

Step two

Now you know your heart rate reserve you can calculate your training heart rate. At the upper end of the training zone you should be working at 85 per cent of your heart rate reserve.

At the lower end of the training zone you should be working at 50 per cent of your heart rate reserve.

The formula for this calculation is:

(HRR × 85%) + RHR = upper end of the training zone
(HRR × 50%) + RHR = lower end of the training zone

Example

24-year-old person with resting heart rate of 65. We have already calculated their heart rate reserve to be 131.

Upper end of training zone = (131 × 0.85) + 65 = 177 bpm
Lower end of training zone = (131 × 0.50) + 65 = 131 bpm

So, when this person exercises they should aim to reach their training heart rate zone which is between 131 and 177 beats per minute. This should be maintained and can be monitored during exercise to ensure they remain in the target range.

The action of the heart

When the cardiac muscle contracts, it squeezes blood out of the heart into the arteries (**systole**). When the cardiac muscle relaxes it fills with blood from the veins (**diastole**). The action of the heart can be described in six stages:

1   **Deoxygenated blood arrives at the right atrium via the vena cava; it is a dull red and contains waste products. The blood has little oxygen left in it; this has been used during the blood's journey around the body**

2   **The atrium contracts to pump the blood through the tricuspid valve into the right ventricle**

3   **The blood is now transported to the lungs via the pulmonary artery in order to be stripped of carbon dioxide and to be supported with oxygen. It then returns to the heart via the pulmonary vein**

4   **The oxygenated blood, now bright red in colour, enters the left atrium**

5   **The ventricle muscles contract, forcing the blood out of the heart via the aorta**

6   **The blood is transported around the body via the aterioles and capillaries as the cycle starts again**

Diagram of the action of the heart

See Figure 7.6 and follow the arrows which show the action of blood travelling around the heart.

Cardiac output

The **cardiac output** is the amount of blood pumped into the arteries by contraction of the ventricles in a given time. It is the product of two components, the **heart rate** and the **stroke volume**. At rest this will be around 5,000 cm^3 per minute; it may rise to 30,000 cm^3 per minute in an athlete undergoing training.

Stroke volume is the volume of blood ejected by each contraction of the ventricle. At rest the ventricles do not eject all the blood completely when they contract; they only expel 40–70 per cent. During exercise the maximum stroke volume will be achieved at a heart rate of 110–120 beats per minute.

You may be able to work out the stroke volume for an athlete during exercise using the following formula:

Cardiac output = Heart rate per min × Stroke volume

Let us assume that an athlete is training at the upper end training zone (85 per cent).

They are 21 years old and have a resting heart rate of 65 bpm. Their cardiac output is 22,000 cm^3 when they are training at 85 per cent.

Using the formula above, work out the stroke volume when they reach their upper end training zone. This should be shown as a percentage.

Caridac output   = 22,000
High end training heart rate = 184
                          Maximum heart rate (220 − 21) = 199
                          HRR = 199 − 65 = 134
                          (134 × 0.85) + 65 = 184
Stroke volume %   = 22,000/184
                          = 120%

Effects of exercise on the cardiovascular system

Aerobic exercise will increase the efficiency of the heart; blood is pumped around the body with minimal effort as the coronary arteries are smooth and levels of fat in the blood are reduced. Cardiac capacity is increased by exercise although only by a maximum of 20 per cent. We are all born with varying cardiac capacities and pulse rates; as a result, training can improve our efficiency but not improve the overall capacity of the heart. Our fitness programmes must aim to maximise the efficiency of the cardiovascular system.

Structure and function of the respiratory system

The function of the respiratory system is to take in air from the atmosphere, deliver oxygen to the blood and return carbon dioxide to the atmosphere. Our bodies need oxygen for aerobic energy production and for life to continue.

Lungs

The organs involved in respiration are the lungs. The lungs are sited in the thorax, which is separated from the abdomen by the diaphragm. The lungs are protected by the rib cage. We have two lungs; the right lung is slightly larger than the left.

Breathing cycle

We breathe in air containing oxygen from the atmosphere via the nose. From the nasal capacity the air is transported to the **pharynx**, by the **epiglottis**, and to the **larynx** or the voice box (see Figure 7.8). It is then transported down the **trachea** or windpipe to two main branches of the respiratory system at the entrance to the lungs; these are called the **left** and **right bronchus**. The air then moves through each bronchus to smaller tubes called the **bronchi** and then even smaller tubes called **bronchioles**.

At the end of each tiny branch or bronchiole are **alveolar ducts** which are attached to **alveolar sacs** which contain **alveoli**. The alveoli are covered in capillaries.

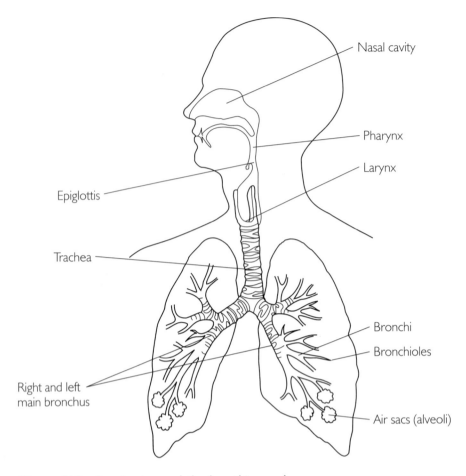

Nasal cavity

Pharynx

Larynx

Epiglottis

Trachea

Bronchi

Bronchioles

Right and left
main bronchus

Air sacs (alveoli)

Figure 7.8 *Respiration and the breathing cycle*

Gaseous exchange

It is at the capillaries that the deoxygenated blood, sent from the heart, is reoxygenated and carbon dioxide is discharged. The blood of the capillaries is low in oxygen and high in carbon dioxide. The opposite can be said of the air we have breathed in, which is high in oxygen and low in carbon dioxide. Therefore the oxygen is transferred to the blood by diffusion and carbon dioxide moves from the capillaries into the alveolis for discharge. The blood is then transported back to the heart.

Effect of exercise on the respiratory system

The capacity of the lungs changes as a result of exercise; exercise has a beneficial effect on the respiratory system and is indeed one of the reasons we are encouraged to exercise.

Lung capacity

Capacity	Definition	Increased or decreased during exercise
Tidal volume	The volume of air inspired or expired per breath	Increases during exercise
Inspiratory reserve volume	The maximum volume of air we can breathe in after a quiet inspiration	Decreases during exercise
Expiratory reserve volume	Maximum volume of air we can breathe out after a quiet expiration	Decreases during exercise
Vital capacity	Maximal volume of air that can be forcibly expired after maximal expiration	Slightly decreases during exercise
Residual volume	Volume of air remaining in the lungs at the end of a maximal expiration	Slightly increases during exercise

Stamina

As mentioned with respect to the cardiovascular system, exercise encourages our bodies to perform more efficiently and so allows us to exercise or perform everyday tasks for longer with reduced levels of effort. This is as a result of increased aerobic efficiency and stamina.

Activity 7.4

It will help to demonstrate the effects of exercise on the respiratory system by carrying out an experiment on your own body.

You will need a piece of equipment used to measure the flow rate of air.

Take three measurements:

1   Before beginning 20 minutes' exercise

2   After 10 minutes

3   At the end of the exercise period

What was the volume of air expelled before, during and after the exercise? What conclusions can you draw from this experiment?

Energy systems

In order to move and exercise we need to produce energy. Energy in the body is produced by creating adenosine triphosphate; this process is shown in Figure 7.9.

There are three ways in which the body produces adenosine triphosphate:

1   **Through anaerobic exercise using the creatine phosphate system**
2   **Through anaerobic exercise using the lactic acid system**
3   **Through aerobic exercise**

Aerobic and anaerobic exercise

During **aerobic exercise** energy needed is supplied by aerobic respiration of energy-rich substrates such as glucose, using the oxygen that is breathed in. Such exercise can be sustained for long periods. Examples include marathon running, rowing, cycling, swimming.

Anaerobic exercise demands more oxygen than can be supplied at the time. This results in the depletion of energy (ATP) stores and the incomplete oxidation of glucose with the accumulation of **lactic acid**. Such exercise cannot be sustained for long periods and examples include 100 metre sprint, javelin throwing and weightlifting.

Lactic acid is formed in exercising muscles anaerobically. The production of this acid causes muscular pain and it is the result of insufficient oxygen to muscles.

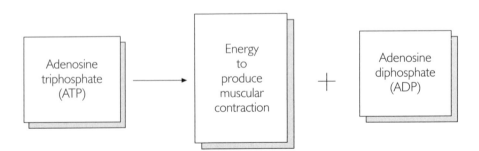

Figure 7.9 *Energy production*

Energy production through anaerobic exercise

Creatine phosphate system

$$ADP + CP \rightarrow ATP + creatine$$

Creatine phosphate (CP) is a substance stored in the muscles to produce energy. Muscular contractions can take place without the presence of oxygen for a limited time. Stores of CP are used up within 30–60 seconds, so if exercise is to be maintained another source of energy must be found. Activities that may use this energy system are sprinting and throwing events.

Lactic acid system

$$ADP + glycogen \rightarrow ATP + pyruvic\ acid*$$

* Lactic acid is produced when there is insufficient oxygen

This energy system also produces ATP without oxygen, but this time ATP is formed by the breakdown of glucose. Glucose is stored as glycogen in the muscles and liver. The glucose and then glycogen is obtained from the diet through the consumption of carbohydrate.

When ATP is produced, a substance called pyruvic acid is also produced: if there is insufficient oxygen then the pyruvic acid is further converted into a substance called lactic acid.

Lactic acid can be debilitating in the extreme, causing muscles to seize up completely. More often there is a burning sensation and a heavy feeling in the muscle. Exercise cannot be sustained without oxygen and eventually lactic acid will be converted back into pyruvic acid which will be converted into ATP, with by-products of carbon dioxide and water.

The oxygen debt

When you exercise anaerobically you are breathless – you are in need of oxygen. This deficiency is known as the **oxygen debt** and this debt must be repaid as soon as possible. The heart rate and respiratory rate remain elevated for some time after exercise has finished in order to repay this debt. In other words, the oxygen debt is the extra oxygen required if the task were to be completed anaerobically.

Fitness levels will affect the body's ability to exercise anaerobically and the speed at which lactic acid is produced or CP stores are diminished.

Energy production through aerobic exercise

ADP + glycogen → ATP + pyruvic acid*

* With oxygen produces carbon dioxide and water

During aerobic exercise, sufficient oxygen is available for the production of ATP and so exercise can be maintained indefinitely. This type of exercise is the least intense and there is no oxygen debt to be repaid. The body maintains a steady rate.

During the oxidation process that produces ATP, pyruvic acid is produced: this is converted to carbon dioxide and water which is removed through the lungs.

Diet and nutrition

In order for the human body to perform effectively it needs the right sorts of food to provide fuel for exercise.

Think of the human body as a car engine – without fuel it will not start and if you use the wrong type of fuel it will not perform to its full potential, if at all. So, if you fill your body with the wrong type of fuel (food) it will not perform effectively and without food we would die.

Nutritional requirements of the human body

Nutrition is the study of the food we eat and how the body uses it. Nutrients are those essential elements in food that we need for life and growth, but which our bodies cannot manufacture.

There are six groups of nutrients that our bodies must consume for efficient functioning:

✪ **Carbohydrates**
✪ **Fats**
✪ **Proteins**
✪ **Vitamins**
✪ **Mineral salts**
✪ **Water**

Each group has a recommended level of consumption and each plays a vital role in the 'balanced diet' and general well-being.

Carbohydrates

Carbohydrates are composed of carbon, oxygen and hydrogen and are the primary source of energy in the body. They provide energy for exercise, for transmitting impulses through nerves and for the formation of new compounds in the body.

There are two types of carbohydrates

✪ *Starch*: **Major sources include potatoes, bread, flour, pasta, rice**
✪ *Sugars*: **Major sources include fruits, honey, confectionery, jams, table sugar**

Carbohydrates in the form of sugars are in reality 'empty calories'; although they do provide energy, they are also the cause of tooth decay and obesity. We should aim to take 80 per cent of our carbohydrates in the form of starch as these foods also tend to be rich in vitamins, minerals and dietary fibre.

The simplest form of carbohydrate is the monosaccharide, which is a sugar such as that found in fruit (fructose) and in honey (glucose). The process of digestion breaks down disaccharides (for example, lactose found in milk and sucrose which is table sugar) and polysaccharides (which are starch carbohydrates) to monosaccharides, which are then ready to be used by the body as energy.

Fats

Although it is recommended in the developed world that we decrease our fat intake, fat is not 'bad for us'; it does serve a vital purpose within the body. It is excess fat intake that is unhealthy.

We need fat to keep us warm, to act as a buffer against injury, to protect vital organs and as a secondary source of energy for muscular activity.

- ✪ *Saturated fats*: **Major sources of saturated fats include milk, cheese, butter and red meat. It is recognised that this type of fat increases cholesterol levels in the blood and so should account for only 10 per cent of our fat intake**

- ✪ *Unsaturated fats*: **Major sources of unsaturated fats include oil and margarine. It is argued by some that this type of fat actually helps reduce cholesterol levels in the blood and so our fat intake should be mainly made up of unsaturated fats. There are two essential fatty acids that we have to consume through the diet: linoleic and linolenic fatty acids, which are both provided by unsaturated fats**

- ✪ *Cholesterol*: **Cholesterol is a fatty substance found mainly in animal produce. It is actually produced naturally by the body but any excess gained from the diet tends to line the walls of blood vessels and prevent efficient circulation of the blood, thus increasing the risk of heart disease**

Proteins

Proteins are made up of amino acids, the building blocks of all tissues in the body. An adult person needs 21 amino acids, of which nine need to be consumed from our diet – these are known as essential amino acids. Proteins can be obtained from both animal and vegetable sources. Animal proteins – meat, fish and cheese – all contain these essential amino acids.

Protein is used by the body to build cells and tissues and so is particularly important during periods of growth such as childhood, adolescence and during pregnancy. It is never the primary source of energy and so the theory of a 'steak before a fight' is actually of little value to an athlete.

Vegans have to ensure that they supplement their diets in order to consume all the essential amino acids as these are not provided in all vegetable protein. Vegetables usually provide one or two essential amino acids and so a broad range must be consumed to ensure that the body receives an adequate supply of all nine.

Vitamins

Vitamins are organic compounds that are needed for the efficient functioning of muscles and nerves, the growth of body tissue and for the release of energy from foods. They are required only in small amounts and are not stored in the body, so it is essential that our diet supplies all of these vitamins. Table 7.1 lists specific sources and details of vitamins needed in the diet, and the effects that deficiencies cause.

Vitamins are divided into two groups:

- ✪ **Fat soluble vitamins**
- ✪ **Water soluble vitamins**

Mineral salts

Minerals are basic elements that account for 4 per cent of our body weight; they assist in many body functions, for example calcium aids the formation of healthy bones and teeth. There are fourteen minerals we need in minute quantities, called trace minerals, and seven we need in larger quantities, called macrominerals.

Water

Water is an essential nutrient; it is second only to oxygen in importance for the body. It transports nutrients; it removes waste and regulates body temperature. We would all survive a number of weeks without food but only a number of days without water. Water accounts for two-thirds of an adult's body weight.

Factors contributing to a healthy diet

The diet we consume affects our overall well-being and performance. Current guidelines recommend that our diet is balanced; all the nutrients

Vitamin	Source	Functions	Effects of deficiency
Vitamin A (retinol) Fat soluble	Animal: butter, eggs, cheese Vegetable: carrots, greens, tomatoes	• Necessary for the health of mucous membranes of the throat, digestive and excretory tracts • Resistance to infection • Growth of bones and teeth • Helps vision	• Blindness – ulcerated cornea
Vitamin B_1 (thiamine) Water soluble	Wheatgerm, yeast, oatmeal, nuts	• Liberation of energy to form glucose (enzyme system) • Growth and good health	• Arrested growth in children • Loss of appetite, nausea, fatigue, constipation, nervous irritability • Beri-beri
Vitamin B_2 (riboflavin) Water soluble	Yeast, liver, cheese, cereal goods	• Release of energy from goods by oxidation (enzyme system) • Utilisation of food fats and amino acids	• Arrested growth in children • Inflammation of mouth and tongue • Nervous depression, unhealthy skin and digestive tract (disturbances) • Cornea misted and vision impaired
Vitamin B_{12} (nicotinic acid) Water soluble	Yeast, peanuts, liver, beef	• Release of energy from carbohydrate foods	• Arrested growth in children • Diarrohoea, digestive trouble • Rough, red, raw skin • Mental disorders – pellagra
Vitamin D (cholecalciferol) Fat soluble	Animal: fish liver oils, fish, eggs, dairy fat Sunlight	• Formation of bones and teeth (+ calcium + phosphorous)	• Rickets • Dental decay
Vitamin E (tocopherol) Fat soluble	Wheatgerm oil, eggs, milk	• Used to treat women who have had miscarriages	
Vitamin K	Obtained sufficiently in well-balanced diet, including green vegetables	• Enables blood to clot	

Table 7.1   *Vitamins needed in the diet*

listed in the previous section are essential; we all need them in differing quantities and it is only when they are consumed in either insufficient or excessive amounts that our diet becomes unbalanced and our bodies do not perform maximally.

In a balanced diet, it is important to consider the quantities of fat, salt, sugar and fibre that we eat.

Generally we are recommended to

✪ **Reduce our intake of fat, particularly saturated fats, as this is linked to obesity and heart disease**

✪ **Reduce our consumption of salt, as this is linked to an increase in blood pressure and heart disease**

✪ **Reduce our intake of sugar, as this is linked to problems of excess weight gain and to tooth decay**

✪ **Increase our consumption of fibre, as this aids digestion, controls blood sugar levels, reduces blood cholesterol levels and promotes a general feeling of well-being**

Nutrients required at different life stages and by individuals with different lifestyles

The amount of energy and the different nutritional requirements we need depend on our lifestyle, our life stage or age, and whether we are male or female.

Calorie

The **calorie** is used to measure energy production in the body; this is defined as the heat required to raise one gram of water by one degree centigrade. Measurements are usually made in kilocalories as the calorie unit is too small for any practical use (1 kilocalorie = 1,000 calories). A more recent measure of energy production is the **joule**, which is the energy expended when one kilogram is moved by a force of one newton.

Basal metabolic rate

The more energetic we are, the more energy we need and so the more calories we use. However, whatever our lifestyle, we all need a certain amount of energy to maintain the life processes. This is called the **basal metabolic rate (BMR)**. This is normally 50–70 per cent of our daily caloric expenditure. It is influenced by size and composition of the body, for instance a muscular person uses more energy than a fat person. Age is known to lower the BMR.

In order to calculate your daily caloric expenditure, you need to add the caloric costs of the activities of your day. This is measured by the amount of oxygen used to perform the activity. Energy expenditure is only an estimate as it will depend on such factors as skill and body weight.

Lifestyle

Lifestyle affects an individual's energy requirements. A sedentary lifestyle has few extra activities and generally involves a 'sit down' office job. An active lifestyle includes regular exercise and perhaps a manual or labour-intensive job. Other influences on energy expenditure include pregnancy, lactation and other medical conditions.

Life stage or age

Energy requirements change, depending on age. Energy requirements are shown in Table 7.2. Peak requirements are during the ages of 15–18, due largely to rapid growth through puberty. After this time energy requirements fall. This can account for 'middle age spread' where people continue with the same diet but tend to acquire a few unwanted pounds in weight.

Age	Estimated average requirements MJ/day (kcal/day)	
	Males	Females
Months		
0–3	2.28 (545)	2.16 (515)
10–12	3.85 (920)	3.61 (865)
Years		
1–3	5.15 (1230)	4.86 (1165)
4–6	7.16 (1715)	6.46 (1545)
7–10	8.24 (1970)	7.28 (1740)
11–14	9.27 (2220)	7.91 (1845)
15–18	11.51 (2755)	8.83 (2110)
19–50	10.60 (2550)	8.10 (1940)
51–59	10.60 (2550)	8.00 (1900)
60–64	9.93 (2380)	7.99 (1900)
65–74	9.71 (2330)	7.96 (1900)
75+	8.77 (2100)	7.61 (1810)

(*Source:* Statistics from COMA: Committee on Medical Aspects of Food Policy)

Table 7.2 *Energy requirements by age and sex*

Sex

The BMR of a man is higher than that of a woman because of the differing body compositions — men have more muscle and women have more fat. The BMR for a man weighing 65 kg is 7,650 kJ/day and the BMR for a woman weighing 55 kg is 5,960 kJ/day.

Obesity

You often read in the newspapers about a number of eating disorders and the health of the nation. It is claimed that in the developed world, the number of obese people, that is, those carrying excess fat, is ever increasing. Obesity causes high blood pressure, which is associated with an increase in the risk of heart disease. The cause of obesity is generally social. Our society encourages overeating, often rewarding success with high calorie/low nutrition snacks. Obesity can be caused by the malfunctioning of the thyroid gland but this is extremely rare.

Anorexia nervosa

There is also a general raising of awareness of the disease of anorexia nervosa. This is an eating disorder where the victim refuses to eat to the point of starvation as a result of a poor body image and fear of being fat. The extreme consequence of this illness is death. This condition tends to affect young women but is not limited to this group. Anorexics need medical help in order to return their diet and lifestyle to the accepted norm for their age and weight.

Conversion of food into energy

Carbohydrate, fat and protein are all energy providers; our primary source is carbohydrate, followed by fat, and protein is never our most immediate source of energy. Carbohydrate provides 17.1 kJ; fat provides 38.9 kJ and protein provides 18.2 kJ of energy. So how can a potato become the fuel that allows our bodies to perform everyday and elite activities? The process of digestion and absorption ensures that our food provides sufficient energy to keep us warm and to provide movement.

This process takes place in the mitochondria of every cell and, by the process of oxidation, a chemical compound called adenosine triphosphate (ATP) is produced. This is the energy currency of the body and supplies energy for muscular contraction.

Carbohydrate, fat and protein are burned in the presence of oxygen and adenosine diphosphate to produce ATP — other by-products include carbon dioxide and water. Any surplus energy is given off as heat.

Creatine phosphate is another high energy substance stored in the muscles; this allows muscular contractions to take place without the presence of oxygen.

Healthy living

Our ability to perform depends greatly on our lifestyle; we all have the option to pursue healthy living yet a great number of people abuse their bodies. This abuse includes excess alcohol consumption, smoking, drug dependency, overeating and malnutrition.

Our life stage affects our demand for nutrients; the fitter and (more importantly) more active we are, the more energy we expend, therefore the more calories and nutrients we need. An active lifestyle will require more fluid intake due to increased loss of fluid through sweating; this can include a manual or active occupation as well as exercise. The diet of a child is different from that of an adult; a child has to sustain growth and so too does a woman's body during pregnancy.

Pregnant women

It is important that the diet of a pregnant woman should be nutritionally sound, so that she produces a healthy baby and at the same time maintains her own health.

Even before pregnancy, it is vital that a woman of childbearing age has a balanced diet so that she is able to cope with the demands of pregnancy, once this occurs.

There used to be a popular saying that a pregnant woman should 'eat for two'; in one sense this is true, but it does not mean that she should double her daily amount of food. This is unnecessary and can lead to excessive weight gain. What it does mean is that her diet should provide sufficient nutrients to cope with the demands of the growing baby as well as the needs of her own body. The increased requirements for the individual nutrients are shown in Table 7.3.

	Non-pregnant	Pregnant	Lactating
Energy (kJ/kcal)	9,000/2,150	10,000/2,400	11,500/2,750
Protein (g)	54	60	69
Vitamin A (μg)	750	750	1,200
Vitamin B$_1$ (thiamin) (mg)	0.9	1.0	1.1
Vitamin B$_2$ (riboflavin) (mg)	1.3	1.6	1.8
Vitamin B$_{12}$ (nicotinic acid) (mg)	15	18	21
Vitamin C (mg)	30	60	60

Table 7.3 *Nutritional requirements during pregnancy*

The foetus receives nutrients from the mother; these nutrients are carried from the mother's bloodstream through the placenta and umbilical cord into the baby's bloodstream.

Nature ensures that if a particular nutrient is in short supply, it is the foetus who receives the nutrient, not the mother.

If the mother's diet lacks some nutrients, here are the possible effects:

✪ *Lack of calcium*: **If the diet is deficient in calcium or vitamin D, then some of the calcium from the mother's bones and teeth will be removed and passed on to the foetus. This will weaken the mother's bones and teeth and she may develop adult's rickets**

✪ *Lack of vitamin A*: **If the diet is deficient in vitamin A, then any that is stored in the mother's liver will go to the foetus. This may result in the symptoms of a vitamin A deficiency. Often the foetus' store of vitamin A does not build up sufficiently; once born, many babies develop a vitamin A deficiency which in extreme cases can lead to blindness in these babies**

✪ *Lack of iron*: **A deficiency of iron can lead to anaemia in the mother and a failure to build up a store of iron in the foetus. This store is important because both breast milk and cow's milk are poor sources of iron, and the newborn baby has to rely on the store of iron that it builds up as a foetus for the first three months of life. In the UK most pregnant women are prescribed iron tablets**

General advice during pregnancy

In the UK a careful check is kept on both the mother and her developing baby in order to ensure that an adequate diet is maintained. Low income families can get statutory help with this. During antenatal clinics, mothers are given plenty of advice on diet and well-being during pregnancy.

It is generally recommended that the following nutrients should be increased in the daily diet:

✪ **Vitamin D**

✪ **The minerals iron and calcium**

✪ **Folic acid**

✪ **Dietary fibre as constipation is an unpleasant side-effect of pregnancy**

It is important not to increase the consumption of energy through high calorie foods such as chocolate and biscuits, as this can lead to excess weight gain.

After the birth the mother's nutrient requirements increase to enable the body to cope with breastfeeding and with the increased activity associated with rearing a baby; fluid intake during breastfeeding should also be increased. The following nutrients should be increased:

✪ **Protein for body growth**

✪ **Calcium for bones and teeth**

✪ **Fluoride for teeth**

✪ **Iron for red blood cells**

Infancy (up to one year)

An infant's diet for the first few weeks of life consists solely of milk. Human breast milk is specifically designed to feed human beings and it follows that it is therefore more suitable than other milks for consumption. The reasons for this are:

✪ **The correct composition and proportion of nutrients are provided automatically**

✪ **The milk is at the correct temperature and consistency**

✪ **Virtually all the milk is digested by the baby**

✪ **The baby takes only what is needed and is therefore less likely to become overweight**

✪ **Immunity from some diseases is passed to the baby from the mother**

✪ **There is a reduction in gastric infections as the milk is sterile**

Bottle-fed babies do also thrive: however, they do not benefit from the advantages above. Bottle milk is manufactured to be as close to breast milk as possible.

Children

When babies have been weaned on to solid food they can enjoy the wide range of foods on offer. A broad-based diet should be followed; children do tend to grow quickly and the following nutrients should be increased to supply this extra demand for energy:

✪ **Protein for body growth**

✪ **Calcium for bones and teeth**

✪ **Fluoride for teeth**

✪ **Iron for red blood cells**

Children should be limited in the amount of sugary foods they eat as these serve little nutritional benefit and do cause tooth decay. Babies and young children should not be given nuts, which can cause them to choke, and they should not eat foods containing nuts, as these can lead to severe allergies when they are older.

Adolescents

Adolescence is a period of rapid growth and body development; consequently, nutrient requirements increase at this stage of development.

The hormones for adulthood are produced at this stage and this may cause skin disturbances. It is important for adolescents to eat plenty of fresh fruit and vegetables and avoid eating fatty foods that may aggravate these conditions. The diet should provide plenty of protein. Girls particularly need sufficient iron to avoid the symptoms of anaemia, which may develop with the onset of menstruation.

Adults

Once body growth has declined in adulthood, food is required to maintain and repair the body and keep it healthy. Nutrient requirements will to some extent be determined by the body size of the individual and the amount of daily activity. Women need less food than men in general.

The type of job will affect the balance of the nutrients required:

- ✪ *Very active jobs*: **Sufficient energy must be provided for this sort of occupation but in the form of carbohydrate, not fat as this can increase the risk of heart disease. Fluid intake must increase, particularly if the job is in a warm atmosphere**
- ✪ *Sedentary jobs*: **Careful attention should be paid to the energy intake of meals for this type of worker, as it is easy to exceed energy output and therefore lead to weight gain. Meals should be kept simple and less bulky as these are more comfortable to digest during inactive periods**

Old age

As age increases, activity slows down, especially after retirement from an active job. Food is required to maintain the health and state of the body as in the younger age group but there is an increased requirement for calcium and vitamin D to prevent decalcification of the bones and teeth, and for iron to prevent anaemia.

The size of meal should decrease with levels of activity but the quality should not. Often the diet of elderly people is affected for social reasons, such as a reduction in income. The death of a partner can mean that there is no motivation to cook meals for one person, or possibly the bereaved partner lacks the domestic skills required.

Advice on diet

For each of the life stages there are huge amounts of literature regarding diet. Advice given can conflict, both currently and over time as research increases knowledge and opinions change.

Diet is a specific aspect of a fitness programme and is totally individual, through social, physiological and environmental causes. When discussing a specific diet, all facts must be noted first and preferably referred to a qualified dietician or doctor.

Revision questions

1 What are the four main functions of the human skeleton?

2 Name the two main parts of the skeletal system.

3 Name the three main muscle groups.

4 Define the term smooth muscle, giving two examples.

5 How are muscles attached to the bones?

6 Identify and give examples of five muscle groups.

7 In what ways do muscles produce actions?

8 What the main characteristics of the synovial joints?

9 Explain how levers work to produce muscle action.

10 What are the major effects of exercise on the muscular and skeletal system?

11 What is the main purpose of the circulatory system?

12 What are the functions of blood in the circulatory system?

13 How is blood transported through the body?

14 Name the largest vein in the body and explain its function.

15 Define the terms Resting Heart Rate, Maximum Heart Rate and Heart Rate Reserve.

16 What is the optimum heart rate zone for training?

17 How would you calculate the training heart rate of a 42-year-old with a resting heart rate of 70?

18 Define cardiac output.

19 Define the term stroke volume; at what point does this reach maximum efficiency?

20 What are the main effects of exercise on the cardiovascular system?

21 Explain the processes of the breathing cycle and gaseous exchange.

22 What are the benefits of exercise in relation to the respiratory system?

23 Explain how a tri-athlete will produce energy during a competition.

24 Explain how an athlete will produce energy during a 100 metre hurdles race.

25 What is the oxygen debt?

26 How does a lack of oxygen contribute to muscle fatigue as a result of exercise?

Assessment activity

You have been appointed to a new position as a Sports Coach Supervisor in a local leisure centre called *Fitness Forever*. It has come to your attention that the induction process for customers using the fitness suite needs to be updated and revised. Of particular concern is the lack of information given to new clients during induction.

You recently raised this matter with your manager who sent you the following e-mail:

Following our conversation about induction for new clients in the fitness suite I think it would be a good idea to produce an information pack for new clients, which will explain the physiological effects of exercise. I'd like you to work on this asap.

I would suggest that the following sections need to be included in the pack:

- ✪ **The use of the skeletal and muscular system during exercise.** In this section I would like to see a clear description of the skeletal and muscular systems – this should be related to their use during movement
- ✪ **The efficiency of the cardio-respiratory system during exercise.** In this section I would like to see a clear description of the structure and function of the system
- ✪ **The energy requirements related to different types of exercise**
- ✪ **Nutritional requirements of exercise**
- ✪ **Physiological adjustments made by the body during exercise**

You should attempt to analyse how the structure and functions of each system are inter-related and present this information in a clear and easy to understand format – remember that this is designed for new clients who may have little knowledge of exercise.

I would strongly suggest that you demonstrate the effects of exercise on the physiological systems by the use of a case study on a particular individual – this will make the information pack much more user friendly.

I'd like you to give me a plan of how you will produce this information pack and how you will research the pack along with details of specific resources to be used. I need this plan by the end of next week.

1 Reply to this e-mail with details of your action plan for the information pack. Be sure you are thorough when producing this plan and identify potential sources of information, including verbal and written sources.

2 Produce the information pack in a suitable format for new clients at the fitness suite. Remember to use the correct terminology and demonstrate the inter-relationship of different systems during exercise. Don't forget to include a suitable case study to evaluate the effects of exercise and how these systems have affected their ability to exercise.

Fitness, testing and training

8

Objectives

- **Develop and improve your understanding of the components of physical fitness**

- **Examine some of the theoretical and practical aspects of training**

- **Identify a range of procedures that are used to assess levels of fitness**

- **Review the design of individual training programmes**

- **Identify the benefits of exercise and training**

- **Examine the long-term effects of exercise on the body**

The past twenty years have seen a major growth in the health and fitness industry, and subsequent employment opportunities. Through education, publicity and advertising, by government and the fitness industry, individuals have become more aware of the benefits of maintaining their level of fitness.

If you are interested in working in the fitness industry, for example as an instructor or coach, this chapter will provide you with the background on the practical aspects of fitness and fitness testing. This chapter will also provide you with underpinning knowledge on the benefits of regular training and how the body improves and adapts to this training.

Please remember, however, that poor techniques, poor instruction or badly designed training programmes can lead to injury, so please make sure you check with a teacher, lecturer or fitness professional before carrying out any physical activity yourself, or with others.

Fitness, testing and training has close links with other units of the VCE in Leisure and Recreation. These are: Unit 2 Safe working practices, Unit 3 The sports industry and Unit 7 Exercise physiology.

Components of physical fitness

Every individual is different. They often have different concepts of what it is to be fit. They will usually have different ambitions as to how fit they want to be. The body shape and structure that they have will respond to different forms of exercise, or fitness training, in different ways. However, there are common components that make up overall physical fitness, and it is important that you have an understanding of these.

When we ask someone how fit they are they sometimes flex the muscles in their upper arm, or pat their stomach to show how flat it is; they may try to show you they can touch their toes, or even challenge you to watch how many press-ups they can do. Though a little simplistic, they are demonstrating some of the basic elements of fitness: Endurance – Strength – Flexibility – Body composition. Some basic definitions of these components could be stated as:

- ✪ *Endurance*: **This is the ability of the body to work/exercise repetitively over a period of time**
- ✪ *Strength*: **This is the ability of a muscle, or muscle group, to exert a force against a resistance**
- ✪ *Flexibility*: **This is the ability of the limbs at the joint to move through all the movements that the limb would normally be expected to achieve**
- ✪ *Body composition*: **This is the proportion of fat in the body compared to bone and muscle. Please note, *not* weight in kilos or individual body shape or physique**

Aerobic fitness – cardiovascular and cardio-respiratory endurance

The function of the cardiovascular and the cardio-respiratory systems could be described as the ability of the heart and lungs to supply oxygen-rich blood to the muscles. If we break the terms down it will be more clearly understood.

Cardio = of the heart
Vascular = the circulation of blood through the blood vessels
Respiration = taking in oxygen and giving out carbon dioxide

Cardiovascular and cardio-respiratory fitness is usually known under the title of aerobic fitness – aerobic meaning 'working with oxygen'.

Aerobic activities are those that make us breathe harder, at a steady rate, over a period of time. These could include jogging, cycling, swimming or dance. The more efficient our aerobic system is, the longer and/or more intensely we will be able to sustain activity.

Activity 8.1

In a small group, try to draw up answers to the following questions. When you have done this, discuss your answers with the group as a whole.

1   What determines how efficiently the heart is able to pump blood around the body?

2   What determines how much oxygen the lungs can take in?

3   What might determine how fast the oxygen in the blood gets to the muscles?

4   What might determine the efficiency of the muscles in using oxygen?

Muscular endurance

If we watch a person exercising, we will notice muscles in their body contracting and pulling a limb, to give movement. If we were to examine a muscle and look at how able it was to continue to contract repetitively over a period of time, that would give us an indication of the 'endurance' of that muscle.

Muscular endurance is important to our health and well-being. Training to achieve good muscular endurance is also important for sports and physical activities that involve repetitive muscle use, such as distance running.

You may have studied in previous chapters that the muscles of the body are made up of different muscle fibres. Muscular endurance requires the ability of the muscle/muscle fibres to carry out continuous contractions, and will therefore require a continuous supply of energy. The muscle fibres best suited for this are slow twitch oxidative, or **type I**, fibres. These fibres are red in appearance, and contend with fatigue well.

Muscular strength

We need muscular strength in everyday activities – to get up from a chair, to lift a bag of shopping, to open a tightly sealed jar. If we do not maintain our muscular strength, these activities will become gradually more difficult with time. Training to improve or maintain muscular strength will enable us to maintain muscle mass.

Activities that are associated with strength, such as weightlifting, pumping iron in a gym or throwing the shot or hammer, are usually associated with one short burst of activity. Muscular strength can be classified in a number of different ways:

✪ If the activity involves little or no motion of the limbs, this is known as **static or isometric strength**

✪ If the activity involves moving the limbs using the maximum effort, in one movement, this is known as **explosive strength**

✪ If the activity involves the movement of the limbs a few times, usually for a short period of time, until the muscles tire, this is known as **dynamic or isotonic strength**

Within the muscle structure are muscle fibres that help us perform strength activities. Fast twitch glycolytic, or **type IIb**, fibres contract quickly and can produce great amounts of force, but they tire quickly. These fibres are white in appearance.

Many of the physical activities that the human body performs cannot be categorised only as a strength activity and do have elements of muscular endurance within them. A good example of this would be the 100 or 200 metre sprint. Here there is a burst of activity, but this is maintained over a period of time. Within the muscle structure, we have fibres that combine the characteristics of Type I and Type IIb fibres; these are known as fast twitch oxidative, or **type IIa**, fibres.

Flexibility

Flexibility is the normal range of movement at a joint. The range of movement of joints will vary depending on the structure of the joint.
If a joint is moved beyond its normal range of movement, injury will occur. Flexibility allows us to take the joint to the limit of its range of movement.

Factors that can *limit* flexibility include:

- **Genetic inheritance, age and gender**
- **Connective tissues**
- **Body fat**
- **The elasticity of the muscles and tendons**
- **Disease such as arthritis**

Flexibility is important to both muscular strength and muscular endurance. The ability to achieve the full range of motion, to be flexible, is significant in most sports. We are able to reach or stretch or jump that much better. In many activities, such as gymnastics, hurdling and dance, flexibility is a central element.

Flexibility is also important because the better the muscle's ability to stretch over a supple joint, the less likely we are to have a muscle tear, or pull, and become injured.

Body composition

The body is composed of a wide variety of things: organs, muscles, blood, bone, fat and so on. There are even some things in the body, such as the appendix, that we don't use. How we treat our bodies in terms of the exercise that we do, and the food that we eat, will have a direct effect on its composition.

The body's composition should be considered separately from the weight of the body or the body's physique. When we weigh the body, we weigh everything in it. People involved in fitness training often point out that muscle weighs more than fat, so, if we were to put on weight, it could just mean that we were becoming more muscular. Equally, our physique, our natural body shape, is predominantly determined by the genetic make-up we inherit from our parents. Try as we might, the only way of becoming taller, apart from natural growth, is to wear shoes with a larger sole.

The body in its most healthy state will always contain fat. If we lose essential body fat, this can be a risk to our health, in just the same way as surplus levels of body fat can be. Many animals put on fat when food is abundant, so they can survive leaner times – this is perfectly natural. However, we are very lucky in that the majority of us have access to food all year round, so we don't really have any excuse.

Essential fat totals, approximately, 3–5 per cent of body weight in men and 11–14 per cent of body weight in women. For men an acceptable level of body fat can be as high as 20 per cent, and for women as high as 25 per cent of body weight.

Putting on extra weight means that the body has to work that much harder. If we put on this weight through training, we are preparing the body to cope with that extra weight. If we put on extra weight through over-eating, and lay down fat, this just places extra strain on the organs and joints of the body.

Activity 8.2

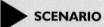

▶ **SCENARIO**

You have been asked to give a short presentation as part of your interview for a job at a local health and fitness club.

▶ **TASK**

Prepare a presentation on 'The components of physical fitness', and give this to the rest of your group. You should try to use visual aids where appropriate.

Principles of training

The body will always try to adapt to any exercise that we do. If we start a new activity, we will normally feel some form of discomfort such as shortness of breath or muscle soreness, but after carrying out the activity a number of times, these feelings will normally disappear. This is because the body has adapted to doing the activity. Some of these adaptations are discussed at the end of this chapter.

Even the smallest amount of activity can lead to improvements in physical fitness. However, just as the body will adapt to different levels of physical activity, so it will revert to a 'less fit' state if that activity is stopped, and a more sedate lifestyle followed. It is therefore important to carry out, and encourage regular participation in, physical activity by individuals. But it should also be remembered that individuals are different.

Factors affecting individuals' physical fitness and their ability to train

Heredity

Our genetic make-up, what we inherit from our parents and grandparents, will often predetermine the physical attributes that we have. Just as we may look like our parents, or have the same-coloured hair, so we will inherit things such our heart or lung size.

Age

Our physical capabilities change through our life. As we grow from a baby, unable to walk or talk, so we become more able to carry out physical activities, until a time when our body begins to go into a state of decline. Though our body clock is constantly ticking, it should be remembered that we could maintain our body, and offset decline, through regular physical activity.

Lifestyle

What we eat – our diet. How much sleep we get. How often we walk somewhere as opposed to getting in the car. If we smoke and drink alcohol. If we are stressed. The type of job that we do. If we use our free time watching television. All these factors can be thought of as making up our lifestyle, and have a direct effect on our level of physical fitness. If we wish to improve our physical fitness through training, we will have to take our lifestyle into account.

Illness

If we are lucky, we will progress through life without any major illnesses or debilitating injuries. However, it is likely that at some point we will get a bad cold, or influenza. Even the simplest virus, or a slight pull in a muscle, can affect our ability to perform the simplest physical activity or task.

Level of fitness

The individual's level of fitness at any given time, the point from which they start to train, will determine how often and how intensely they are able to train, and the improvement they can expect to make. If a person is reasonably fit, they will be able to train quite intensely, but it is unlikely that they will experience anything but marginal changes in fitness levels. Equally, if a person is very unfit, they will need time to get used to exercising on a regular basis, at which time major changes will usually be observed.

Activity 8.3

LOOKING AT LIFESTYLE I

Over the next week keep a diary, or record, of all the the activities that you do. When your body is actually in motion, doing something, walking somewhere, participating in sport. Also, when you are not being physically active, sitting in class, watching television – and don't forget sleeping time (in bed and in class). Record the times, e.g. 5 mins, 10 mins, 1 hour, of these activities and at the end of the week calculate the percentage of time that you were physically active as opposed to being inactive.

Check with some of your friends to see how your lifestyles compare.

LOOKING AT LIFESTYLE 2

Design a small display that will show the effects of smoking on physical activity. You will find information on the effects of smoking in local health centres or doctors' surgeries. As part of your project you may want to organise a visit by a health professional to give a talk on the effects of smoking.

Training to improve physical fitness

Overload

If we wish to train to improve physical fitness, then we must be aware that we always need to challenge the body and gradually increase the amount of effort; this is known as overload. We 'overload' a muscle, for example, by using a weight or a resistance against it. The muscle adapts/strengthens/grows, and the exercise becomes easier. If we wish the muscle to strengthen more, we must increase the weight, or the resistance that the muscle is working against – this is known as **progression**, or **progressive resistance**.

Progression through 'FIT'

We can overload in order to induce the gradual progression of physical fitness in a number of ways. We could train more times a week or month. We could work harder during the time when we train. Or we could increase the length of time that we train. This is usually known as the **FIT** model of progression:

> **F** = Frequency
> **I** = Intensity
> **T** = Time

Frequency – Whenever we train it is always important to let the body have time to recover. If we do not allow time for recovery, this can lead to fatigue and loss of motivation. Also, if we are training towards activities such as sports matches or a competition, it is important to take those into account when deciding how frequently we train. However, increasing the number of times we train, i.e. increasing frequency, will help improve our progression.

For the less physically active this may just mean increasing from one 20-minute session a week to two 20-minute sessions. With a more advanced person this may be increasing from three two-hour sessions per week to four, or even five, two-hour sessions. But, whatever the physical condition of the person, it is important to see increasing frequency as part of the overall training programme and to remain aware that rest and recovery are just as important as the activity. This is sometimes known as the **training cycle**.

Intensity – We can make the exercise that we do harder, or more intense, in a number of ways. We could try to do the same exercise in a quicker time, or repeat the exercise again, while keeping the length of time the same – increasing repetitions or sets of the exercise. We could increase the resistance involved in the exercise; this could mean working against a greater weight. We could increase the range of movement involved in the exercise – this means that the limbs have to move through a greater distance and the muscles have to contract with greater force.

Time – The time taken for an exercise session falls into three basic parts: the time that we 'warm-up' in preparation for the activity, the 'main component' or the activity itself, and the 'cool-down, or warm-down' after the main activity. As well as increasing the overall time of the exercise session, we can vary the times of the three elements of a training session. So, for example, with a less physically active person it is important to spend more time in the warm-up element. As their fitness improves, it will be possible to transfer some of this time to the main component. Also, if we are concentrating on a particular aspect of fitness, such as flexibility, it is recommended that we allocate more time to this within the cool-down/warm-down element.

Progression – adding another 'T' to the FIT model: 'Type' of exercise

Just as our body adapts to different levels of exercise, so it will adapt to the type of exercise that we do. Each sport or activity has different characteristics, and places different demands on different parts of the body. Even within the same sport, playing in different positions will vary the effect on different muscle groups, or components of fitness. This is also known as **specificity**.

So, as we are training, the body changes and makes specific adaptations in response to that training. An extreme example of this would be if we decided to do strength training, say by doing bicep curls with only one arm; that arm would become more muscular in appearance, while the other arm remained the same. Equally, if our exercise programme consisted mainly of jogging, so our body would adapt to doing that well, or if we concentrated on weight training, it would adapt to that.

We can introduce progression, if we are training for a particular sport or activity, by adding to our programme activities that concentrate on the groups of muscles, or element of fitness, that we are trying to improve for that sport.

If we are involved in a sport that involves sudden bursts of running, we may want to introduce weight training in the gym into our training programme, to improve the strength of the muscles in our legs. If we are involved in a sport that involves steady running over 80 or 90 minutes, then we may want to do some additional running, or jogging, over distance. Alternatively, if we are trying to develop all-round fitness, and retain the motivation to train, it is important that we vary the type of activity that we do, and try to introduce new activities that we will like and enjoy, as part of our training programme.

Activity 8.5

1   Form a small group.

2   Choose an individual sport and a position within a team sport.

3   Try to answer the following questions:

★   How do the components of fitness for the individual sport differ from the team sport?

★   How do the components of fitness for your chosen position in the team sport differ from other positions in the same sport?

★   What additional type of training would help the performance of a person playing the individual sport?

★   What additional type of training would help the performance of a person playing in the position of the team sport that you have identified?

The principle of reversibility

Unfortunately, as was discussed above, all the good work that we put into training can be reversed. Just as our body will adapt quickly to doing more physical work, so it will adapt even quicker to doing less. A general rule is that it will take three times longer to achieve some progression than it will for the body to return to its original state or condition. Also, we may not be quick to notice this reversal in our physical condition as our physical strength takes longer to reverse than our stamina.

This is why it is important to see our approach to exercise as a longer-term one, even a lifetime-long approach. Being able to maintain regular exercise is as much psychological as it is physiological. It has to be something that we enjoy and that is part of our everyday life. There should also be times, perhaps after a period of intense training for a competition, when we allow some reversibility. The important thing is that we do incorporate exercise as a fun thing into our life together with all the other, sometimes not so healthy, fun things.

Over-training

Yes, we can over-train. The body is far more likely to start 'telling you' that it is being overworked than that it is being underworked. It is important to watch out for the symptoms that the body is displaying. Over-training can lead to:

- ✪ **Repetitive stress injuries to the bones and joints**
- ✪ **Injuries to the muscles and tendons**
- ✪ **Fatigue and lethargy**
- ✪ **Mood swings**
- ✪ **Less resistance to infection**

Over-training can occur in even the simplest of circumstances; if these are not addressed, then, in some extreme conditions, over-training can lead to physical breakdown.

If we are training, and including progression within that training, the body will take time to adapt to the new load or strain that we are putting upon it. If we push the body beyond its adaptive capabilities, this will limit our ability to perform and no real progression will come about.

Over-training is something that can affect anybody. With a person who is in very good physical condition, any progression will be quite minor, so there is often a temptation for them to over-train. It is important that we work with a coach, or have our training approved by a coach. It is more important that if we do feel that we are displaying the symptoms of over-training, we take notice of these, reduce training, and if they persist consult a medical professional.

Rest and recuperation

Rest and recuperation should be introduced:

- ✪ **Within a training session**
- ✪ **Between training sessions**
- ✪ **Immediately, should any injury occur**

During a training session we will be using up energy, and our bodies will be dehydrating through water loss. We will need to have periods of rest in order to allow the body to recover, to take on water, and in some circumstances have a small amount to eat such as a piece of fruit or a cereal bar.

After training, we need to cool down slowly, and let the body's metabolism return to a normal state. We will need to replace water loss, and we will need to give the body nutrition, both to allow it to recover from the exercise and to help it adapt to any progression that we are trying to train it towards.

Sleep is the best form of rest. Through our lifetime, we may find that our sleeping patterns change. We should be aware of this. Regular exercise should help us get a good eight hours' sleep at night. However, we may find that, when training, an additional nap or rest may make us feel better and more able to train.

Because training stimulates us mentally as well as physically, we may have to learn relaxation techniques in order to calm us down before rest and sleep. If we do not have enough rest and sleep, this will directly affect what we are trying to achieve through training. Persistent problems with sleep should be referred to a medical professional.

If we become injured during a training session, or even if we feel the smallest niggle, we should rest immediately. We should also bring the injury to the attention of the coach, or the person in charge of the session. If we do not rest, we could risk permanent damage. If we do have a more serious injury, we must rest for an even longer time, working with a coach, or sport injury specialist, to ensure full recovery.

Key point

'Pain equals gain' – THIS IS WRONG: Pain is your body telling you **stop!**

Physical training and exercise programmes – keeping the individual as the central focus

Any training programme should be designed to meet the needs of the individual. Each individual is different; they are different both physically and mentally, they have different levels of fitness and they have different goals that they wish to achieve.

Initial screening

Before a person begins an exercise programme, it is important that they are screened, and that they are medically able to carry out the exercise programme. An exercise programme can be beneficial in most cases. Special programmes can be devised to help individuals recover from illness or an operation. But, in these circumstances, they should be carried out under medical supervision, or in consultation with the person's doctor. If there is any doubt about a person's health and their ability to carry out a training programme, always advise them to consult their doctor.

When we screen a person before they begin physical activity, we would normally ask them a series of questions, including:

- ✪ **Do you have, or have you had, heart problems?**
- ✪ **Do you feel pain, dizziness or breathlessness when you are physically active?**
- ✪ **Do you have any bone or joint problems that could be made worse by exercise?**
- ✪ **Are you using any medication, either prescribed by your doctor or under your own volition, that may affect your exercising?**
- ✪ **Are you aware of any reason why you should not do physical activity?**

If a person answers yes to any of the above questions, you should advise them to discuss the matter further with their doctor before exercising.

Knowing the individual

Because a training programme should be tailored to meet the needs of the individual, it is important that you get to know the individual. You need to known how they will respond to physical exercise – this was discussed earlier in this chapter. You will need to know the time they have available to train. You will need to know what motivates them to train and why they become bored. You will need to know the type of training they enjoy, and the training that they dislike.

Setting goals

Goals need to be realistic, measurable and agreed.

- ✪ *Goals need to be realistic:* **If a goal, or a target, is set too high, a person can become demotivated. If a goal is set too low, it will be easily achieved and the person may become bored,** stop short of where they should be, or even become over-confident and make mistakes in future training

✪ *Goals need to be measurable*: **We need to know at what point a person reaches a goal that is set, so we should only set goals that can be measured in some way. Introducing a measurable element is important, so that an analysis can be made of the individual's progress in reaching the set goal. This will be beneficial in monitoring the individual and will be helpful in setting future goals**

✪ *Goals need to be agreed*: **In order for an individual to be motivated to reach a goal, they must agree that goal in the first place. A person may need professional help in the setting of goals, as they might set them too high, or wish to try to achieve them too quickly. Goals need to be agreed that will allow the individual to reach them, while retaining motivation to go on and set new goals**

Screening during an activity session

If we know the individual well, we learn quite quickly what to watch out for during training sessions. If they have a medical condition, or have had an injury in the past, we should be aware of any indicators that will show any aggravation of these. If we know the individual, we should also soon get to know when they have reached their limit of activity – even if they don't.

Wherever possible, those who are involved in the supervision of physical activity should have first aid training. When an injury or a medical problem occurs, the session should be stopped immediately and professional help sought.

Though physical activity involves exertion, we need to observe the individual participant for signs of over-exertion and either reduce the intensity of the activity or stop it altogether. Warning signs include:

✪ **Shortness of breath, or heavy breathing**

✪ **Vomiting and feeling sick**

✪ **Loss of focus or dizziness**

✪ **Poor coordination**

✪ **Pain**

Field tests of physical fitness

Field tests of physical fitness are a way of collecting information about the individual's level of fitness. This information can then be used to help in the design of a fitness programme, or to monitor the individual's progress during or at the end of a programme.

Some of the advantages of field tests are that we can:

✪ **Identify specific areas for improvement**

✪ **Highlight any weaknesses to be taken into account**

✪ **Set targets**

✪ **Measure improvement**

✪ **Adjust training programmes**

✪ **Select appropriate training partners for the individual**

✪ **Help with the motivation of the individual**

Field tests are normally quite specific, and they should not be viewed in isolation. A person's level of fitness involves the summation of a number of elements and there is no one test that can tell you what this total summation of fitness is. Field tests should be used only as a guide. Also, field tests can be dangerous. If you carry out a test, make sure that the individual doing the test is physically able to carry it out. When in doubt, consult a tutor or a professional health/fitness instructor. When unable to consult – don't do it.

Before planning any testing, make sure that:

✪ **You know how to carry out the test**

✪ **The facilities and environment where the test is to be carried out are appropriate**

✪ **The test that you are to carry out is appropriate for the person that you are testing**

✪ **You know how reliable the test is, and its margin of error**

✪ **You record the results of the test accurately**

✪ **You can interpret the results of the test accurately**

✪ **You take all necessary safety measures**

Activity 8.6

The tables below outline tests that can be used to indicate levels of fitness. The best way to become familiar with these tests is actually to carry them out.

1   Form a group of two or three

2   Read through the tests, and in consultation with a tutor, decide how you are going to carry out one of the tests on each other

3   Carry out one of the tests

4   When you have recorded the results of your tests, you and your partner(s) should design a poster, or display, showing details and outcomes of the test. You should include tables of results and graphs as appropriate

5   Decide when you are going to carry out the test again

Field tests of aerobic or cardiovascular endurance

These are the performance levels of the cardiovascular and muscular systems for endurance (Table 8.1). In other words: (1) the ability to take in oxygen, (2) the ability to transport it through the body, (3) the ability to use that oxygen efficiently in the muscles.

Name of test	Details and information about the test	How the test works
The Harvard Step Test	• The test indicates the fitness of your cardiovascular system • The test can be performed on most individuals • To carry out the test you will need a gym bench and a stopwatch • A heart rate or pulse rate monitor would be useful to help you take readings during the test	• Resting pulse rate is taken • Individual being tested begins stepping onto bench once every two seconds for three minutes. After finishing, note the pulse rate every minute until it returns to normal • The information on the 'Recovery rate', which you now have, will help establish the person's cardiovascular efficiency
The Multistage Fitness Test	• The test measures the maximal oxygen uptake (VO2 max), the body's capacity to use and consume oxygen • The test may be difficult for the untrained individual • Though the test can be carried out by a number of individuals at the same time, competition should be discouraged • To carry out the test you will need: a flat non-slip surface to run on, two markers 20 metres apart, a prerecorded 'bleep tape' and an efficient tape player	• Go through a warm-up exercise with the individual to be tested • Start the tape and follow any instructions • When the bleeps begin, start the run between the two markers • The run should be at an even pace so a foot is placed over the marker line as each bleep sounds • As the frequency of the bleeps increases, so the pace should be increased, until the person being tested cannot reach the line, or becomes over-tired • The level and number of shuttles that the individual reached can be used in conjunction with a Multistage Fitness Test table to assess their VO2 max

Table 8.1 *Field tests of aerobic or cardiovascular endurance*

Field tests of anaerobic ability

This is the assessment of performance levels in activities where there is no, or little, oxygen use (Table 8.2). The muscles are used in short bursts at high intensity. These tests are for both muscular strength and muscular endurance.

Name of test	Details and information about the test	How the test works
Grip Test	• The test measures the muscular strength • As the name suggests, the test is a measure of the grip of the muscles in the hand and lower arm • To carry out the test you will need a specially designed grip meter	• Check that the grip meter is measuring zero • Adjust the grip on the machine so that the person being tested is holding it with the fingers and thumb in a normally relaxed grip • The grip meter should be by their side • As much force as possible should be exerted through the grip in a continuous squeeze • Repeat the test two or three times and take the highest reading • The reading indicates the kilogram force that the person is normally able to exert
The One Rep Maximum Test	• The test is a measure of muscular strength • The test can be used to measure the strength of muscle groups • The test should only be performed on muscle groups that are reasonably well trained • You should use fixed weight machines to perform the test • The test can be used to help design weight training programmes for muscular strength and muscular endurance	• Decide on the muscle group to be tested and select the appropriate machine e.g. if you were testing the chest and upper body, you would use a bench press machine • Make sure the person being tested is warmed up • Allow them to use the machine on a lighter weight so that they can get used to the machine and the resistance • Set the weight at a level that the individual can move through its range of movement **once** • Alternatively set the weight that allows several reps and estimate one rep maximum
Muscular Endurance Test	• The test measures the strength endurance of different muscle groups • The test can be performed on most people, but a reasonable level of fitness is desirable • To carry out the test you will need: a well-ventilated area, gym mats and a stopwatch	• The test involves an individual repeating an exercise over a minute • The test can involve a series of exercises such as press-ups, leg extensions or sit-ups • The person being tested should be allowed to recover between each individual exercise • Avoid testing similar muscle groups • Record the number of exercises completed during the minute and keep for comparison with future tests

Table 8.2 *Field tests of anaerobic ability*

Field tests of body composition

The composition of the body can have a direct effect on the individual's level of fitness and on their ability to carry out exercise. These tests should be used only as a guide (Table 8.3). Remember, if the same information is taken from two different individuals, two totally different conclusions might be drawn.

Name of test	Details and information about the test	How the test works
Skinfold test	• The test is used to give an indication of the percentage of body fat • To carry out the test you will need: a pair of skinfold callipers, and the manufacturer's instruction booklet with body fat tables • Make sure you follow the manufacturer's instructions in carrying out the test	• The callipers are used to take a series of 'pinch' tests at different parts of the body • Measurements are normally taken on the biceps, the triceps, the shoulder-blade and the thigh • The readings taken are compared with the body fat tables
Measurement of height and weight	• The test is undertaken to make a comparison with the averages of age and gender • To carry out the test you will need an accurate height measure and weighing scales, and height and weight charts	• Measure the weight and the height of the individual to be measured • Remember, training shoes and excessive outdoor clothing do not aid the accuracy of the test • When you feel you have accurate test results, compare these with the tables for the expected results for an 'average' person of their age and gender
Girth measurements	• These are used to measure changes in body shape • To carry out the test you will need a flexible 'tailor's' tape measure	• Carry out a series of measurements of the different circumferences of the body • You can take measurements of the chest, thigh, waist or upper arm • Decide how you want to take the measurement, e.g. inhale/exhale, before a training session/after a training session • Record the information and use this to compare with future measurement

Table 8.3 *Field tests of body composition*

Field tests of flexibility

The level of flexibility is important in designing training or fitness programmes, because they will give an indication of the range of motion around the joint(s) that the individual has (Table 8.4). Remember that, unless we retain a good level of flexibility, this will limit our ability to perform.

Name of test	Details and information about the test	How the test works
Sit and reach test	• Indicates level of flexibility • The test should not be carried out by a person with back problems • A warm-up should be completed before the test • To carry out the test, you will need a 'Sit and reach box' and gym mats	• The person to be tested places the soles of their feet against the box • They then reach forward as far as possible along the scale on the top of the box • They should not perform any sudden movement or lunges • Repeat the test two or three times and record the best score • Store the information to be compared with future results
Range of movement tests	• These tests can be used to measure the range of movement at a single joint, or a number of joints • They can be performed on most people • The joint(s) to be tested should be thoroughly warmed during a warm-up session • To carry out the test you will need to be familiar with the range of movement at the joint to be assessed • To carry out the test you will need a tape measure	• Decide on the joint(s) and range of movement(s) to be assessed • Allow the person being tested to carry out the range of motion and make a written note of any discomfort • Decide how you are going to measure, with the tape, the range of movement, from which starting point to which finishing point and/or compare the degree of movement to that of a 'normal' person • Record the information to compare with future results

Table 8.4 *Field tests of flexibility*

Activity 8.7

Explain the following joint movements:

★ Flexion

★ Abduction

★ Rotation

★ Circumduction

The tests that are discussed in this chapter deal with physical fitness. There are a number of health tests for which equipment is now available, such as blood pressure, blood cholesterol levels or lung function. The type of information that we get from these tests can be a good starting point to measure the general level of health and development of the individual. But, again, check with a tutor or health professional about how best to obtain this type of information.

Training programme design and methods of training

When designing a training programme, the key aspect to success is planning. We need to get to know the individual for whom the programme is to be designed. The correct screening and appropriate testing need to take place before a programme is planned and drawn up. A training plan involves setting goals and objectives for the individual, in consultation with them, to ensure that motivation is maintained. The implementation of the programme is normally a learning process for both trainer and trainee.

Goals that are set for the programme must be clear and realistic. This is important, because when designing a programme we need to consider if the programme/plan:

- **Includes progression**
- **Is clear on how and when overload is incorporated**
- **Accounts for reversibility**
- **Allows adaptations which are measurable**

When deciding on what to include within a training programme, we need to decide:

- **Which aspects of physical fitness we are seeking to improve**
- **What balance we wish to have between the elements of fitness**
- **The activities that will be most appropriate in meeting our goals**

A training programme should include elements that maintain, or improve:

✓ Aerobic Fitness	✚ Stamina
✓ Anaerobic Fitness	✚ Strength
✓ Anaerobic Fitness	✚ Speed
✓ Flexibility	✚ Suppleness

As has been discussed previously, when a person does a particular activity, adaptations occur. If a person follows a particular training programme, the body will adapt to that training programme. We are fortunate in that a range of training methods have been developed over the years, which are designed for the improvement of the different elements of fitness. The validity of these training methods has been established.

It is important that we now look at these different training methods, so that you are better placed to incorporate them within your future fitness training programmes.

Training methods for aerobic fitness

Steady-state training

Steady-state training seeks to raise the heart rate to a pre-determined level, and attempts to maintain a reasonably steady rate of heartbeats per minute. This type of activity can include walking or jogging, or using cardiovascular machines such as a jogger, stepper or rower.

Table 8.5 shows the intensity of steady-state aerobic training in relation to heart rate:

Level of aerobic intensity	Training zone – percentage of maximum heart rate
Low	55–65%
Medium	65–75%
High	75–90%

Table 8.5 *Intensity of steady-state aerobic training in relation to heart rate*

Steady-state training, then, seeks to maintain the heart rate, usually with the aid of a heart rate monitor, within one of these percentage bands. The maximum heart rate is directly related to a person's age, and reduces over time. Figure 8.1 shows the relationship between age and the target aerobic training zones.

A quick way to estimate the maximum heart rate, taking into account age, is to use the formula:

220 – Age = Maximum Heart Rate

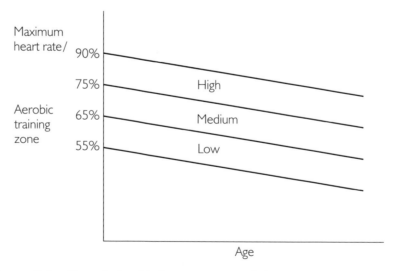

Figure 8.1 *The relationship between age and the target aerobic training zones*

For a person who is 40 years old, their estimated maximum heart rate could be calculated as:

220 – 40 = 180

So if you wished the person to train in the middle of the low-intensity zone, at 60 per cent of maximum heart rate, you could estimate the desired beats per minute of the heart as:

Target Heart Rate (beats per minute)
= 220 – Age × Desired Percentage Heart Rate
= 220 – 40 × 60%
= 108 beats per minute

(Please remember that this is only an estimate and there are more detailed methods available for calculating maximum heart rate and for relating the capacity of the heart to the intensity of the exercise. You may wish to discuss these with your tutor, or carry out some research on your own in a group.)

Activity 8.8

Steady-state training is often recommended as part of a weight management programme. Carry out some research in a small group:

1   Establish if this would be a valid recommendation

2   Write a short report to explain the relationship between steady-state aerobic training and weight management

Interval training

Interval training, as its name suggests, consists of training, at higher and lower intensity, with rest periods, split into a series of intervals. If you went out for a jog, the chances are that you would be doing interval training naturally. As you run up a hill, down a slope or on the flat, so the intensity with which your body is working varies. Interval training programmes exist on most cardiovascular machines, and it can easily be incorporated within a training programme.

The level of intensity of the intervals in the exercise can be monitored by the changes in the heart rate with the use of a heart rate monitor. A person following a low-intensity training programme, which included interval training, could well have results similar to Figure 8.2.

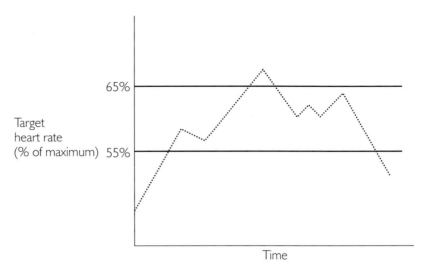

Figure 8.2 *Results of a low-intensity training programme including interval training*

The diagram shows a person doing interval training as part of a steady and continuous exercise. Intensity or rest times could be increased, but should never be increased until a person becomes over-fatigued, or the rest period becomes a total stop. Also, interval training should never be seen as the sole method of training, but as part of an overall training programme.

The key to interval training programmes is in the relationship between the periods (and level) of intensity, and the length of rest periods in between. A good guide is to allow twice the amount of time in low-intensity periods as in high-intensity periods.

Interval training is a very good way of achieving progression in aerobic capacity. It is also a useful method for controlling and monitoring the adaptations of the body.

Fartlek training

Fartlek training was originally developed in Sweden. Fartlek is a Swedish word that means 'speed play' or 'playing with speed'. Fartlek training is similar to interval training in that it involves periods of high- and low-intensity exercise, but the periods are usually far more random, and it is often likened to the physical activity patterns of children during playtime.

A Fartlek jogging/running activity could follow a pattern such as:

- ✪ **Jog gently for ten minutes**
- ✪ **Run at a quick pace for two minutes**
- ✪ **Resume jogging for three minutes**
- ✪ **Sprint for one minute**

- **Resume jogging for two minutes**
- **Walk briskly for two minutes**
- **Resume jogging for five minutes**

Fartlek training is very flexible, and can be based around time, intensity, distances, heart rate targets, and a variety of activities. It allows the person training to work at their own pace and get used to periods of greater speed, or more intense activity, such as they may experience in a game of sport or a race.

Fartlek training can be used, much like interval training, to push back thresholds and develop aerobic fitness. But Fartlek training should be used in allowing the participant to work at their own pace, feeling for themselves the limits and thresholds in their bodies. The participant should always finish a Fartlek training session feeling motivated because they know they still have something 'left in the tank'.

Training for anaerobic fitness – speed/speed endurance

The body can be said to be working anaerobically when it is not using oxygen. This normally takes place when the body is working more intensely. The anaerobic system is used for short bursts of activity by using energy stored in the muscles. When we are training, or participating in a game of sport, our body often needs to work faster. We breathe faster, our heart rate increases, we become short of breath. If we have to do a sudden sprint, our body may well be going through the anaerobic threshold as shown in Figure 8.3.

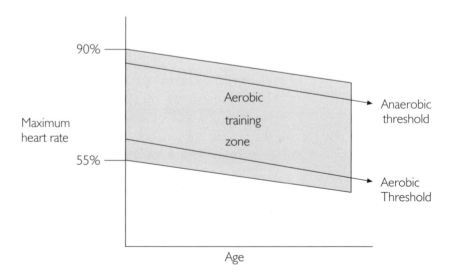

Figure 8.3 *Going through the anaerobic threshold*

As can be seen from the diagram, when our bodies are working at the highest part of the aerobic zone, our bodies are working in an anaerobic way. We should only do this if we already have a good level of fitness. Training the body beyond the anaerobic threshold contributes very little to improving the body's aerobic capacity. Training the anaerobic capacity will only mean that we are improving the ability of the body to work at a greater intensity for (marginally) longer periods of time.

The ways in which we could devise training to improve anaerobic speed training have already been discussed within the section on aerobic training. What we would seek to do is to design training plans that would include a programme of progressive short/intensive activities. These could be incorporated as:

✪ **Interval training**

✪ **Sprinting or speed drills**

✪ **Hill sprinting, or sprinting incorporating resistance**

Activity 8.9

Form a small group and discuss the ways in which a 30-minute interval-training programme aimed at aerobic fitness would differ from a 30-minute programme designed to improve anaerobic fitness. Once you have done this, discuss this with the whole of your group.

Training methods for anaerobic fitness – muscular strength, power, endurance

Fixed resistance machines and free weights

Training to improve muscular strength and muscular endurance can be carried out by developing a training programme, or including within a training programme, 'progressive resistance training' with specially designed machines, or free weights. Free resistance machines are found in most gyms and include bench press, 'pec dec', leg curl and leg press machines. Free weights include barbells and dumbbells, which either have a fixed weight at the ends, or weights that can be removed or added to.

When deciding which method to use, or how to combine the use of fixed and free weights, it is useful to consider their advantages and disadvantages:

Fixed resistance machines	Free weights
✪ Safe – especially for beginners, or if training without a partner	✪ Their use develops greater balance and coordination
✪ Easy to use and quick to adjust the resistance/weight	✪ Accommodates the uniqueness of the individual's limb movements
✪ Good for developing major muscle groups	✪ Ancillary, 'fixator' muscles are also developed in training
✪ Designed for the 'average' person	✪ Gains in strength usually more rapid than with fixed weight machines

Though weight training can be used to develop a particular muscle or muscle group, this should never be done in isolation; muscles should always be worked in pairs, and weight training should be completed as part of a 'total body' programme.

When planning a programme for fixed or free weights we need to consider:

✪ The physical condition and the needs of the individual
✪ The number of '**reps**' within each exercise – how many times they will repeat the movement
✪ The weight/resistance that will be used in the exercise
✪ The number of times they will repeat a set – '**sets**'
✪ The rest period between sets
✪ The ordering of the exercises, e.g. arm vs. leg, upper body vs. lower body

Also, when planning a programme, you will need to decide if you are training to achieve more muscular strength, or muscular strength/endurance. This is because of the factors contained within Table 8.6.

To improve muscular strength	To improve muscular strength/endurance
✓ Lower repetitions 5–10 reps	✓ Higher repetitions 10–15 reps
✓ High weight/resistance used	✓ Moderate/low weight/resistance used
✓ Longer rest periods between sets	✓ Shorter rest periods between sets

Table 8.6 *Training goals*

There are a number of training methods that can be used within weight training to develop progression. If you are interested in weight training, it may well be worth your while, individually or within a group, to try to find out some more information about the following:

★ Set training
★ Pyramid training
★ Eccentric training
★ Split training

Plyometrics

Plyometric training is used to develop and improve speed, agility and power. The plyometric training method uses explosive jumping, leaping, bounding and hopping, normally performed with only body weight. Exercises are used that rapidly stretch and then contract the muscle. This type of training helps the muscles produce a powerful force quickly.

Plyometric exercises can include:

✪ **Jumping off an elevated platform and then bounding forward**
✪ **A push-up exercise with a hand clap**
✪ **Single leg hopping or bounding forward**
✪ **Hurdle hopping**
✪ **Bunny hops**

Plyometric training can be dangerous and should only be used after a thorough warm-up. This type of training is often used to develop a muscle movement used in a particular sport or exercise. It can be very effective, if incorporated within a weight-training programme. But it should not be undertaken by untrained, injured or unfit individuals, and it should always be used with the greatest of care.

Circuit training

Circuit training involves carrying out activities or exercises at a series of 'stations' with rest periods between each station. Completing a weight training session in a gym is a form of circuit as one goes through a series of exercises at weight training 'stations'. Though a circuit of activities can be incorporated within a training session, circuit training is normally thought of as a separate activity usually carried out in a gym or a sports hall.

Circuits can be designed to incorporate a great variety of activities and could include stations for:

- **'Free-hand' exercises such as press-ups, squats or sit-ups**
- **Anaerobic exercises such as short sprints or shuttle runs**
- **Small free weight exercises such as a bicep curl or a lateral raise**
- **Skill activities such as dribbling with a ball**
- **Stretching between activities**
- **A plyometric exercise**

Circuit training can be very useful, as it can

- **Be designed to help improve fitness for a particular activity**
- **Be adapted for different fitness levels**
- **Be used to develop different *types* of fitness**
- **Incorporate skill training**
- **Be performed with little equipment**
- **Be changed quickly to provide variety and maintain motivation**

When designing a circuit we need to decide:

- **If the circuit is appropriate for the individual**
- **What stations to include**
- **How the stations are ordered**
- **How the stations interlink, e.g. work different muscle groups/provide variety**
- **How many times the circuit is to be completed**
- **The time spent at each station**
- **How rest periods are to be incorporated**
- **How we are to warm up the participant appropriately to meet the demands of *each* station**
- **How we are going to cool down the participant**

Activity 8.11

Choose a sport that you play, or are interested in. Design a short circuit of activities appropriate to this sport. Once you have done this, explain to a colleague, or to your group, your reasons for choosing the activities, and how the circuit would benefit the sportsperson involved.

Training methods for flexibility

Stretching of the muscles should always be carried out as part of a warm-up session to prepare the muscles for the main activity. However, developmental flexibility, to improve flexibility and mobility, should be carried out when the body is fully warmed up, or as part of a cool-down session. In a flexibility training session you should attempt to stretch most muscles, but particularly those around the more mobile joints, and the muscles that you have been using during the activity.

You should always be careful not to overstretch. When we stretch a muscle, a stretch reflex occurs, and we feel a slight discomfort in the muscle; this is our bodies' way of telling us to be careful. However, we must learn to distinguish between this slight natural discomfort and actual pain.

Static stretching

Static stretching involves gradually stretching the muscle, moving into a fully stretched position, and holding the stretch. You can use gravity or a partner (who is aware of their role) to help you move into a stretch position. Once you achieve the stretch, it should be held for at least ten seconds. As you feel more comfortable in the stretch, the length of time that you hold it should be increased. Once you complete the stretch, you should slowly release it, and stretch the opposite muscle.

Ballistic stretching

Ballistic stretching is dynamic stretching. It involves a rapid bouncing and swinging movement of the limb around a joint. The muscles and joints should always be thoroughly warm and mobile before any ballistic stretching. Ballistic stretching is normally only performed after static stretching.

Ballistic stretching is usually used to help trained athletes develop specific flexibility for their event, such as hurdling, 'kicking' activities, dance or martial arts. For most other activities ballistic stretching should be avoided.

PNF stretching

PNF, or proprioceptive neuromuscular facilitation, stretching is when:

- **The joint is gradually stretched to the limit of its natural range of movement, or until a stretch reflex occurs.**
- **The stretch is held for ten to thirty seconds. If the stretch reflex has passed, the muscle is contracted in the stretch position, then allowed to relax, and an attempt made to stretch further until another stretch reflex occurs, when the stretch is held again**

The person carrying out the stretch, once they feel confident they have stretched the muscle adequately, should slowly release the stretch. They should next stretch the muscle that acts as the opposite muscle to the one just stretched. As the flexibility improves, the time for which the stretch is held should be gradually increased.

PNF stretching can also be done with the help of a partner or coach, but always make sure that they are experienced and respond to the instructions of the participant.

The benefits of exercise and fitness training

It has generally been agreed that regular exercise throughout your life can be beneficial. Unfortunately, because of the principle of reversibility these effects cannot be stored up. However, regular exercise in early life will help the body to develop to its full potential and create good habits of physical activity for later in life.

The benefits of regular exercise include:

✪ **Reducing the risk of disease**

✪ **Improving health for specific conditions**

✪ **Improving mental or psychological well-being**

Regular exercise can reduce the risk of disease by:

✓ **Controlling obesity**

✓ **Reducing the likelihood of smoking**

✓ **Maintaining the heart**

✓ **Controlling cholesterol levels, which helps to offset coronary heart disease**

✓ **Controlling high blood pressure**

✓ **Helping to reduce the risk of diabetes and strokes in adulthood**

✓ **And there is increasing evidence that regular exercise is associated with a reduced risk of some cancers**

Regular exercise can help improve specific conditions such as:

✓ **Arthritis**

✓ **Osteoporosis**

✓ **Back problems**

✓ **Heart disease**

✓ **Recovery from an illness or surgical operation**

✓ **Recovery from a physical injury or accident**

Regular exercise can help improve mental or psychological well-being by:

✓ **Reducing anxiety and depression**

✓ **Improving self-esteem**

✓ **Controlling stress**

✓ **Reducing likelihood of addiction or eating disorders**

Long-term effects of exercise and the body's adaptations

As was stated at the beginning of this chapter, the body will always (at least try to) adapt to the exercise and work that is placed upon it. When we design fitness programmes that work the body aerobically, or anerobically, or try to improve strength, stamina, speed or suppleness, the body will try and adapt accordingly.

The adaptations that the body makes to exercise can be seen in three areas:

✪ **Circulation**

✪ **Respiration**

✪ **Muscular**

The circulatory system adapts to exercise by:

✓ **Increasing the volume and muscular strength of the heart, allowing more blood to be pumped around the body**

✓ **Improving the efficiency of the blood in carrying oxygen to the muscles**

✓ **Increasing the number and strength of capillaries that transport the blood**

The respiratory system adapts to exercise by:

✓ **The lungs' volume increasing**

✓ **The lungs utilising more of the oxygen that they draw in, and becoming more efficient at expelling carbon dioxide**

✓ **The respiratory muscles becoming more efficient**

The muscular system adapts to exercise by:

✓ **Improving its ability to store and produce energy**

✓ **Improving its ability to use oxygen**

✓ **Improving its ability to offset fatigue**

✓ **The muscles growing in size and becoming stronger**

The key to developing a fitness programme, and to help the body become and stay fit, is to remember that the body is one unit, and 'bits' of it cannot be seen or trained in isolation.

Revision questions

1 What are the four components of physical fitness?

2 What is the difference between cardiovascular and cardio-respiratory functions?

3 What action does isotonic strength involve?

4 Give three factors that could limit flexibility.

5 What is the recommended essential body-fat level for women?

6 How might heredity affect a person's ability to train?

7 What is the difference between 'overload' and 'progression'?

8 In relation to training, what does 'FIT' mean?

9 How can you use 'FIT' to improve physical fitness?

10 Explain 'the principle of reversibility'.

11 Give two outcomes of 'over-training'.

12 'Pain = Gain': is this true?

13 Give examples of two questions that should be asked during initial screening.

14 Why do goals need to be measurable?

15 Give three reasons for carrying out a test of physical fitness.

16 Give an example of a field test for aerobic fitness.

17 Give an example of steady-state training.

18 What is a 'set'?

19 What are the differences between static and ballistic stretching?

20 State two benefits of regular physical activity.

Design a six-week training programme for yourself, or a colleague with whom you will work, making and keeping appropriate records.

Make sure you:

★ Carry out initial screening

★ Plan the activities within the programme

★ Identify goals

★ Identify and carry out appropriate tests

★ Fulfil the programme

At the end of the programme, carry out any necessary activities which you may need to present your programme and the results of the programme in a report.

Prepare a display of your findings. This should include appropriate tables and graphs.

Sport and recreation leadership

9

Objectives

- Explore the role and qualities required of a sports leader
- Prepare how to lead activities in a safe manner and in accordance with legal and approved working practices
- Learn how to plan and prepare activities
- Learn how to lead and deliver activities
- Understand the importance of providing feedback to the group
- Learn to evaluate how the activity went
- Find out where you can obtain support from organisations both locally and nationally

Participation in sport is fun, exciting and extremely rewarding. For many, becoming a sports leader is the next stage of personal development, helping others to enjoy the benefits of taking part in organised sports and recreation activities.

Introduction

Sports leaders work with children, adults, senior citizens or those with particular needs, usually in a voluntary capacity with local clubs or organisations. Increasingly, however, private clubs and leisure centres are employing people with sports leadership qualifications to lead sports and recreation sessions.

Being a good sports coach is one of the many roles played by a sports leader, and so it is important that you also study the principles of coaching in Unit 10 Principles of sports coaching. You will also find it useful to read Unit 11 Sports psychology as many of these principles will be relevant in your capacity as a sports leader.

Careful attention should also be paid to the safety principles that you learn about in Unit 2 Safe working practices. Safety will underpin all that you do and you should be aware of both moral and legal issues.

David Cave Photography

Figure 9.1   *Coach giving a demonstration during a session.*

Further reference should also be made to Unit 5 Customer service as it is important to realise that your participants are using your service and so their needs as customers need to be met or even exceeded.

You are encouraged to work towards achieving a sports leader or coaching qualification. Your tutor can advise you how this can be attained; however, a list of useful contacts will be provided at the end of this chapter.

Completion of the activities will help provide assessment evidence for your portfolio.

Role and qualities required of a sports leader

Sports leaders are in a position of responsibility and influence and so it is vital that you are aware of the qualities and attributes that will be expected of you.

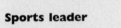

Sports leader
Someone who will plan, organise and lead an activity session that meets the needs of a particular group of people

Types of leadership

Different situations require different types of leadership styles, according to the needs of the participants at any moment in time. Let us look at typical situations:

- ✪ **The need to quieten down a noisy group**
- ✪ **Deciding on which route to take on a country ramble**
- ✪ **Discussing the long-term objectives of a sports group**
- ✪ **Organising relay teams at the end of an activity**
- ✪ **Controlling a group immediately following an accident**

Each of these situations requires leadership – but each will be handled in a different way.

Autocratic leadership will involve you exercising complete control of the situation without any discussion or debate. Such control is usually required when discipline is needed or during an emergency when an immediate decision is taken and the leader takes action without delay.

There is no time to seek the views of the group or indeed to allow any member of the group to disassociate themselves from the group or from your instructions.

Democratic leadership on the other hand follows a period of some discussion and is generally carried out with the agreement of the group. It may be that different members of the group will carry out different activities subject to your approval.

It is most unlikely that your style of leadership will be totally democratic or even autocratic, but on a continuum somewhere between the two styles.

For example, when considering the situations mentioned earlier we might place the style of leadership as follows:

Quietening a noisy group will require a more autocratic style as shown:

Democratic ◀┄┄┄┄┄┄┄┄┄┄┄┄┄ ×┄┄┄▶ Autocratic

On the other hand, your actions in a state of an emergency following an accident or when evacuating a building will require even greater control:

Democratic ◄--x--► Autocratic

Organising relay teams will require an assertive approach but may involve you listening to the advice of others. An element of democracy is then introduced:

Democratic ◄----------------------x----------------► Autocratic

When discussing which route to take on a country ramble, it may be appropriate to consider the views of those who are going; however, as the leader you will still need to make a final decision – such a leadership style would be considered more democratic:

Democratic ◄--------x----------------------------► Autocratic

Agreeing a longer-term strategy with a participant will require a considerable amount of negotiation with their coach if they are to be committed to achieving a goal. This will need more time for discussion and may need some direction from you, but it is essentially democratic in style:

Democratic ◄---x-------------------------------► Autocratic

You will have to decide, throughout the session that you are taking, what the best style of leadership should be, and this is likely to change depending on the situation that you are in. Adopting the wrong style of leadership can have serious consequences. Taking too long to make decisions and implement them quickly may lead to further problems – causing further indiscipline and even causing injuries. However, if you are too autocratic when it is not appropriate to be so, this might result in your participants being resentful even to a point where they might ignore or lose respect for you.

Clearly it is important to consider your style of leadership carefully. Seek the views of your tutor and those who took part in your session as to whether your style was right for each situation.

Activity 9.1

Describe four different situations that you might find yourself in when leading an activity. Show on a continuum, as described earlier, the style of leadership that you feel might be most appropriate in each situation.

You may wish to reconsider your answer once you have experienced the situation in practice.

Communication

Communication is made in so many different ways, again depending upon the situation.

Consider the following forms of communication.

Verbal communication

- ✪ Issuing instructions, to organise the session
- ✪ Providing guidance or direction, when introducing a new skill
- ✪ Providing feedback, letting the participant know how they are doing
- ✪ Discussing tactics, goals and strategies
- ✪ Listening and responding; answering any questions or clearing up any misunderstandings
- ✪ Speaking to a group, i.e. a committee, a group of parents etc., in order to present your proposals

David Cave Photography

Figure 9.2 *The coach lets the student know how he is doing.*

UNIT 9 SPORT AND RECREATION LEADERSHIP

It may be appropriate to use various forms of technology that will help you communicate more effectively. Consider also the use of a portable microphone or loudhailer when operating in a large or noisy area. The benefits of mobile telephones or radios when maintaining contact with others can also be essential to the smooth running of events.

- ✪ **When communicating verbally, make sure that what you say is clear and understood by the audience – this means using terminology that is appropriate:**

    'Accelerate off the blocks' may be understood by you but not by a group of ten-year-olds. 'After leaving the blocks, increase your speed' may be a more appropriate instruction.

    'Get in a line' is not obvious either. 'Form a line behind one another – here!' is clearer.

- ✪ **Check for understanding, by asking questions or observing closely, to make sure that your instructions are being followed**

- ✪ **It goes without saying that what you say needs to be accurate. Always read up on the rules of activities or games beforehand, or if you are unsure ask someone**

- ✪ **Consider the timing of your intervention:**

    - **Wait until the group is quiet before speaking**

    - **Make sure that you have the group's attention and try to establish eye contact**

    - **Be brief, and give only one point of information at a time**

    - **Reinforce skills where appropriate**

    - **Offer feedback as soon as it is appropriate to do so – this can be during the activity or immediately afterwards**

- ✪ **Make sure that you can be heard. Position the group so that you are facing them – if you are unsure, ask if everyone can hear you (by a show of hands). You will need to adjust your tone according to the situation – and avoid shouting all the time; it is not necessary and you will only lose your voice!**

- ✪ **Be positive with your feedback ('do this', as opposed to 'don't do this') and reinforce your comments with visual demonstrations. Avoid being sarcastic and look and sound enthusiastic – 'let's get into groups', said with your hands in your pockets, is not likely to provoke an enthusiastic response!**

David Cave Photography

Figure 9.3 *The coach needs to correct any faults during a demonstration.*

Visual communication

'A picture is worth a thousand words.'

- ✪ **Provide a demonstration – either by yourself or by a competent performer (live or on video). This can be so much clearer than telling someone. When teaching a new skill, or providing feedback, visual reinforcement is vital. Make sure that it is clear, accurate and can be seen by everyone**

- ✪ **Use video playback to provide feedback or analyse a team or individual performance**

- ✪ **Show videos of successful performances to highlight particular skills or tactics or even to motivate**

- ✪ **Use a white/blackboard or flip chart to write down or reinforce instructions**

- ✪ **Posters and leaflets used effectively can promote your activities**

- ✪ **Consider how you intend to distribute posters and leaflets and if you are using a notice board keep it tidy and up to date**

David Cave Photography

Figure 9.4 *Coach giving a demonstration.*

✪ **Computer technology can be used to enhance visual images, which can be used to produce newsletters or presentations**

No form of communication should ever be used to offend or insult anyone. There is no place for this in sport and care should be taken when working with young children, people with special needs, or those from ethnic minorities.

Special arrangements may need to be made with those who have visual or audio impairment or who have language difficulties.

Working with others

Good sports leaders will call upon others for help or advice, when required.

Working with assistants makes it easier to supervise your session, allows for more feedback to be given to the participants and provides a tremendous opportunity to introduce others to the role of a sports leader. Assistants can help in the following ways:

- ✪ **Checking and setting up equipment**
- ✪ **Dealing with parents, collecting forms or money**
- ✪ **Helping those with special requirements**
- ✪ **Driving a minibus**
- ✪ **Preparing drinks or refreshments**
- ✪ **Taking small groups – giving feedback or refereeing**
- ✪ **Helping to put equipment away**

Having an assistant will also be valuable in the event of an emergency:

- ✪ **Notifying the emergency services**
- ✪ **Controlling the remainder of the group if someone is injured**
- ✪ **If qualified, providing first aid treatment**

As a sports leader you should be encouraging more assistants to help you, but remember to offer support and guidance, particularly if the assistant is new to the role.

It can also be useful to call upon other sports leaders for help – perhaps as a referee in a tournament, or if you need specialist support at any time (i.e. when working with someone with special needs), or if you are working with particularly large numbers. You might also wish to discuss aspects of your activity programme, or seek new ideas.

You should also maintain links with the coaches or instructors in local clubs.

Sports leaders have an important role to play in guiding those who may have a particular desire or talent to progress further – many coaches will be delighted to come along and help out at one of your sessions and talk to those who may wish to consider pursuing their interest further.

Your role as a sports leader

You are now in a position of responsibility.

Up to now you will have been the one receiving the support, playing the games, practising the skills and having a laugh. But now it is you who is in charge!

People will now look to you to make decisions, give direction and take control. You are a role model to those in your charge (you may not even be aware of it) and others will look to you to lead by example. So, what does this involve?

- ✪ First of all, you need to be well organised, having thought carefully about the objectives of the session, the resources required and the content and structure of your programme. This means having to **plan** what you do. (We will look at this in more detail later)

✪ You will gain respect for your knowledge, and your ability to pass it on to others (again this means being prepared in advance)

✪ Enjoy what you are doing, be enthusiastic and encourage others as much as possible by being positive, and rewarding with praise. Your influence can encourage or discourage participation in sport for life

✪ Finally, and it should go without saying, your own behaviour should be a good example – dress appropriately, be on time for your sessions, avoid smoking or drinking in the presence of young children. And watch your language!

As the person responsible for the safety of those in your group, you have a 'duty of care' to ensure that you have taken all reasonable precautions to avoid an accident happening, and above all, remain vigilant at all times.

The personal rewards of being a sports leader are intrinsic, in that encouraging others and seeing the results of your efforts can be extremely satisfying. Your enthusiasm will have a huge influence on others. This should still be the case even if you are fortunate to receive payment for your work as a sports leader.

Safety

Your main concern at all times is the safety of yourself and others. Sports activities by their very nature are extremely hazardous – some more than others; but by taking sensible precautions accidents can be avoided or minimised.

By law you have a 'duty of care' to those for whom you are responsible – this means being able to demonstrate, if required to do so by a Court of Law, that you have taken all reasonable steps to minimise the risk of an accident. In the unfortunate event of an accident, you will need to prove also that you had taken all steps to provide the best possible treatment and aftercare.

Of course you do not have just a legal obligation but also a moral one, to ensure that those in your charge are safe.

The law

It is beyond the scope of this chapter to cover all the relevant Acts, Regulations and Codes of Practice that apply to sports leaders. You should, however, be familiar with those referred to in Unit 2 Safe working practices, in particular:

- ✪ *The Health and Safety at Work Act*: **This will have implications on those who employ sports leaders in ensuring that they operate safely, but also in making sure that sports leaders do not endanger themselves or other employees (i.e. by leaving equipment lying around)**
- ✪ *Fire Safety and Safety of Places of Sport Act 1987*: **As a sports leader, you, your assistants and your participants should be familiar with the means of escape and the procedures involved in evacuating in an emergency. Make sure that fire escape routes are not blocked**
- ✪ *Data Protection Act 1998*: **If you do hold information on individuals, you need to comply with this Act**
- ✪ *Children Act 1989*: **This will apply to most sports leaders as it affects everyone who has responsibility for planning, managing and delivering services to children. Child protection issues are extremely important in sport, and sports leaders can obtain advice from National Governing Bodies of Sport, the National Coaching Foundation, and the Sports Council**
- ✪ *Codes of Practice*: **Sports leaders should endeavour to keep up to date with their training in order to be aware of codes of**

practice advised by various bodies in respect of operating safely. It goes without saying that all sports leaders should keep their qualifications as up to date as possible

Risk assessment

One of the first aspects of planning for any activity is to conduct a risk assessment. You will learn how to complete a full risk assessment in Unit 2 Safe working practices. Example forms are given in Figure 9.5. The same principles apply:

1   **Identify all hazards**
2   **Establish the risk**
3   **Evaluate existing controls and if necessary state additional measures to reduce the risk**
4   **Record the likelihood of an accident occurring**
5   **Record the severity if an accident were to occur**
6   **Implement further measures where required**
7   **Monitor and amend measures as appropriate**

Activity 9.2

▶ **TASK 1**

With the aid of a word processor, devise a suitable form that you can use to conduct a risk assessment.

▶ **TASK 2**

Conduct a risk assessment on an activity that you are going to be leading or assisting with.

Gathering information on the participants

The more information that you have on your group, the better prepared you will be in:

○ **Planning appropriate activities**
○ **Ensuring that you have the right equipment**

Hazard	Severity Score (1–5)	Probability Score (1–5)	Total Risk Score (Severity Score × Prob score)	Measures taken to reduce risk	Reduced risk store as a result of action

Evaluating health and safety hazards

(a)   Hazard Severity

Score	Category	Examples of consequences
5	VERY HIGH	Causing multiple death and widespread destruction
4	HIGH	Causing death or serious injury to an individual
3	MODERATE	Causing injury or disease requiring more than three days off work
2	SLIGHT	Minor injury which would allow individuals to continue work with First Aid
1	NIL	No risk of injury or disease

Evaluating health and safety hazards

(b)   Hazard Probability

Score	Category	Examples of consequences
5	VERY LIKELY	Almost 100% certainty if work continues
4	LIKELY	Needs additional factor such as wind, vibration or carelessness
3	QUITE POSSIBLE	Needs additional factors such as vehicle left running, failing to replace light bulb when it is the only source of lighting etc.
2	POSSIBLE	Needs other factors such as worn steps, cracked window, frayed or damaged cables etc.
1	NOT LIKELY	Only a risk under freak conditions and all reasonable and practical precautions have been taken

Figure 9.5   *Sample risk assessment form*

- ✪ **Having the correct number and appropriately trained assistants**
- ✪ **Dealing with medical issues**
- ✪ **Contacting parents or guardians in the event of an emergency**

This will mean collecting information such as

- ✪ **Numbers and ages of children**
- ✪ **Emergency contact numbers**
- ✪ **Name and address of doctor**
- ✪ **Details of any medical condition, or prescribed medication**
- ✪ **Resources and equipment available**

You should keep a register of all children in attendance and maintain an awareness of your group at all times.

Activity 9.3

With the aid of a word processor, design a form that can be given to potential participants to gather all the relevant information necessary for planning a safe activity programme.

▼▼▼▼▼▼▼▼▼

Emergency Action Plan

A document that shows the layout of the building and the position of fire bells, fire extinguishers and emergency exits. Procedures for emergency evacuation will also be included

First aid provision

A first-aider should be in attendance at all sessions.
A first-aider is someone who has a recognised, up-to-date qualification

▲▲▲▲▲▲▲▲▲

Emergency procedures

Make sure that you, your assistants and the participants are aware of procedures in the event of an emergency and, if indoors, how the building should be evacuated. Make it your business to find out where the nearest telephone and first aid box are. Leisure facilities should provide you with a copy of the Emergency Action Plan, which you need to study carefully.

Prevention of injury

Warm-up

Always warm up prior to starting any activity. The colder the environment, the longer and more vigorous the warm-up should be. And remember to keep warm while you progress into your main activity. A common fault of leaders is to have the participants standing around (getting cold again) while they get the groups organised and explain the next activity.

David Cave Photography

Figure 9.6 *A class warming up by stretching: the coach should be able to see the pupils at all times.*

The warm-up should involve whole body movements with no undue stress on the joints. The activities should *gradually* increase the pulse rate with the participants feeling a *progressive* increase in temperature.

This means starting off slowly and gradually increasing the tempo.

It is useful to carry out some mild static stretching across the main joints, holding the stretch for around 10–15 seconds. (More information on this later.)

Cool-down

You should allow the participants the opportunity to cool down following strenuous activity, at the end of the session. This can be done by carrying out some light exercises or jogging/walking followed by some stretching. This will bring the body's core temperature down and assist in eliminating any waste products built up during exercise.

Observation and awareness

Keep vigilant at all times and avoid excessive fatigue – remember children in particular will often try their hardest all of the time. Ensure that fluid intake is maintained at regular intervals to avoid dehydration.

Children are particularly sensitive to temperature change – they get very cold or hot much faster than adults. Often you may feel all right, but the child can be suffering quite badly – and will probably mention it to you.

Correct clothing

Participants should be wearing clothing that is appropriate to the activity and change into their everyday clothing afterwards. Quite apart from reasons of hygiene, incorrect clothing may restrict movement, which could in turn cause an injury.

Some sports will require proper safety clothing, i.e. shin pads, gloves, mouth guards, helmets, life jackets etc. Do NOT ignore the advice of the Governing Body and make it your business to be aware of the proper safety clothing.

For most activities and games it is not safe to allow pupils to wear jewellery (rings, necklaces, watches, earrings, etc.), so make a point of asking them to remove these prior to the activity. Where they cannot be removed, the items should be covered by tape.

Outdoor activities need to consider the weather conditions and both you and your participants should be prepared accordingly. This needs advance planning, with guidance given to parents on the expected conditions and what will be appropriate to bring. Give plenty of advance notice as parents may need to buy certain items. It is often possible to hire items such as boots and jackets.

Equipment

Use only equipment that is

- ✪ **Appropriate to the age and ability of the participants**
- ✪ **Properly maintained**
- ✪ **Meets approved safety standards (Governing Body can advise)**

Always store equipment tidily and supervise closely the erection and dismantling of large or awkward items.

Changes in conditions

Outdoor activities require close attention to be paid to the weather conditions and light. In the event of deterioration in either, cease the activity, regardless of the disappointment. There can be no compromise on safety.

Activity 9.4

Design a safety leaflet that can be given to participants (and parents if appropriate) in relation to the activity that you are involved in. The leaflet should make clear the clothing and equipment needed for safe participation, safety rules, and any other information relating to their safety.

Unless you are fully qualified, having achieved the appropriate National Governing Body qualification, you should NOT allow yourself to be left to take a group on your own. Your tutor or other qualified person should always accompany you.

Organisations or individuals that offer any outdoor adventure activity are required by law to have an Activity Licence. The contact is listed at the end of this chapter. This involves meeting certain safety criteria.

Insurance and public liability

If you organise activities that are paid for by customers, you should have proper insurance cover that also covers you (or the organisation and its members) for public liability.

Public liability insurance will cover any costs incurred as a result of a claim for damages made against you. Solicitor's costs to defend a claim can be very expensive and so it is reassuring to leave the arrangements for this with your insurers.

Most Governing Bodies will be able to advise on how you can obtain insurance cover. In many cases you will have to satisfy certain criteria before being accepted, and you should read the conditions carefully as certain activities may have restrictions on them. If you do work (even voluntarily) for an organisation, check with them that you are covered by their insurance policy.

Of course, being insured does not avoid the possibility of criminal charges being made against you in the event of you being negligent. You need to demonstrate vigilance at all times.

The planning process

Find out as much as you can about the group that you are to lead.

What are their reasons for taking part?

- ✪ **Fun?**
- ✪ **To get fit?**
- ✪ **To make friends?**
- ✪ **To learn new skills?**
- ✪ **A leisure pursuit?**
- ✪ **Give mum and dad a break?**

Your aims and objectives must be compatible with theirs. If not, you will soon lose all credibility and will probably see a drop in numbers.

Good planning and preparation can help ensure that you run safe, enjoyable activities that achieve their objectives. A sample session plan is shown below. The key stages in planning a sports or activities session are as follows:

SAMPLE SESSION PLAN

NAME OF COACH_____

VENUE _____ DATE _____ TIME _____

Objectives:	No. of Participants: Ages: Ability Level:	Special Requirements:	Equipment Needed	Space Available: Duration of session:
	Content	**Teaching Points**	**Organisation**	**Time Allocation**
Warm-Up				
Activities				
Games				
Relays				
Cool-Down				

1 Setting objectives

Objectives of the sports leader

The principal objective will be to successfully organise and deliver a session (or series of sessions) that meets the needs of the group, and individuals within the group. This will involve

- ✪ **Ensuring effective communications before, during and after the session**
- ✪ **Knowing about the rules of the activity (if any)**
- ✪ **Being clear about the structure and organisational requirements of each session**
- ✪ **Knowing about the correct warm-up procedures**
- ✪ **Understanding how to use the equipment correctly**

This will require some preparation by you, as sports leader, and may involve you contacting your tutor or other sports leaders or coaches for advice.

Objectives of the group

Your principal aim here is for your group to get to know one another, make friends and work together as a team. A happy group is usually easy to work with and achieves an enjoyable and successful outcome.

Objectives of the individuals

Each individual must feel that the activity is worthwhile and will achieve his or her objectives. It is helpful if all of the individuals have similar objectives. For example, if a few in the group just want to enjoy themselves and not take any of the activities seriously, those who do will soon get fed up.

Proper planning of the groups beforehand may avoid such mismatches.

Individual objectives may include:

- ✪ **Improving fitness**
- ✪ **Learning new skills**
- ✪ **Improving co-ordination**
- ✪ **Meeting a particular challenge**
- ✪ **Having fun**

Indeed it is likely that many will have more than one of the above objectives, perhaps even all of them!

Figure 9.7 *Improving co-ordination: the use of basic equipment can help structure a practice.*

Objectives of the organisation

Whilst all organisations will wish to meet the needs of its members, they will have obligations in terms of making sure that resources are used effectively, that costs are kept to a minimum and that there are sufficient members to make the organisation viable.

2 Having knowledge of the participants

We discussed earlier the importance of knowing about your participants for safety reasons and this will involve the collection of medical as well as other important information, but in order that you can plan to meet the needs of each participant you will also need to find out:

- ✪ **Their reasons for participating. Your objectives must match up with the group and the programme of activities planned accordingly**

- ✪ **The level of ability of the members of the group. Your session will need to challenge the group sufficiently for it to be rewarding. If the challenge is too hard or too easy, the group will soon become bored. You may also need to plan for having a mixed ability group by having a range of suitable activities prepared**

- ✪ **Their age and gender; so that you bring along the right equipment and plan the most appropriate activities**

- ✪ **Any special needs. There should be no barrier to participation in your sport or activity programme; however, this may need you to prepare more thoroughly to ensure that you have the correct resources (assistants, equipment, transport, access etc.) to meet the needs of those who require additional support.**

  Special needs may include:

  - **Visual or audio impairment**

  - **A physical or mental disability**

  - **Religious or cultural barriers**

  - **Transport or financial difficulties**

3 Having knowledge of the facilities and equipment

The type of venue and the space available will dictate the activities that you will be able to carry out. You will need to check the following.

Booking the facility

- ✪ **Has the facility/space been reserved or confirmed in writing?**

- ✪ **Do I need to produce a confirmation letter on arrival?**

- ✪ **What are the arrangements for paying?**

- ✪ **What agreement is there for early access, use of equipment, changing, first aid cover etc.?**

- ✪ **What are the arrangements for notifying you or checking for cancellations (due to bad weather conditions/frozen pitch etc.)?**

Unawareness of these factors can often lead to conflict between the facility management or staff and yourself. For example, you may think that you have the facility booked up until a certain time – then it turns out that this is the time the caretaker needs to lock the doors and go home for his tea – meanwhile 20 kids still need to get showered and changed! With advance planning you could have finished the session earlier (or negotiated for extra time).

Equipment

✪ **What type of equipment is available?**

✪ **How much of it is available for my use?**

✪ **Will I need to bring along any additional equipment?**

✪ **Do I have access to the equipment or do I need to obtain a key or notify the caretaker?**

✪ **How long will it take me to set up the equipment? Do I need to get early access to do this?**

✪ **Is the equipment in good condition?**

✪ **What safety equipment is available (e.g. in a swimming pool, or at an outdoor activity centre)?**

Failure to check on the above can lead to awkward difficulties if the type and amount of equipment is not available, or part of your session is taken up looking for the caretaker to open a storeroom.

For most sports activities, the following need to be considered.

Space available

This will dictate the numbers attending your session and the type of activities that you can do. Other considerations will include:

✪ **Are we indoors or outdoors? Can we have the choice?**

✪ **If outdoors, what facilities are available if the weather is bad – can we use the indoor facilities?**

✪ **Are there any markings that will help me organise the groups (i.e. grids, badminton/basketball/five-a-side marked-out areas)?**

✪ **What type of surface area is it? You will need to advise your participants on appropriate footwear**

✪ **How much space do I have available for use? Are there any restrictions?**

- ✪ **Am I sharing with other groups? This may restrict your use of a whistle and you will need to consider how to position your group so that their attention is not diverted when you speak to them**

Changing facilities

- ✪ **Which changing facilities can I use? (if more than one)**
- ✪ **Are there separate changing facilities for coaches and officials?**
- ✪ **Are there lockers? If not, provision will need to be made for securing personal belongings**
- ✪ **Can the changing rooms be locked?**
- ✪ **Are there rules about showering?**
- ✪ **What supervision will be required in the changing areas?**

Personal equipment

This will depend on the type of activity you are running, but generally the following items are useful:

- ✪ **Whistle**
- ✪ **Clipboard/pen**
- ✪ **Stopwatch**
- ✪ **Chalk/board marker**
- ✪ **Water bottle**
- ✪ **Outdoor activities may require specialist equipment such as a compass, maps, refreshments, specialised clothing etc.**

Depending on the equipment and the facilities, other items such as a mobile telephone and an emergency first aid box may be useful to have in your possession. The phone is for emergencies – do NOT let it distract you whilst you are leading the session.

Prior checks

When using a facility for the first time, it is a good idea to check out the venue beforehand for:

- ✪ **Suitability**
- ✪ **Directions on how to get there**
- ✪ **Confirmation of many of the items listed**

As a sports leader it is YOUR responsibility to check all of these factors. Never assume that someone else has done it for you.

4 Knowledge of activities

Your training as a sports leader will include knowledge of the activities that you will teach. It is beyond the scope of this chapter to cover them; however, there are a number of courses and qualifications that you should achieve to help you gain the knowledge and help you apply it as a sports leader. These will include:

- **Sports Leaders' Awards**
- **National Governing Body Coaching Awards**
- **National Coaching Foundation Awards**
- **NVQs in Coaching, Teaching and Instructing (in a specific sport or in an Exercise and Fitness discipline)**
- **NVQ in Activity Leadership**

Many colleges will also offer accredited courses in sports coaching and leadership that support these qualifications. You should also consider obtaining a first aid award and the National Pool Lifeguard Qualification.

Essentially you will need to know how to plan and construct a session in order to achieve particular goals, which meet the needs of the group. Knowledge of the following is required.

Warm-up

Warming up serves the following purposes:

- **To prepare the person mentally for the effort to come**
- **To raise the pulse and respiratory rate**
- **To raise the body temperature**
- **To increase the mobility in the joints**

The warm-up is an important feature of the session and will reduce the chance of injury since the muscles become more elastic, thus reducing the risk of sprains and tears.

The more severe the work or competition and the colder the weather, the more extensive the warm-up should be.

There are two main stages to warming up:

1 **Cardiovascular work, to increase the pulse and breathing rate gradually. Jogging and skipping are common exercises; however, an imaginative leader will introduce some variety by doing dance-type exercises to music and enjoyable games involving all members of the group (i.e. tag games). Such**

games can also be used to get groups into smaller numbers ready for the next activity

2   **Stretching exercises carried out smoothly without speed or jerks. Two to four repetitions of each exercise should be done with the position held for approximately 10–20 seconds**

If the participants are going to embark on a specific activity that will stress a particular joint and muscle, then some light work mimicking the movement patterns to follow will be useful. For example, tennis or badminton players would play a number of easy shots with a partner, and practise a number of serves; golfers may practise a few swings; canoeists will start paddling slowly before increasing the intensity; games players may involve activities which involve dribbling and passing a ball.

The warm-up will therefore be dependent on the activities to follow and the conditions of the environment.

The cool-down

A cool-down is a valuable method of gradually allowing the body and mind to recover to its normal state. It is also a pleasant way of rounding off the session.

Essentially a cool-down is similar to a warm-up, where the exercises are of a general nature mixed with some light stretching. The intensity, however, should decrease gradually. Clothing needs to be kept on throughout the cool-down period to avoid a sudden drop in temperature.

Activities and small-sided games

These will form the largest part of your session and need to be carefully planned in order to consider:

✪ **The equipment needed**
✪ **The most effective use of space**
✪ **The number and size of the groups**
✪ **The sequencing of activities**

Everyone in the group should be involved as much as possible – try to avoid activities that involve a lot of standing around or waiting 'to have a go'.

Keep rules to a minimum, especially with beginners; however, you should apply them rigorously otherwise you will soon have a battle on your hands.

Adapted games

Adaptations of adult versions of the game are necessary for children or those with special needs. Consider, for example:

Football: Smaller-sized pitch
            Smaller goalposts
            Smaller ball (a bright coloured ball or one with a bell can be
            used for visually or audio impaired participants)
            Smaller numbers in the team
Tennis: Smaller rackets
            Smaller-sized court
            Reduced height of the net

Short tennis is an excellent example of an adapted tennis game for children.

Question

How many other adapted games can you name? (Tip: have a look in a sports equipment catalogue.)

Small-sided games

Numbers in teams should be kept low in order to involve all of the players more often. Very often, players in teams with large numbers can go a whole game with very little or even no contact with the ball.

Potted sports or games offer groups the opportunity to participate in competitive, yet fun activities. For example:

- ✪ **Crab football**
- ✪ **Bench ball**
- ✪ **French cricket**
- ✪ **Beach ball**
- ✪ **Indoor athletics**

Relays

Relays can be a fun way of practising skills under pressure (e.g. dribbling a hockey ball with a stick, round cones). With a little imagination, relays can offer variety and excitement to a session. Teams of three or four will ensure that everyone has a go – but try to group teams as evenly as possible.

Activity 9.5

 TASK I

With the aid of a word processor, design an information sheet that will gather additional information from your participants that will inform you about:

★ What their objectives are. What they wish to achieve from the sessions

★ What activities they enjoy most

★ What their current level of ability is

★ What their current level of participation is

Complete the remaining tasks with reference to taking adults, aged 16 years and over, AND to a group of children aged under 16 years

▶ **TASK 2**

1 Based on information received from each of the two groups, outline *your* objectives for a sport or recreation activity session. What do you want to achieve?

2 Now, state what your objectives are for the session and how they meet the objectives of the participants

▶ **TASK 3**

1 Devise a checklist that will help you check that all arrangements are in place with regard to the facility/venue and equipment required

2 Justify why the facility/venue and equipment is appropriate to meeting the needs of the group and why it will help you achieve your objectives

Leading and delivering activities

Planning is not just about stating *what* you are going to do but *how* you are going to do it. It is a poor sports leader who trots off to take a session with just a list of activities in mind.

Careful consideration needs to be given to the application of the following skills.

Organisation and control

Real leadership is demonstrated when you are there in front of the group communicating the ideas and plans you have prepared earlier. Control starts at the very beginning of the session:

David Cave Photography

Figure 9.8 *Ask the class to help lay out equipment.*

David Cave Photography

Figure 9.9 *Working with small groups enables you to give specific feedback.*

✪ **Arrive early and get the equipment ready – if you are not able to lay it out then place it neatly and safely to one side.**

✪ **Selecting groups and teams has to be done quickly**

Random teams can be allocated by issuing everyone with a number – how many you give out will result in that number of teams, each of a size determined by dividing the total by the number of groups. For example, if you have 16 in the group, number the students '1', '2', '3', and '4'. You will now have four groups of four.

Activities that require the participants to get quickly into groups of a certain size when that number is called out are fun and will also produce random teams. Shout 'four' and everybody quickly gets into groups of four. Shout 'six' and everyone gets into groups of six – anyone left over has to do 10 press-ups! Then shout out the number indicating the size of group you want – this will be quickly formed.

If you are unsure of the levels of ability then progression through a range of skill practices will mean you can, by observation, spot the stronger pupils and group them accordingly.

Your planning should indicate what size you want the groups to be. Consider also the progressive nature of your session, i.e. for a group of 18 pupils a hockey session may progress as follows:

✪ **Divide into 6 groups of 3 (each group working in a grid)**

 1   **Passing in 3s**

 2   **Passing between 1 and 3. No. 2 trying to intercept.**

✪ **Set up 3 groups of 3 vs. 3 game, each using 2 grids**

 3   **Adapted game progression:**   **No goals – aim to pass without interception**

    Aim to hit a cone – one-touch passing only

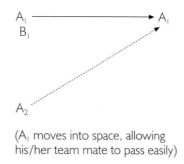

(A$_1$ moves into space, allowing his/her team mate to pass easily)

Figure 9.10 *Diagram of 2 vs. 1 passing practice*

✪ **Two teams of 9**

 4   **Full game to finish with:**   **Smaller goals – minimum of six passes before a shot at goal allowed**

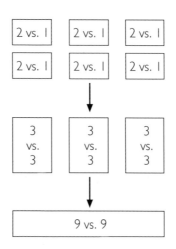

Figure 9.11 *Game progression*

The numbers don't always divide quite so evenly, so you need to consider how you might split up the groups of different numbers to achieve the same effect. This should form part of your planning.

Activity 9.6

Plan a games skill session for a group, showing the progression of practices used.

Indicate the methods you would use to select the groups for each practice and the size of the groups at each stage.

Structure

Your programme should have a planned structure to it with a definite beginning, middle and end. Each stage of your plan should indicate a time allocation. A one-hour games practice session may be timetabled as follows:

2 mins	Introduction
10 mins	Warm-up
10 mins	Skill practices in pairs
10 mins	Small group practices/game
15 mins	Game (whole group or round-robin tournament involving smaller groups)
5 mins	Relays
5 mins	Cool-down
3 mins	Feedback/Information

Sessions involving different activities or potted sports still need to be planned in similar detail.

Improvisation

This means responding to changes in your plans. Reasons for this might include:

- **Change in numbers due to absences**
- **Behaviour/attitude of participants**
- **Reduced space**
- **Unavailability of or insufficient equipment**
- **Change in facilities**
- **Change in weather conditions**

These may happen for all sorts of reasons outside of your control, but nonetheless you need to adapt accordingly. It may mean changing the nature of the activities planned, having improvised rules or working with different group sizes.

Motivation

You are probably familiar with the phrase 'success breeds success'. An exciting programme of activities should in itself be intrinsically rewarding; however, setting goals or challenges either for individuals or for the group will add further incentive to try harder.

As a sports leader your job is to make *everyone* feel like a winner.

✪ **Set challenging goals**

Remember – goals should be

Specific	E.g. learn to serve over-arm in volleyball
Measurable	E.g. achieve 8/10 serves in the opponent's area
Agreed	Both sports leader and coach agree
Realistic	The individual is capable of achieving this
Time specific	E.g. to be achieved within four sessions
Evaluated	Review the goals regularly
Recorded	Write them down so you remember them

✪ **Organise competitions that measure improvement**

✪ **Arrange tournaments between the group and against other groups**

✪ **Reward those who: try hard, are punctual, have improved the most, for best team player, for best supporter – there is something good in everybody which can be rewarded!**

✪ **Give positive feedback: 'Strike the ball with your wrist' is much more effective than 'don't strike the ball with your arm', and also informs the participant how to improve**

✪ **Praise achievement at all levels**

Any of the above methods will inspire confidence and encourage effort. You may recall yourself how much more motivated you were when *you* were successful and it was acknowledged.

Feedback

As a sports leader you will be communicating regularly with your group and with your helpers. Just as they need direction, instruction and feedback about their performance, so do you.

You will need to evaluate your session. The success, or otherwise, should be measured against your objectives.

Ask your participants:

- **Have you any comments on the venue or the equipment?**
- **What part of the session did you enjoy most?**
- **Is there anything that could have been done differently or better?**
- **What help did you get to improve?**
- **Are there any future activities that you would like to do?**
- **Were any special requirements catered for?**

You may wish to ask more specific questions but it is better to keep them brief. A useful method of obtaining feedback is to bring the group together at the end of the session. This will give you the opportunity to give feedback on the session, ask questions of them and vice versa – you can also use this opportunity to advise them about future sessions, tournaments etc.

Written evaluation forms can ask people to circle a number on a scale to indicate their response – this can save a lot of time, e.g.

> Circle the number that you feel describes the session
> 1 = Excellent, 2 = Good, 3 = Poor, 4 = Very Poor
> 1   The organisation of the session   1   2   3   4
> 2   The warm up   1   2   3   4
> 3   The passing practices, etc.
> Comment on any part of the session that you have awarded a '3' or a '4'

Ask your assistants:

- **Were the session objectives met?**
- **What aspects of the session went well?**
- **What went badly?**
- **Have you any recommendations for future sessions?**
- **Was there sufficient equipment – if not, what else do we need?**
- **Were there any behavioural problems?**

If there were any injuries you may need to revisit your risk assessment.

Always finish on a positive note so that everyone leaves the session feeling good about themselves.

Activity 9.7

Design an evaluation form that can be handed out to participants and a second one that can be given to your helpers. Some of the responses should be in the form of circling a number on a scale.

Finding help and support

There are many organisations on a national and local level that can offer valuable advice or support. These will include:

- ✪ *Local Authority Leisure Services Department*: **Organise local sports development activities and coaching courses**
- ✪ *Local Sports Councils*: **Often administered by the Local Authority, they provide support and grant aid for local sport initiatives**
- ✪ *National Governing Bodies of Sport*: **Administer the rules and regulations for their respective sports, and organise coach education qualifications**

Useful Websites

www.asksport.com is an extremely useful site providing names addresses and contact numbers for local authority sports development units, governing bodies of sport and other useful organisations.

Adventure Activities Licensing Authority	**www.aala.org/**
Association for Outdoor Learning	**www.adventure-ed.co.uk**
British Olympics Association	**www.olympics.org.uk**
British Association of Sport and Exercise Sciences	**www.bases.co.uk**
British Wheelchair Sports Foundation	**www.britishwheelchairsports.org/**
Disability Sport England	**www.euroyellowpages.com/dse/ dispeng/html**
English Sports Association for People with Learning Disabilities	**www.esapld.co.uk**
Institute of Leisure and Amenity Management	**www.ilam.co.uk**
Institute of Sport and Recreation Management	**www.isrm.co.uk**
Institute of Sports Sponsorship	**www.sports-sponsorship.co.uk**
National Coaching Foundation	**www.ncf.org.uk**
National Council for School Sport	**www.schoolsport.freeserve.co.uk**
Physical Education Association of the United Kingdom	**www.pea.uk.com**
SPRITO (The National Training Organisation representing Sport and Recreation and Allied Occupations)	**www.sprito.org.uk**
Sports Aid	**www.sportsaid.org.uk**

Sportsmatch	www.sportsmatch.co.uk/
Women's Sports Foundation	www.wsf.org.uk
Youth Sport Trust	www.youthsport.net

Sports Councils

Sports Council for Northern Ireland	www.sportni.org
Sports Council for Scotland	www.ssc.org.uk
Sports Council for Wales	www.sportscouncilwales.co.uk
Sports Council for England	www.english.sports.gov.uk
UK Sports Council	www.uksport.gov.uk

Revision questions

1 What is the difference between autocratic leadership and democratic leadership?

2 Name five positive qualities which a good sports leader should demonstrate in terms of being a good role model.

3 What obligations does the Health and Safety At Work Act place on an employee?

4 Name a Code of Practice which a leisure centre might adopt in order to improve safety in a swimming pool.

5 Name three actions a sports leader can take to improve safety.

6 Name four possible objectives of individuals participating in a sports activity session.

7 State two ways in which an organisation can increase its membership.

8 Why is it important to know the level of ability of your group beforehand?

9 What personal equipment might you take with you to a sports games session that you are leading? Name four items.

10 What checks might you make at a facility/venue prior to organising a session there?

11 What is the name and telephone number of the National Governing Body for the following sports:

> Badminton
> Hockey
> Athletics
> Tennis
> Football
> Basketball

12 Who might you contact for advice on disability sports?

13 What is the purpose of a warm-up?

14 Why is it important to group players of similar ability together when grouping for skill practices?

15 Name three situations when you may have to improvise in a session.

16 Name four ways of motivating bored participants.

17 Why is self-evaluation important?

18 What role do the following organisations play in sport?

> UK Sports Council
> Youth Sports Trust
> National Coaching Foundation

Assessment activity

You must produce evidence of planning, leading and evaluating activities for two selected groups – one for adults (16 years +), and one for children (under 16 years). Activities should be different for each group.

► **TASK 1**

Outline a plan for each group, identifying your objectives, which should take into consideration the facilities, equipment and the sport or activities you will be leading for each session.

► **TASK 2**

Structure a programme of activities, showing how you would organise each activity.

► **TASK 3**

Lead each of the sessions planned above, ensuring that the activities are conducted safely and that they meet the needs of individuals taking part.

► **TASK 4**

Evaluate your performance as a sports leader for each of the sessions.

You should note the criteria that will enable you to obtain a higher grade

Principles of sports coaching

10

Objectives

- Study the roles and responsibilities of the coach

- Learn about the qualities and skills needed to plan a session

- Know what to look for when observing techniques of a sports performer

- Understand the principles of training and how they affect performance

Introduction

Sports coaching offers exciting opportunities to help individuals or teams realise their potential in sport. This may include those who simply wish to participate in a sport for recreational purposes (for whom applying advanced skills will enhance their enjoyment), those who are being introduced to a sport (i.e. school children or adults seeking to learn new skills), or those who aspire to excellence in competition.

It can be extremely rewarding to share in the enjoyment of an individual or team that has just achieved a successful outcome, either in the learning of a new skill or following a successful performance in competition.

Many coaches have themselves been competent performers and retain their involvement in the sport by coaching, keen to 'put something back into the sport' and / or spurred on by the desire to achieve excellence in the sporting arena. Clubs will also 'recruit' helpers from parents and this too can spark off many years of enjoyable participation in coaching.

Most coaches work on a voluntary basis helping out in clubs or youth organisations; however, there are a growing number of opportunities to obtain part- or full-time paid employment coaching in advanced clubs, schools or local authority sports development schemes. Successful coaches may also work with individuals or national teams competing internationally at the very highest level.

SPRITO, the National Training Organisation for Sport and Recreation, has stated that sports coaching will soon be regarded as a recognised profession.

This chapter will help you learn about the qualities and skills you will need to become a sports coach and provide guidance which will prove invaluable when undertaking the practical elements of this course. The principles will also provide a sound foundation that can be used later when embarking on a governing body coaching award or NVQ in coaching.

Whilst you should be encouraged to gain as much practical experience as possible, you should at all times coach under the direction and control of a fully qualified coach. Take every opportunity to observe successful coaches and performers in action, asking questions and taking careful note of aspects that will help you in your role as a coach.

You will need to read Unit 9 Sport and recreation leadership, Unit 7 Exercise physiology and Unit 11 Sports psychology in order to gain a full understanding of the various aspects of sports coaching.

Role of the coach

The roles of a coach are many and varied and even the most experienced coaches say they continue to learn something new each day as they are presented with new and exciting challenges presented by the sport or the athlete.

You have probably selected this unit because you already have many of the qualities needed to be a successful coach – let us have a look at these two important qualities:

✪ **Communication**

✪ **Leadership**

Communication is an essential skill exercised by most of us in our daily lives and is a critical element of successful coaching. No matter how good you are in the theoretical or technical aspects of a sport, success will depend on your ability to communicate effectively with a range of people, including:

✪ *Performers*: **giving feedback, providing guidance, direction and motivation in training and in competition**

✪ *Parents*: **explaining your plans, reporting on progress, advising on their role or even justifying selection**

✪ *Officials*: **checking on rule decisions or making an official protest**

✪ *The media*: **reporting or commenting on results, promoting your sport or in some cases yourself!**

✪ *Other coaches*: **asking advice, seeking guidance or just enjoying the company of those who have similar interests to yourself**

✪ *Committees*: **presenting plans, asking for resources, or reporting on coaching matters in general**

It is not what you know, but how well you can communicate information to others.

You should try some of these tips when next communicating with someone, or with a group.

✪ *Non-verbal communication*:
  – **Establish eye contact: it tells the other person that *you* are interested in *them***
  – **Gestures and body language create positive impressions: smile, look interested, listen when spoken to, lean forward *facing* the other person and above all acknowledge their presence!**

David Cave Photography

Figure 10.1 *The coach lets a pupil have a go.*

— **Give visual demonstrations: performers seeing the correct action are more likely to understand better. Demonstrations, however, should be should be accurate and clearly seen**

✪ *Verbal guidance*: **Coaches will have important key points to stress during a session. It is important that the message is understood and that the appropriate impact is made. Consider your:**

— **Tone of voice: Sarcasm, praise and criticism can easily be detected and often misinterpreted. Take care!**

— **Volume: You don't always have to shout, but there again you have to be heard. The volume has to be appropriate to the situation. Remember, if you are coaching for long periods of time your voice can soon wear out. Use your voice sensibly**

— **Choice of language: It must be suitable for the situation, age-group and level of ability**

Above all, it is important to check that instructions have been understood and that they have been acted on.

You do this by asking questions and then WATCHING to make sure that they are carrying out your instructions.

You should be positive when issuing instructions and giving feedback: 'keep your head still' sounds much better than 'don't move your head' and of course it provides clear guidance as to what to do. The latter comment doesn't!

Leadership provides structure, motivation and direction – vital ingredients in any coaching programme.

- ✪ **Coaches are leaders who know where the individual or team is going and will provide the direction and resources to help get there**
- ✪ **They will seek to ensure that their athletes have the maximum opportunities to achieve success**
- ✪ **Successful team coaches will ensure that individual success helps achieve team success**

There will be evidence of leadership in many aspects of coaching, including decision-making processes, motivational techniques, giving feedback, establishing interpersonal relationships and directing the coaching programme confidently.

You can adopt different styles of leadership depending on the situation you are in and the relationship you have with the person/team you are coaching.

You can be **autocratic** and make all the decisions, with little consultation from those being coached, or you can be **democratic** and have considerable dialogue between the athlete and yourself to agree on the way forward (Figure 10.2).

Different situations call for different styles of leadership.

Autocratic ◄·····························► Democratic

Figure 10.2 *Autocratic–democratic continuum*

Coaches use a style which will lie somewhere between the two extremes and will often vary it depending upon the situation.

You should read Unit 9 Sport and recreation leadership to learn more about the qualities and skills necessary for effective sports leadership.

List the different situations in which either of the two styles would be best adopted in order to achieve the most successful outcome.

Remember – good communication and outstanding leadership are two qualities that underpin all aspects of the coaching process.

Key roles of a coach

Whilst the primary role of the coach is to develop and improve the performance of others in their chosen sport, the coaching process incorporates a number of key roles (Figure 10.3).

Teaching new skills and techniques which can be adopted to achieve a successful outcome in a variety of situations

For example, a skill such as passing a basketball, once learned, needs then to be practised in real game situations where the pass may need to be made quickly, following a dummy, with force or lobbed. Decisions need to be made quickly depending on the situation. Your job as a teacher is to make sure that the learner has all the skills to be able to decide on the correct course of action and then be able to carry it out. This requires the participants to understand what they are doing and why.

Showing the learner what to do by demonstrating a skill is extremely valuable and should be attempted where possible.

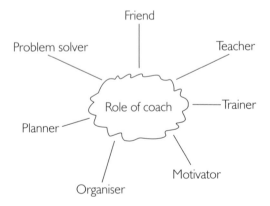

Figure 10.3 *The coach has many roles*

David Cave Photography

Figure 10.4   *Demonstrating exactly how to hold the ball.*

Continually observing and analysing other performers in action will develop a trained eye and an increasing understanding of the technical as well as tactical demands of the sport. You will then teach the skills to meet these demands.

Training the performer to apply techniques that meet the specific demands of the sport

This will involve giving information in the form of directions and reasons which apply sound physiological and psychological principles that will improve skilful performance. Knowledge of these (and the ability to impart it to others) is clearly necessary and the coach should continually seek to improve their knowledge of the sport.

The learning never stops!

Developing interpersonal skills of others

It should never be forgotten that it is the individual who is being coached and not the sport.

Figure 10.5 *Confidence building: another example of a coach demonstrating.*

Participation in sport can enhance so many qualities in a person, such as self-confidence, how to overcome obstacles, co-operation with others, and the development of self-control even in the face of defeat.

Coaches have a moral and ethical obligation to ensure that the best interests of the individual are always considered and should maintain integrity at all times (and encourage it in their athletes).

Motivating others to learn and to perform to the best of their ability

This is a quality which is evident in all successful coaches and which most performers usually respond most positively to.

This invariably involves establishing a relationship which creates confidence and credibility but also entails the coach stamping his or her own personality on to the whole coaching process – a quality which should never be underestimated.

Organising resources essential for the effective delivery of the coaching session and for competitions

These will include

- ✪ **Facilities – ensuring that they are open and available and that there is access to changing rooms, equipment cupboards, first aid, emergency telephones etc.**
- ✪ **Equipment, including personal items such as whistle and stopwatch, and any necessary kit or apparatus**
- ✪ **Time – ensuring that there is the proper allocation given. Management of time is an important quality of all coaches**
- ✪ **Assistant coaches or helpers – how can they best be utilised?**
- ✪ **Travelling and accommodation arrangements**

Example

A basketball coach asked to take a session at the local school may use the following checklist:

1   **Will the sports hall and changing rooms be open?**

2   **What equipment is available and is it accessible? What equipment will I need to bring with me?**

3   **Is there access to a first aid kit and a telephone?**

4   **How much time have I got?**

5   **Who do I need to help me and what instructions do I need to give them?**

6   **Do the players know when the session starts and finishes?**

There is a danger, however, that coaches take on too much of the organisation in a club, anxious to ensure that everything is right for their athlete or team. This can distract the coach from their primary role.

Good coaches will actively recruit parents and officials to assist them (demonstrating some of the leadership qualities referred to earlier) – they will also provide support and guidance, whilst at the same time allow them the opportunity to make decisions for themselves and accept responsibility for their own actions (and credit for any success). Poor coaches often don't think they need help, or if they are offered it provide no support and leave assistants to work in isolation, often ignoring pleas for guidance. An example of tasks carried out by the coach and assistant is shown below.

COACH'S TASKS

- ✪ Welcome the players and talk to them
- ✪ Commence warm-up
- ✪ Divide into groups and set programme of training
- ✪ Check on the progress of the whole group
- ✪ Control cool-down and talk to players about the session

ASSISTANT'S TASKS

- ✪ Set out equipment needed for the session
- ✪ Assist the coach with carrying out instructions
- ✪ Assist by taking one group/monitor performance and give feedback to both the player and the coach
- ✪ Put equipment away

Coaches need to consider the resources that are available in relation to the group age, size and ability.

Equipment designed for adults is not appropriate for children and should never be used 'to make up the numbers'.

Either the session needs to be adapted around the equipment available or additional equipment found.

Activity 10.2

Cut out from a catalogue examples of equipment which can be used for coaching adults and that which can be used for coaching children. You should try to cover at least six different sports. Paste the sections into a notebook to form a catalogue of equipment for each of the sports selected.

Most importantly, the coach has to be organised: arriving punctually for sessions, keeping people informed of arrangements and being prepared for most eventualities. Coaches who have planned well are usually well organised.

Planning carefully to ensure that sessions are delivered in a structured and progressive manner

Coaches need to consider:

- *The age and ability of the group*: **Without this information you will not know how much equipment will be needed or the level at which the sessions should be aimed**

- *The aims and objectives of the session*: **Is it to improve a specific skill or technique, fitness or to work on tactics? The objectives of each session should form part of a longer-term aim. For example, the long-term aim is to improve the front crawl stroke – the specific objective for a session might be to improve the leg action. A good leg action is essential for a good stroke, and so achievement of this short-term aim forms part of the overall long-term objective**

- *The numbers participating and the space and equipment available*: **Knowledge of this will ensure that you can prepare properly for the session ahead and that you can best use the resources that will be available to you**

- *Assistance required and available (consideration should be given to individuals who have particular requirements)*: **Knowledge of the assistants means that you can plan how you intend to use them most effectively. If you have participants in your session who have particular requirements, e.g. have visual impairment, then you will need to ensure that you have the necessary assistance to be able to offer them a safe and productive session**

- *A suitable warm-up and cool-down*: **This will be dependent upon the environment and the type of activity – for example, if the sports hall is cold, a more intense and longer warm-up will be required. If the session is of light intensity, only a small amount of time will be allocated to a cool-down**

- *Practices and key teaching points appropriate to the individual or group and which allow for progression*: **Unplanned sessions may lead to practices being too hard or not challenging enough. If the coach has considered the practices carefully, allowance will have been made for a range of abilities within the session and also for progression for those students who are ready for a more challenging activity**

- *Training content and principles which might be necessary to improve fitness*: **A key aspect of improving fitness is to apply overload in a progressive manner, building on the work of** previous sessions. Planning and monitoring will ensure that this aspect of training is effective

✪ *The most appropriate sequencing of activities and the organisation of groups to ensure the smooth running of the session*: **For example, a session for which the objective is to improve dribbling skills in hockey might follow the format below:**

> **Warm-up (whole group)**
>
> **Dribbling practices round cones – walking then running (working in groups of three)**
>
> **Dribbling around players who are stationary, then moving (working in pairs)**
>
> **Relays (four teams of six)**
>
> **An adapted game – when receiving the ball the player must dribble for at least 5 m before passing**
>
> **Cool-down (whole group)**
>
> **Consideration will need to be given as to how the groups are going to be set up – this should be evident in the planning**

✪ *Competitions which will provide the most appropriate preparation*: **It is important that preparation is given to competition – this may mean attending several 'unimportant' competitions in order to test new techniques and tactics prior to the major competition(s). This should form part of the coach's long-term planning**

✪ *Contingencies, in the event of unforeseen circumstances*: **For example, bad weather, fewer numbers than expected, shortage of equipment, variable improvements in the group etc. Once a session is under way, the coach will need to adapt the session accordingly, but some pre-planning will have been useful**

Solving problems

This is perhaps the most exciting aspect of coaching.

What changes do we make when things are not going well? Interest is being lost, how can we inspire a losing team? Some members of the team are being disruptive – how do we best deal with them? Illness or injury has affected individual or team plans – how do we handle the situation?

These are problems that need to be overcome and if not resolved can lead to conflict, deterioration in performance and even withdrawal from the sport. Coaches can learn from their experience and by watching and learning from others. Mistakes will no doubt be made, but good coaches will learn from them and use it to their advantage in the future.

Activity 10.3

Consider someone you think is a good coach or teacher. You may wish to choose your lecturer. Analyse what makes them successful or otherwise. Work in pairs for this activity and compare notes with your partner.

Why coach?

As stated at the beginning of this chapter, reasons for participation in a sport are different, as are the reasons for coaching.

Reasons for participation	Reasons for coaching
Fun	Enjoy seeing the students succeed
Make friends	A boost to the ego – enjoying the
Keep fit	personal reward and the glory
A leisure pursuit/hobby	A leisure pastime/hobby
(family involvement)	To help out at the local club
Learn new skills	Employment – financial remuneration
Compete	The challenge – the will to be successful
Excel at the highest level	The buzz associated with competition at an elite level

It is important that the aims and objectives of the coach match those of the individual being coached.

An enthusiastic and highly motivated coach who wants to coach successful athletes or teams to an elite level is unlikely to gain any satisfaction from working with those whose aims and objectives are otherwise – and so should seek to coach in that type of environment. The opposite is also true! Trying to push people to achieve levels higher than they are capable or willing is likely to result in conflict and coach or participant (or both) dropping out of the sport.

Many people are keen to receive coaching so that they can enjoy participating in a sport, without a desire to compete seriously – in this case, much of the emphasis will therefore be on technique.

It also has to be recognised that some do not wish to be coached at all! There is nothing wrong with this.

An ongoing role of the coach is to assess the level of ability of the performer and to constantly review the appropriateness of the training programme. The long-term needs of the individual performer always need to be considered over and above any short-term gain.

Self-evaluation

Finally, and perhaps the most important of all, is the ability of a coach to evaluate themselves and continue to find new ways of improving their own performance. This will involve seeking feedback by talking to athletes, coaches and others whose views are respected and by being prepared to respond positively to criticism.

Attendance on National Governing Body coaching courses will provide you with an opportunity to have your skills as a coach tested and weaknesses identified and improved. Seminars and conferences also provide useful opportunities to keep up to date with topical issues and the latest coaching techniques. The sport's governing body or the National Coaching Foundation will provide information on these.

The coaching process

Unlike most projects which require an element of planning, the coaching process involves a rather complex inter-relationship between the coach, the performer, those who have influence on the performer and the team.

There are many potential conflicts, with other goals or interests held by each of these, and invariably the desired long-term outcome is never achieved!

The coaching process begins when both athlete and coach form a partnership, with an agreed aim in mind.

The athlete may form part of a group (i.e. a club, a lesson programme etc.) or in some cases may be receiving individual tuition.

The partnership may last for just one session or for many years. Many successful athletes will have developed a close friendship with their coach and will attribute their achievements to their hard work and dedication.

Very often athletes will feel that their coach has taken them as far as possible and will wish to change coaches, or ask specialist coaches to assist them with aspects of their performance. Indeed some coaches will specialise in teaching only the early stages and will then pass the athlete on to a coach who has expertise at another level.

The process for the athlete is often a long-term one with one or more coaches being involved along the way.

This section is going to focus on the processes involved with one session; however, it should be realised that the long-term coaching process involves this being repeated many times.

We are now going to look at three stages of the coaching process:

1   **Planning the session**
2   **Conducting the session**
3   **Evaluating the session**

1 Planning the session

The first stage of the process is to gather information that will enable you to plan properly. This will involve finding out about your students, the facility or venue where the session is to be delivered and any other resources that are available to you. Information from the previous session will also provide valuable information as to what the level of ability of the students is and what the next progression should be.

Make a checklist of all information that will be required to enable you to make informed decisions about the content of a session plan.

Once the demands of the student have matched the resources available, the coach is ready to plan the delivery of the session. It is this process that will test the coach's knowledge of coaching methods to ensure that the session is appropriate to age, level of ability and motives of the student(s) being coached.

The plan will have a short-term objective but will be central to the achievement of a longer-term aim.

Knowledge of this is more likely to motivate the student to train well. The plan should be structured to include:

- **A warm-up, appropriate to the environment and the activities to follow**
- **Practices for technical development or reinforcement of previously learned skills**
- **Conditioning sets to bring about physiological adaptation**
- **An adapted game selected to practise the skills taught earlier or to work on tactical set pieces. This may be followed by a proper game (for team games only)**
- **A cool-down appropriate to the session**

Of course the emphasis on each will vary, depending on the motives of the group. A novice group, for example, will spend more time on technical development than physical conditioning. Coaches may also plan time for psychological preparation (e.g. imagery training – see page 177).

Consideration also needs to be given as to how each section of the plan is to be delivered:

- **The division and organisation of groups where appropriate**
- **Relevant coaching points to be stressed**
- **Safety factors**
- **Most appropriate use of equipment**
- **Time allocated to each section**
- **Use of assistant coaches or helpers**
- **Catering for the needs of those with particular requirements**

2 Conducting a session

A lot can be learned by observing other coaches in action. Look out for:

- ✪ *How the session is introduced*: This part of the session will set the tone for what is to follow. The coach should always arrive first and welcome their students; introduce themselves if new to the group and get to know their names

- ✪ *How the objectives of the session are explained*: This will focus on the purpose of the session, stressing the key points that the student will have to think about. Students who are focused and have a clear purpose are more likely to be motivated to work hard during the session. Explanations should be brief and students encouraged to ask questions

- ✪ *How directions are given to the students*: The coach should be positioned so that all the students can

  - Be seen

  - Be heard

  - Watch demonstrations clearly

  - Ask questions

  Positive feedback with clear directions on how to improve or to reinforce the correct action will ensure that the student remains focused. Coaches should avoid using negative statements about the performance of the student, as this is unlikely to bring about any improvement and will probably just demoralise the student

- ✪ *When instructions are given*: No student should set off on a practice without clear direction and a task to focus on, or complete the practice without receiving feedback. The best time to give feedback is during the performance, if it is appropriate to do so – this is known as **augmented feedback** and is useful when introducing a new skill. **Terminal feedback** is given immediately the performance has finished and can reinforce key teaching points and provide a positive direction for subsequent performances.

  Sometimes it is difficult to give feedback immediately afterwards and so every effort should be made to provide it as soon as possible afterwards. This is known as **delayed feedback** and whilst it is least effective it is better than no feedback at all. Just think how you have felt when you have tried your best at something – at the request of somebody else – and it has not even been acknowledged

When working with a group there are times when it is appropriate to stop the whole group and other times when only part of the group should be stopped, in order to give general feedback or direction. There is no point in stopping the whole group if only a small section of it needs guidance.

David Cave Photography

Figure 10.6 *The coach watches closely to check that the action is being carried out correctly.*

Activity 10.5

Misunderstood instructions will only confuse. What are the different ways in which a coach might check for understanding?

Coaches should encourage their students to self-evaluate and to make decisions about aspects of their performance. Asking questions such as 'How did that feel?' or 'What do you think is causing that problem?' is a useful way of eliciting a response from your student.

Establishing a two-way dialogue between coach and student throughout the whole process is critical to achieving a successful outcome.

Activity 10.6

Watch a session conducted by three different coaches (it would be courteous to ask permission first) and make notes on each of the following:

★ The introduction to the session

★ Aims and objectives of the session

★ Directions given (note the actions of the coach, not just the words)

★ Feedback given

The coach will probably be happy to discuss your comments and treat it as a useful evaluation!

Compare and contrast the sessions delivered by each of the coaches and comment on any strengths and weakness that you may have identified. It would not be appropriate to discuss any weaknesses other than with your tutor or the coach themselves.

3 Evaluating the session

Coaches need to evaluate two things. The first is the performance of their student, where the coach must have the expertise to identify faults and then to correct them. The second is the ability to analyse themselves and evaluate their own performance as a coach and the methods that they have used.

Evaluation of technique requires a good knowledge of the sport and the ability to break down actions into smaller components, where possible, for analysis, tracing the source of the fault and making recommendations for improvement. (This will be investigated in more detail later in this chapter.)

When evaluating a session, coaches should make make notes on their analysis and make recommendations for improvement and progression.

The evaluation of physiological or psychological improvements will require testing to be carried out under proper test conditions. The tests should be specific to the sport and determine where any weaknesses are.

For details on fitness testing and training you should read Unit 8 Fitness, testing and training.

Psychogical testing is covered in some detail in Unit 11 Sports psychology.

Activity 10.7

> ▶ **TASK 1**
>
> Find out what tests are conducted by coaches observed by you and make notes on what aspects were being measured, the method used and the frequency of them.
>
> ▶ **TASK 2**
>
> Assist a coach while a test is being conducted. Record the results. Use your computer skills to present the results in tabular and graphic format.

When analysing and evaluating their own performance, coaches need to take a detached look at themselves and be prepared to listen to feedback from others, such as students, other coaches and parents.

Accompanying the session plan should be an evaluation checklist, which might include the following items:

- ✪ **Date/time/venue**
- ✪ **Activity**
- ✪ **What went well with the session**
- ✪ **What did not go well during the session**
- ✪ **Whether the objectives of the session were met, and if not, what was achieved**
- ✪ **How future sessions could be improved**
- ✪ **Safety and disciplinary issues**
- ✪ **Any other comments**

The most important thing is to complete the evaluation as soon as possible after each session.

What makes a good coach?

Some of the qualities and skills were identified earlier in this chapter. Specific knowledge of the sport and other important aspects must underpin these if they are to be delivered effectively.

A coach will generally be expected to have a coaching qualification verified by the governing body of that particular sport. Qualifications are available at different levels, allowing you to progress as you gain more experience. The qualification will ensure that the coach practically understands the theoretical aspects and their application of them. However, as in all cases, added experience gathered over the years along with the qualifications will ensure that all of the areas are covered in detail. Many good coaches will tell you, however, that they never stop learning – the more they find out, the more questions there are to ask!

Activity 10.8

▶ **TASK 1**

Find out what qualifications are available from three different National Governing Bodies of Sport.

▶ **TASK 2**

What prerequisites are required (age/entry requirements, etc.)?

▶ **TASK 3**

Where and when are examinations for these qualifications held and what costs are involved?

▶ **TASK 4**

Put together a leaflet which can be distributed to your class, providing them with information on the qualifications that you have researched.

What does a good coach need to know?

Areas of knowledge should be specific to the sport or event and include:

- ✪ **Exercise physiology**
- ✪ **Nutrition**
- ✪ **Safety factors**
- ✪ **Psychology**
- ✪ **Techniques and tactics**
- ✪ **Rules of the sport**

Exercise physiology

Exercise physiology is about understanding the workings of the human body with particular reference to its response to exercise and the sport or event involved.

Each sport has different physiological demands depending on its physical intensity; for example, a marathon runner will require a high degree of aerobic endurance whereas a weight lifter will be more concerned about developing strength. Within sports, different events require different physiological demands (e.g. 100 m/10,000 m/high jump, etc.) and even within team games different players have different demands; a goalkeeper's needs will vary significantly from outfield players. You must be clear about the physiological demands of the sport *and* event(s) that you are researching in terms of their demands for:

- ✪ **Strength**
- ✪ **Speed**
- ✪ **Stamina**
- ✪ **Suppleness**

Exercise physiology is discussed in greater detail in Unit 7 Exercise physiology. Because of its relevance to coaching you should study this unit very carefully.

Activity 10.9

 TASK 1

Construct a pie chart that shows the degree of emphasis you think should be placed on each aspect of fitness in relation to your own chosen sport. This will determine the amount of emphasis that will be put on this area of fitness when designing a training programme.

▶ **TASK 2**

Discuss the outcome of Task 1 with an experienced and qualified coach.

Do the plans of this coach show a similar emphasis to your own and, if not, where were the major differences?

Remember that coaching is not an exact science and so there is no correct answer to this task – the answer will lie in the eventual performance of the athlete. By studying the plans of different coaches who have been successful you will be able to establish the approximate weightings given to the different physiological areas and this will help you to design training plans in the future. Remember also that consideration will need to be given to individual differences.

Nutrition

There is little point in having a superb training programme if the athlete does not have the energy to carry it out.

A well-balanced diet will provide the essential nutrients to maintain a healthy lifestyle. For those in training, however, there is a greater than average consumption of calories needed to provide energy.

Many people train early in the morning or straight after school or work, when carbohydrate and hydration levels are probably low, and so consideration needs to be given to the timing of food and fluid intake to enable the athlete to train properly at those times.

Of course, the athlete does not want to train on a full stomach, having consumed a large meal shortly beforehand – this will only cause the body to redirect the blood supply from the working muscles to the digestive processes, affecting performance and increasing the likelihood of cramp. The type of food therefore needs careful thought.

Essentially athletes, like the rest of us, require a balanced diet of fats, carbohydrates and protein which should meet the minimum recommended levels of intake of vitamins and minerals. Regular drinks are also needed to ensure that there is an adequate intake of water.

No two individuals will follow the same diet, however, as it will be vary according their sex, height, body type, level of training, and of course their own personal preferences.

Coaches should encourage athletes to monitor their diet closely and this should form an integral part of their training programme. Intake requirement during the off-season will be less than that taken during heavy training.

Athletes are often prone to putting on excessive weight during this time and so close attention to diet is also important during this period.

Alcohol consumption, if excessive, can result in a number of side-effects which are significant to maximal performance, and so excessive consumption should be avoided at all times. Few successful athletes consume alcohol other than perhaps the occasional social or celebratory drink.

As with physiological principles, the coach needs to know about the importance of the different food groups and other nutritional requirements and be able to advise the athlete in order to achieve the best possible performance both in training and in competition.

To recap – consideration therefore needs to be given to:

- ✪ **Type of food**
- ✪ **Calorie intake**
- ✪ **Timing of eating**
- ✪ **Water intake**
- ✪ **Lifestyle factors such as the consumption of alcohol**

Nutrition is discussed in greater detail in Unit 7 Exercise physiology. Because of its relevance to coaching you should study this subject very carefully.

Safety factors

Participation in sport involves risk. Safety of all those involved in the coaching process overrides all other principles. This includes the safety of the athlete, the coach, spectators and consideration for those who may be using a facility afterwards.

The principles learned in Unit 2 Safe working practices should be applied in this unit. Coaches are now compelled to abide by the Health and Safety at Work Act 1974 and the Children Act 1989 along with other legislation such as Control of Substances Hazardous to Health (COSHH).

Factors to consider are:

✪ *Resources*: **All equipment and facilities should be checked for suitability. Equipment should be stored so that it will not cause injury to others**

✪ *Participants*: **The type of training provided must be right for the individual. Inappropriate training caused by ignorance of the coach can cause a great deal of damage**

These responsibilities are down to the coach. You should conduct a risk assessment as part of your planning for coaching in order that you can consider all of the risks and take action to minimise the probability and severity of any possible accident.

Activity 10.10

Carry out a risk assessment on

★ The facility being used for a coaching session, including equipment

★ The participants

You should use your word-processing skills to present the risk assessment in proper table format.

It goes without saying that coaches in charge of the session should be qualified and experienced in dealing with the particular student group (i.e. children, adults or those with special needs). Such coaches will have no difficulty in presenting evidence of their qualifications and experience if challenged.

Risk assessment built into the planning process will minimise the risk of injury; however, the very nature of some sports attracts a greater risk than others. You will need to have a knowledge of the types of injury which are common to the sport being undertaken and how to prevent or treat them and provide guidelines for returning to training after injury.

Initial assessment of the athlete

You should obtain as much information as possible about your athlete beforehand to establish any awkward medical condition or previous injury. This should be obtained by using *all* of the following methods:

✪ **Completion of a medical form by the athlete**
✪ **Asking the athlete**

- ✪ **In the case of children, discussing issues of concern with parents**
- ✪ **By watching new athletes very closely for evidence of any worrying medical condition (i.e. pain when executing certain movements)**

The Health and Safety at Work Act 1974 states that you must not place anyone in personal danger.

There is also a moral obligation as you are in a position of responsibility.

If you feel that continuation of the activity either in training or in competition is likely to cause personal injury or harm then you MUST STOP IMMEDIATELY and take the appropriate action to prevent further harm – even if the athlete wishes to contiue.

In order to devise an appropriate training programme you have also to establish other information on the athlete:

- ✪ *Level of physical fitness*: Training programmes should not place excessive stress on the body. Any overload should be progressive, to allow for the appropriate adaptations to take effect
- ✪ *Physique*: The person's physique should suit the activity under the stress it will be exposed to in a comprehensive training programme
- ✪ *Age, gender and psychological factors*: All of these are relevant when considering the intensity levels of training programmes, the type of activities suitable for inclusion in the session and when organising groups or teams. A forty-year-old unfit man will not be too keen to train alongside fit teenagers, for example, or a teenage girl alongside an under-9s group! Similarly, highly motivated athletes will soon become disenchanted if disruptive or 'recreational' athletes are grouped with them during a serious training programme – the latter will also become equally frustrated. Furthermore, such inappropriate grouping increases the likelihood of injury
- ✪ *Influence of drugs or alcohol*: Anyone showing signs of consuming alcohol prior to a session should be prevented from taking part – the influence of alcohol creates additional stress, affects decision making and is likely to result in an action which can cause injury. It would be helpful to discuss the reasons for consumption of alcohol and explain the dangers. Other social drugs should be treated similarly. Athletes using drugs for medicinal purposes should discuss their implications with the coach beforehand and if necessary be referred to a doctor. It goes without saying that drugs taken to enhance performance should be discouraged at all costs. **If athletes you are coaching have, in your opinion, a problem with any of these issues you should refer them to specialists who have greater experience in dealing with them**

- *Technique:* The risk of injury can be increased through poor technical ability. If the body movements are not precise or a muscle is stretched inappropriately, the muscle is placed under stress and this is likely to cause injury, particularly if repeated. It is the coach's job to spot bad habits which may lead to repetitive strain and alter their technique accordingly

- *Proper planning:* As mentioned earlier, coaches must ensure that they are using the correct equipment and that it is safe. Time must also be allocated for a proper warm-up and cool-down appropriate to the activity and level of intensity

Basic procedures for treating injuries

Quick and accurate thinking at the time of an injury will minimise any further damage. The following procedures are useful:

1 **Assess the situation**
    - **What is the nature of the injury?**
    - **What happened?**
    - **Find out the exact details from the casualty and from any other witnesses**
    - **Are other casualties involved?**
    - **Is this a recurring injury?**

    You should immediately contact a registered first aider who will help decide whether further professional assistance is required.

    You should never place yourself in a position where you cannot access a registered first aider quickly. It is always useful for the coach to be a registered first aider but remember that if it is a group of young children being coached, someone will need to supervise the others whilst the injured casualty is being treated. The role of the first aider is to provide reassurance and to minimise further damage whilst waiting for help to arrive.

2 **Treating specific injuries**
    - *Breathing stopped:* **Apply the principles of ABC – airways, breathing, circulation:**
        - *Airways:* **Check the airways are clear**
        - *Breathing:* **Give mouth-to-mouth resuscitation if breathing cannot be detected**
        - *Circulation:* **If the casualty has no pulse, external cardiac compression must be applied**

Once the presence of breathing has been confirmed, place the casualty in the recovery position

- ✪ *Spinal injuries*:
  - – **Never move the casualty; this can cause further damage**
  - – **Call for an ambulance immediately**
  - – **Talk to and constantly reassure the casualty**
- ✪ *Soft tissue injuries*: **These are probably the most common type of injuries you will come across, the aim here is to decrease circulation which will in turn decrease internal bleeding and swelling. Apply the principle of RICE – rest, ice, compression, elevation:**
  - – *Rest*: **Stop using the injured part immediately – further use will simply increase the damage**
  - – *Ice*: **Apply ice to the injured part; this will allow the blood vessels and surrounding tissues to contract and will reduce blood flow to the injured area. This will reduce the swelling. Do not apply ice direct, but through a cotton towel or similar**
  - – *Compression*: **Wrap a bandage tightly around the injured part – this will apply direct pressure and keep swelling to a minimum**
  - – *Elevation*: **Again to decrease circulation, raise the injured body part above the heart. The force of gravity will reduce blood flow and drain any excess fluids away from the injured area**

The recovery programme

A sports injury specialist such as a physiotherapist will be the only person who should advise how much rest is required and when a return to training is possible. The length of time will depend on the severity of the injury and any history of previous injury.

Once the injury has been adquately tested, training can be resumed and this must be progressive. The athlete will not be able to start at the point where they were prior to injury and constant monitoring will be necessary to assess any adaptation.

It is pure folly to continue training with even the slightest injury and as a responsible coach you should advise caution and encourage the athlete to seek specialist help. The slightest tweak can often be building up into a larger, more serious problem.

Sports psychology

Sports psychology is discussed in greater detail in Unit 11 Sports psychology. Because of its relevance to coaching you should study this unit very carefully.

Would *you* want to be the player who steps up to take the penalty that could win, or lose, the World Cup for your country?

Most of us have experienced being nervous, perhaps before an important exam or prior to sitting a driving test!

The real question is whether it had affected your performance – often when we do badly we put it down to 'nerves'.

On the other hand, this nervousness can sharpen your focus and motivate you to do really well. The secret is getting it just right in order to achieve an optimum level of performance – and coaches need to recognise exactly what intervention is required from them, if any, to help their athletes achieve this.

You will find that you are applying sports psychology skills all of the time when coaching, even when you're not aware of it!

You will be applying verbal and non-verbal cues to send positive messages such as approval, satisfaction or pleasure, or depending on the situation or your mood, negative expressions which are completely opposite to this. This can have a huge impact on your athletes – either positively or negatively.

Think of a situation in which a teacher or coach has made a comment or gesture which has had a positive influence on you, resulting in you wanting to try harder or in you performing better.

Now consider a comment or gesture which has had the opposite effect.

Have there been times when *you* have made a comment or gesture which has been mis-interpreted, resulting perhaps in a subsequent breakdown in communication or an argument of some kind?

Remember that when you are coaching you are communicating with your athlete for a great deal of the time.

Learn from your own experiences above to ensure that any impact you make results in a positive outcome.

In your investigations of other coaches, watch carefully how the athlete responds to the coach – and how effective or otherwise the coach has been in achieving the desired outcome.

Of course there are structured and specific techniques which you should be aware of in order to assist the athlete achieve their full potential both in training and competition. These will include:

- **Goal setting: Having an aim, to be achieved in the short, medium and long term**
- **Concentration: Maintaining focus**
- **Imagery: Mentally rehearsing actions**
- **Stress management: Ensuring that stress is just right for an optimum performance**

Do not underestimate the importance of applying sound psychological principles when coaching – they will not allow the athlete to exceed their physical capabilities, only help them to achieve them. Applied poorly, however, they may undo all of the great work which has been done to attain maximum physical conditioning.

Coaching techniques

A sports technique carried out efficiently will ensure that all the energies produced as a result of a good fitness programme are channelled in the right direction. In contrast, poor technique will result in energy being lost in producing unwanted movement.

Time spent on ensuring good technique will pay dividends in terms of performance and should never be forgotten in the quest for ever-improving fitness gains. Your role as a coach is vital in helping an athlete develop a sound, efficient technique.

You need to know your sport well and be familiar with the specific movement patterns required to execute the technique correctly – bear in mind that there will be individual differences depending on physique, strength, flexibility and level of skill.

There are underlying bio-mechanical principles with which you will need to familiarise yourself. These, together with the rules of the sport, will dictate the requirements of the technique. Remember also that techniques, once learned, must be practised and analysed under pressure and in realistic situations.

Principles of movement

Movement involves the study of three important areas:

- **Use of joints**
- **Direction and application of force**
- **Stability**

Use of joints

In every sport the joints of the body need to be controlled so as to work in the correct sequence.

Activity 10.11

One of the best ways to develop a trained eye is to write down your observations of an action. A video is helpful in analysing techniques and should be used wherever possible.

▶ **TASK 1**

Select a particular action or movement in your sport.
    If possible, divide it into smaller, discrete actions.
    Now write down exactly what you see.
    Avoid the use of opinionated terms such as 'good', 'high' or 'weak' – be more specific, quantifying where possible, e.g. when observing the first part of a golf swing: 'the club was lifted to shoulder height, in line with the body / left shoulder dropped at this point / hips rotating slightly / feet hip width apart / head looking down at the ball'.

▶ **TASK 2**

Look again at each phase and write down where the sources of any problems lie – this is your analysis.

▶ **TASK 3**

Make recommendations as to what needs to be corrected and how (practice and teaching point).

▶ **TASK 4**

You should repeat this task with a number of different actions appropriate to your sport and with different students. If you have the opportunity, discuss your analysis with the student.

In effect coaches are carrying out this analysis all the time when watching the performances of their students, but as a training exercise this task will help you develop a trained eye for spotting faults and their causes.

Direction and application of force

As the joint moves, in whatever direction, there is going to be an opposite and equal reaction.

A flaw in technique is usually attributed to a mis-application of force at some point and the use of slow motion video playback can be extremely valuable in detecting such movements. In your activity above you should note down any such problems as this will be useful when you have to decide which corrections will be necessary to improve the technique.

Stability

An important aspect when considering the application of force is the initial stability of the athlete prior to application. Consider, for example, the stance of a tennis player prior to playing a shot, or of a footballer prior to heading a ball.

There are two major factors factors affecting stability: the first is stance, as mentioned above, and the second is the athlete's centre of gravity, usually around the midpoint of the body.

Swimmers at the start of the race will aim to move their centre of gravity as close to the edge of the blocks as possible in order to initiate a fast movement off the block; gymnasts, divers and skaters will move their centre of gravity by opening and closing their limbs, in order to control the speed of rotation.

Stability can be increased by:

- **Increasing the size of the stance**
- **Lowering the centre of gravity**

It is worth remembering, however, that the more stable a body is, the harder it will be to move quickly. For this reason, actions that require rapid and sudden movement tend to have a more unstable starting position.

Question

Consider this when analysing techniques from your own sport – can you think of any examples?

Principles of fitness training

Essentially the athlete needs to develop their physiological systems in order to cope with the anticipated demands that are to be made on them. The aim of this section is to give you a basic understanding of how the body responds to training and links with Unit 8 Fitness, testing and training and Unit 7 Exercise physiology.

You will need a sound understanding of the following principles to help you construct an appropriate training programme.

Adaptation

The body systems will change or adapt in order to cope with the stress that is placed on it.

Work of a low level of intensity (60–85 per cent of maximum heart rate (MHR) carried out over periods of time will bring about improvements to the cardio-vascular and respiratory systems resulting in a more efficient supply of oxygen and removal of any waste products. This will allow the athlete to work harder before becoming uncomfortably fatigued by the production of lactic acid.

Repeated sets of work at higher levels of intensity (greater than 85 per cent MHR) will result in adaptation within specific muscle groups – either to improve muscular endurance or, if exercised at very high levels of intensity (90 per cent + MHR), to deal with lactic acid production.

An understanding of the different energy systems is necessary to ensure that the athlete is training at the correct level to bring about the correct adaptations. These will enhance the athlete's capability to use that system which is necessary to meet the needs of the sport or event.

Activity 10.12

From your reading of Unit 7 Exercise physiology, list the physiological adaptations that will result following a period of aerobic training.

Overload

Adaptation will only occur if the body systems are stressed just beyond their normal working capacity.

This can be achieved by improving the frequency, intensity or duration of training. When applying interval training techniques, overload can be applied by altering one or more of the following variables:

- ✪ **Distance of each repetition, e.g. 10 × 100 m sprints →
  10 × 110 m sprints**
- ✪ **Interval of rest, e.g. 30 s rest → 20 s rest**
- ✪ **Repetition number, e.g. 10 × 100 m sprints → 12 × 100 m
  sprints**
- ✪ **Training intensity, e.g. target time 13 s → 12.5 s for each
  repetition**

Over a period of time, overload can be achieved by increasing:

- ✪ *Frequency:* **the number of training sessions attended each
  week/month**
- ✪ *Intensity:* **the level of effort which is applied when training**
- ✪ *Time:* **the time spent at each session**

The type of training can also be varied to produce overload – for example, doing additional sessions in the gym, jogging.

Progression

A gradual increase in overload will bring about the best improvements. The systems of the body need time to adapt to the increased pressures put upon them. If this is done too quickly injury may result.

Careful monitoring of the coaching programme will ensure that progression is appropriate.

Specificity

As discussed earlier, different sports have different demands and so the training programme devised must be linked to the physical demands of the sport and event for which the athlete is preparing.

For this reason, you must have an in-depth knowledge of the physical requirements of the sport that you are coaching.

Sports make particular demands on specific muscle groups and so it is important that these muscles are conditioned in a manner that mimics, as closely as possible, the movement pattern required by the sport.

Reversibility

If you don't use it, you lose it.

If an athlete stops or reduces training for any reason, the adaptations gained previously will be lost. You need to take account of this when planning for an athlete who is returning to training after a period of absence.

In general terms, cardio-vascular gains will be lost more quickly than strength gains.

A training programme that has been well planned and offers an interesting and varied programme of work is likely to meet its objectives and motivate the athlete to continue training.

Activity 10.13

Investigate three different training programmes in your chosen sport. Give an example from the programme that demonstrates each of the principles outlined above.

Revision questions

1 Give three important points to remember when giving visual demonstrations.

2 Give three important points to remember when communicating verbally.

3 Describe what is meant by democratic leadership and give one example of a situation in which it may be used in coaching.

4 Name three important features of a good warm-up.

5 When planning for a coaching session, what particular factors need to be taken into account when the participants are young children?

6 What resources does a coach need to consider when planning for a coaching session?

7 Why is important to evaluate your coaching?

8 Name three ways in which a coach could evaluate their performance.

9 Describe briefly four of the components of fitness and the role each of them might play in a sports context.

10 Give three factors which an athlete should consider in relation to proper eating habits whilst training, and state in each case why they are important.

11 Identify as many hazards as possible that you might encounter on a coaching session – you may refer to a particular sport in which you are interested.

12 What information does a coach need to have on the participants prior to taking a session?

13 What three points do you need to consider if you suspect someone has a spinal injury?

14 Describe three different ways sports technology can be used to optimise the performance of the athlete.

15 State two ways that an athlete can improve their stability.

16 Describe briefly the ways in which overload can be applied to achieve adaptation.

17 Define the term specificity and explain why it is an important principle of fitness.

18 List the qualities you would expect to see in a successful coach.

19 What would you consider to be the major differences between a coach and a sports leader?

20 State two organisations that might employ a sports coach.

Assessment activity

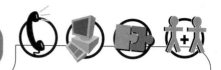

Activities that you have completed throughout this chapter may contribute to this assessment activity. Your tutor will advise of any additions or amendments that need to be made.

Select a sport in which you have a particular interest.

▶ TASK 1

Construct a handbook which can be used by coaches, which outlines:

(a) The main rules

(b) Major techniques which should be taught

(c) Suggested tactics

(d) Common injuries, how they can be prevented and treated. Include guidelines for returning to training after these injuries

▶ TASK 2

Research and analyse the training programme of a performer. Explain the physical and mental training techniques used. Evaluate the effectiveness of this programme following discussions with the coach and the performer and make suggestions for possible improvements.

You should justify your recommendations based on examples used successfully in other training programmes.

▶ TASK 3

Carry out an observation of a performer. Report in detail the actions and movement patterns carried out.

Evaluate the performance and make recommendations for improvement.

Sports psychology

Objectives

- **Understand the concepts of personality and behaviour in the context of sports performance**

- **Analyse motivation as a tool for improving performance**

- **Consider factors which are important in optimising performance**

- **Learn about arousal and the effects of stress in sport**

- **Understand the causes of aggression in sport**

Sports psychology is the scientific study of people and their behaviours in sport and exercise contexts and the practical application of that knowledge. The study of sports psychology will help you to identify principles and guidelines that you can use to help adults and children participate in and benefit from sport and exercise activities.

This unit has links with and supports the practical application of sports psychology in Unit 9 Sport and recreation leadership, Unit 10 Principles of sports coaching, Unit 12 Sports development, Unit 15 Outdoor adventure activities and Unit 16 Play and playwork.

Sports psychologists generally have two objectives in mind:

1   **To understand how psychological factors affect an individual's performance**

2   **To understand how participation in sport and exercise affects a person's psychological development, health and well-being**

The nature of the topic, however, makes it very difficult to obtain conclusive results from research and many psychological theories have been challenged over the years and continue to be so. Part of the fun in studying this unit will be to design a test which will do just that and also help you understand some of the psychological principles which relate to human performance in sport.

Sports coaches and leaders, health and fitness instructors, outdoor pursuits instructors and others working in the leisure and recreation industry will all apply psychological techniques in their careers in order to enhance the performance of those in their charge. Athletes aiming to achieve an optimal performance in competition will also call on various psychological strategies to help them.

Personality and behaviour

If you were asked to describe someone's personality you would probably come up with adjectives such as miserable, happy, outgoing, stable, and so on. Athletes are often remembered for how they react in certain situations and there are many well-known sporting celebrities known as much for their 'personality' as for their sporting prowess.

Whatever definition you come up with for the term personality, one factor is generally agreed on – that it is *unique* to an individual. Wouldn't it be boring if we were all the same!

Personality definitions will also include:

✪ **Characteristics which lead people, when placed in similar situations, to react in different ways**

✪ **Consistent individual behaviour patterns which are unique to an individual**

Of course, what is of interest to us is how someone's personality can influence their performance or even participation in a sporting activity.

Two prominent psychologists, Eysenck and Cattell, have established popular theories relating to personality which are worth looking at.

Cattell's trait theory

Cattell collected information about a range of people from three different sources:

✪ *Life-record (L data)*: **This recorded information such as school grades or work absences, collected through observation and consultation of records**

✪ *Questionnaires (Q data)*: **The completion of pre-set questionnaires**

✪ *Tests (T data)*: **The use of objective tests (different to questionnaires in that the individual is not aware of which aspect of their personality is being measured)**

The L and T data were then analysed using factor analysis (comparing the different pairs of measurements obtained from individuals and then identifying relationships therein). The analysis could then be further extended to determine the strength of correlation between the scores. It was Cattell's belief that if two measures showed a high correlation, they were probably measuring related aspects of personality.

Two distinct personality traits were identified:

✪ *Primary or source traits* **which where inherited and formed the underlying aspects of people's behaviour**

✪ *Surface traits* **which were easily evidenced by our behaviour and influenced by learning and by previous experiences**

Cattell then compared the Q data results with L and T data results and showed that comparable factors could be identified. His conclusion was that there were 16 major personality traits needed to produce a satisfactory description of personality.

The 16 identified traits were:

Reserved... Outgoing
Less intelligent....................................... More intelligent
Affected by feelings.................................Emotionally stable
Submissive...Dominant
Serious... Happy-go-lucky
Expedient... Conscientious
Timid..Venturesome
Tough-minded... Sensitive
Trusting...Suspicious
Practical.. Imaginative
Forthright..Shrewd
Self-assured.. Apprehensive
Conservative... Experimenting
Group-dependent................................. Self-sufficient
Uncontrolled.. Controlled
Relaxed... Tense

Cattell stated that these factors could provide an image of someone in terms of their common traits; however, he stressed that everybody has unique traits which cannot be measured by personality tests.

Activity
11.1

Consider the above traits in terms of your own personality. Compare this with a friend.

Cattell's Sixteen Personality Factor Questionnaire (16PF) is one of the most widely researched personality assessments currently available.

The questionnaire measures 16 underlying personality characteristics that influence the way in which an individual behaves. The information gained can be interpreted to describe likely responses to varied situations and the assessment can be used to provide an insight into:

- ✪ **Aspects of the sporting environment to which the person is more or less suited**
- ✪ **Typical styles of leadership**
- ✪ **Usual team role**
- ✪ **Thinking style**
- ✪ **Characteristic ways of dealing with pressure**

Eysenck's personality theory

Extroversion
Outgoing, forms friendships and socialises easily

Introversion
Quiet and tends to avoid social interaction

Eysenck's major contribution to psychology is his theory of personality. His theory has gained world-wide acceptance and has been studied and assessed on various quantifiable measures. Both Eysenck and Cattell viewed personality as that which permits a prediction of what a person will do in a given situation.

His first research took place at the Mill Hill Hospital and involved over 700 soldiers. He found two dominant general factors: **neuroticism** and **introversion–extroversion** (Figure 11.1). Eysenck established these two factors to be fundamentally important to personality dimensions. He also identified ways in which neuroticism–stability and introversion–extroversion were not only relevant to a wide variety of human performance, feeling and experience, but also identified the importance of the interaction between these two personality factors.

Eysenck's reference to high neuroticism means that person has a tendency for their alarm mechanisms to act too quickly. There are some distinct advantages in that such an individual usually has a lot of 'drive'. The only problem comes about when the person who scores high on the neurotic scale is subjected to a great deal of stress; he or she is then likely to suffer from a neurotic disorder.

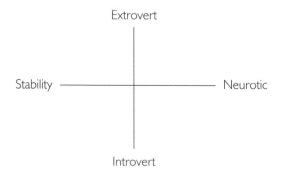

Figure 11.1

The second factor, introversion–extroversion, is viewed as a very important factor. Eysenck suggests that individual variations in introversion–extroversion reflect differences in neurophysiological functioning. Basically, introverts are more easily aroused by events and learn social prohibitions more easily than extroverts. As a result, introverts are more restrained and inhibited. **There also is some evidence that introverts are more influenced by punishments in learning, whereas extroverts are more influenced by rewards.**

Eysenck added a third dimension to his personality theory – **psychoticism**. On the upper level of the psychoticism scale people tend to be insensitive, unconcerned about others, solitary, and against social custom. Hans and Sybil Eysenck described it as troublesome, cruel, lacking in feeling, lacking in empathy, hostile to others, sensation-seeking and liking odd and unusual things.

Eysenck views personality as largely being innate and genetically determined. He bases his view on a considerable number of studies which he has accumulated from the study of twins.

Eysenck maintains that all three factors are found in different studies across cultures and each one has an inherited component.

In studies using Eysenck's Personality Inventory (EPI), Eysenck himself suggested that extroverts and high psychotism scorers are more likely to take up sports and excel in them, because their low arousal levels lead them to seek sensory stimulation and they are more tolerant of the pain associated with sport.

Activity 11.2

Describe the characteristics of players X, Y and Z. Do you know anyone who you think might match this type of personality?

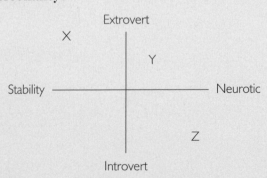

Figure 11.2

Interactional approach

A combination of trait and social learning. Both the environment and an individual's psychological trait need to be considered to understand and predict behaviour, e.g. someone's behaviour on the pitch may be completely different to when they are having tea in the clubhouse afterwards

There are those who are sceptical of such trait theories, however, suggesting that they are too generalised and not directly related to situations. In comparing those who succeed in their chosen sport and those who do not, psychological scales have so far failed to find a significant difference between different traits and performance, or prove that particular sports do or do not attract a particular personality type.

Many sports psychologists now recognise that an interactional approach is the only sensible way to study personality. This takes the view that personality or behaviour is influenced by an individual interacting with the environment or the context in which an athlete is competing. **In other words, different situations will produce different behaviours.**

Activity
11.3

Make a list of the different ways in which you have behaved depending on the situation you are in (e.g. your behaviour when being beaten by a lesser opponent who has continually been aggressive towards you may be different from that towards someone whom you are beating easily).

This interactionist approach is a combination of the trait approach and the social learning approach (Bandura), which suggests that behaviour is best explained as a continuous interaction between current behaviour, thoughts and environmental influences, i.e. **we learn by seeing others being rewarded and punished as well as being rewarded and punished ourselves.**

With sport being such a high profile spectator activity, the importance of inappropriate behaviour (within or outside the sport) being seen to be disapproved of and if necessary punished is extremely important. Inappropriate behaviour is generally regarded as that which has broken the rules of the sport or even the law of the land.

Activity 11.4

Describe three different situations in which sports performers that you know have displayed inappropriate behaviour. What action was taken to punish each individual?

Can you think of any other examples where behaviour has been influenced by interaction with environmental influences?

Case Study
The interactional approach

Two students have enrolled on a Football Coaches Course. Ryan has high self-esteem and Dean has low self-esteem. The group is structured so that each participant takes a turn at leading the practices.

Because he is confident in social situations and about how he looks, Ryan really looks forward to this. He likes being in front of the group, and after leading the class several times has thought of helping out more at the local club. Dean, on the other hand, is not confident of getting up in front of people and feels embarrassed about how he looks. Unlike Ryan, Dean found the experience to be anxiety provoking. All he could think about were the negative comments the class must be making while watching him.

Although Dean likes football, there is no way he wants to get up in front of the group again. Not surprisingly, Dean loses interest in being a coach and drops out of the course.

Activity 11.5

Can you think of similar case studies of people that you know? Describe the situations which affected their behaviour.

Use of personality tests

There are many different ways personality can be tested:

✪ **Interview method: e.g. Inkblot test/Rorschach**

✪ **Discussion method: Discussion with subjects – responses scored and analysed**

✪ **Questionnaires: Cattell/Eysenck**

✪ **Personality profiles: By answering questions and results analysed**

✪ **Observation of behaviour: Recorded, then analysed**

Testing guidelines

✪ **Have well-designed and validated measures, and be able to recognise measurement errors**

✪ **Know your limitations – do not use or interpret results unethically, which can be damaging to people**

✪ **Subjects should be told the purpose of the tests, what they measure, and how the test is going to be conducted – before they actually complete the tests**

✪ **Assure of confidentiality. The results of specific individuals will remain confidential. Fear of exposure may elicit an incorrect response**

Problems with research into personality and sports performance

✪ **Questions can be ambiguous or inappropriate**

✪ **Tests can be subjective – researchers may be biased or different researchers may give different views on the same subject**

✪ **The respondent may reply in the manner s/he thinks s/he should respond**

✪ **Laboratory conditions do not provide a realistic setting**

What can tests tell us about the personalities of top-class sports people?

- Traits of individuals within different types of sport
- Traits of individuals who play in different positions
- Differences between sports people and others
- Differences between team game players and individual sports

Activity 11.6

The assessment brief for this unit requires you to conduct 'research to support or refute your view that personality profiling is a useful tool in predicting sports performance'.

Research the results of at least two types of test that have been published. Comment on the methods used and the conclusions drawn from the study.

> Researchers often publish their work on the Internet. Use a search engine to seek an appropriate site. University libraries will also keep records of published research in the reference section.

With the help of your tutor select one test which you can adopt for use.

Motivation

What kind of grades are you aiming for in your VCE? Why is it that some are just content with a pass at any level and yet others strive to achieve the highest possible grade? Why is it that we may be highly motivated in some aspects of our lives but not in others?

These same questions can be asked in a sporting context.

Motivation is essentially about the direction and intensity of one's effort. This can be identified in terms of:

Motivation
Motivation in sport is the drive to participate or perfom well in a sport or a goal-directed activity

- ✪ **Achievement motivation**
- ✪ **Motivation in terms of competitive stress**
- ✪ **Intrinsic or extrinsic motivation**

This section will consider each of these and determine what factors motivate an athlete to train, compete and succeed. Individuals not only participate in sport and physical activity for different reasons, they are also motivated by different methods and situations.

Achievement motivation

Achievement motivation refers to someone's efforts to strive for success and then experience pride in their accomplishments.

High achievers have a willingness to succeed that will be greater than their fear of failure. There will be a high degree of persistence to succeed – even in the face of failure. Many sports participants will enjoy a challenge as long as it is realistic. Coaches often refer to this as a high degree of **competitiveness** in an athlete.

Activity 11.7

Consider situations in which you have been highly motivated to succeed, even in the face of adversity. What was it that drove you on?
What characteristics would you expect to observe in a person who was motivated to achieve?

There can be a problem with high achievers in that if they don't perceive there to be a challenge they may not become sufficiently aroused or motivated and then not perform to the best of their ability. This can be the case when a good team or player comes up against (what they perceive to be) lesser opposition and fail to become sufficiently aroused to achieve a victory – this perhaps explains why the underdog can 'pull off' a surprising victory.

Low achievers on the other hand, will avoid personal challenges, often giving up, or even attempting unattainable challenges where failure is a distinct possibility and it therefore becomes non-threatening. They will often take the easiest possible route to achieve success, i.e. by playing weaker opposition. With young children, achievement motivation will result if experiences of success or failure are handled well.

Achievement at any level should be rewarded and positive emotions used to encourage future attempts.

If you consider situations when a teacher or coach has praised you for a successful attempt (regardless of how small), your response will probably have been to try harder next time. In contrast, when faced with criticism your willingness to try harder has probably not been as good.

It is important therefore that feedback to individuals who are learning is positive so that self-esteem and confidence remain high.

Activity 11.8

From your own experiences, describe situations when you have not been motivated to try hard. Try to explain the reasons for this.

Bandura's self-efficacy theory

Self-efficacy is someone's belief or self-confidence that they have the necessary ability to meet the demands of a particular sporting situation. It is specific to a particular situation. Factors which influence this include:

- ✪ *Past achievements*: **which if successful led to high self-efficacy or if failed would lead to low self-efficacy – there is nothing like standing on the block when you know you have beaten all the other athletes previously!**

- ✪ *Vicarious experiences*: **observation of others succeeding in a similar skill or activity (particularly where the person is of similar age or ability). You will probably recall feelings of self-confidence after watching a rousing performance yourself**

✪ *Verbal persuasion*: positive encouragement from someone whose opinions matter or from someone of higher status. Again, consider how good you have felt after receiving praise from someone important to you

✪ *Physiological levels of arousal*: a controlled level of arousal which will result in optimising performance – you often see athletes 'psyching themselves up' in a bid to improve their performance

Activity 11.9

A fellow student has low self-confidence in her ability to dive head first into the water. Using each of the factors outlined above, determine how you would raise the girl's self-efficacy to help her learn to dive in.

It is possible that a team player may be quite comfortable in one position, and therefore have high self-efficacy, and yet in another position feel completely out of place and so avoid the situation. This person therefore has low self-efficacy in this situation.

Bandura maintains that a higher level of self-efficacy will result in a higher level of performance. Self-efficacy may deteriorate if:

✪ **Feedback is negative or critical**

✪ **Expectations from others are too unrealistic or the competition is too good**

✪ **The reward becomes more important than the performance**

✪ **The outcomes are rewarded more than the performance (it is perfectly possible to have an outstanding performance and yet be beaten)**

Good coaches can avoid low self-efficacy by:

✪ **Setting short-term achievable targets**

✪ **Providing positive feedback and improving the athlete's understanding of what is a good performance**

✪ **Offering encouragement**

✪ **Setting individual targets rather than focusing on team goals**

✪ **Taking account of the athlete's personality and levels of anxiety when giving feedback**

- **Promoting intrinsic goals – playing is more important than winning**
- **Avoiding comparisons**
- **Identifying with positive role models**
- **Providing opportunities for early success**

Attribution theory

Attributing the reason for success or failure can also affect motivation levels and even affect the desire to continue participation in sport.

It may be useful to refer to the work of Bernard Weiner whose model suggests four major attribution elements (Figure 11.3):

- *Internal and stable factors*: **Ability, skills and physical capacity ('my shooting skills were better')**
- *Internal and unstable factors*: **Effort, current form, level of preparation ('I worked hard in practice')**
- *External and stable factors*: **Task difficulty, standard of the opposition ('they were just too good')**
- *External and unstable factors*: **Luck, weather, referee ('the referee was useless!')**

If it is realistic to do so, the coach should attribute failure to internal and stable factors which are controllable and can be improved on in the next performance. For example, 'The match was lost because your serve was poor' will mean that if this aspect can be improved on then it is possible that the overall performance will improve next time. This is more likely to motivate the player to improve that particular aspect of the performance.

	Internal	External
Stable	Ability	Task difficulty
Unstable	Effort	Luck

Figure 11.3 *Weiner's classification for causal attribution*

External and unstable factors are less controllable but useful reasons to give if the performance is good but the outcome is poor. For example, the athlete finishes the race having achieved a lifetime-best performance but is beaten, simply because others in the race were better.

A poor performance may also be due to other external or environmental factors such as bad weather or faulty equipment, i.e. reasons which are beyond the control of the athlete. The athlete is less likely then to become dejected. Of course, a continued run of bad luck will result in distress and frustration and it will take a convincing coach to make his or her athletes or players believe that they do have the ability.

On the other hand, if the athlete deems success to be due to luck or other external factors which adversely affected the opposition (e.g. the opposition had a bad day, or their key player was injured) then this too can reduce the positive emotions normally associated with success.

Self-confidence can be improved by attributing success to internal factors which were in the control of the athlete.

Many of us will subconsciously make internal attributions and thus reward ourselves for success – even in moments of failure – if only to protect our egos from the psychological consequences of failure! If we don't, our levels of motivation diminish.

This can lead to a feeling of *learned helplessness* caused by constant attribution of failure to internal factors, which may ultimately lead to an almost pre-determined expectation of failure.

In many cases, this may be the reason why some individuals may not participate in sport – perhaps they perceive themselves as being no good and so they avoid taking part, regardless of how much fun it might be.

More specifically, a perceived lack of skill might prevent someone participating in a particular sport (e.g. 'I can't head a ball so I won't be any good at football'). Good teachers and coaches can apply psychological principles discussed in this chapter in order to reverse such feelings of helplessness.

Activity 11.10

Study at least two different performances of an athlete in competition, one successful and one of failure, and try to attribute reasons for the outcome. Compare *your* reasons to those *given by themselves*.

The root of motivation can vary between individuals and, as we have seen, can vary between athletes, the situation or indeed the incentives at stake. We will consider the latter in terms of motivation which is **intrinsic** or **extrinsic**:

✪ **Intrinsic motivation** is generally linked to successful outcomes which have resulted from enjoyable participation in the activity. Participants will feel a sense of self-satisfaction from their mastery over themselves or others, leading to higher self esteem. This type of **internal reinforcement** will result in a determination to succeed on subsequent occasions

✪ **Extrinsic motivation** results from the receipt of external rewards usually linked to the quality of performance. Examples will include:

  – Feedback on results of the performance

  – Praise from significant others such as parents, peers, coaches, team colleagues etc.

  – Tangible awards such as certificates, badges, medals and prize money

Care has to be taken that motivation does not become dependent upon ever-increasing need for greater extrinsic motivation which, if undervalued, loses the motivational effect. This can become the case when athletes receive rewards which don't match the effort or outcome (for example, children who receive praise too often or are awarded badges where the challenge has not been fully met).

Used sensibly, however, extrinsic motivational techniques should complement internal reinforcement to ensure that the athlete is suitably rewarded for their performance *and not just the outcome*.

Activity
11.11

Consider the different ways in which success can be rewarded in the following situations:

★ Individuals who have played well in a team which has just lost

★ A child who finished last in a race but ran a personal best time

★ A marathon runner who has completed his first marathon

★ A swimmer who wins easily every time without having to try hard

Motivation within a team

Individuals who are performing as part of a team are often affected by what is known as **social cohesion**. It is important that individuals who are part of a team are set individual goals which they know are going to be monitored, otherwise there is a danger of what is termed **social loafing**, i.e. hiding within the group when there is a belief that they can rely on others to 'pull then through'. When individual feedback or praise in a team situation is provided it can often serve to generate higher levels of effort. In many cases, athletes competing in a relay race will produce a better performance than when they are competing just for themselves.

A group which interacts with each other positively, working towards the same goal (e.g. to win the league), is more likely to perform better as a team. The converse can also be true, of course, if individuals in a team do not share the team objectives.

Coaches need to consider factors which affect group cohesion when selecting teams. It may not always be the best players who constitute the best team – a fact not always understood by the media when football managers announce their team!

Goal setting

A goal can probably be best described as an aim or a target which you would like to be achieved. Setting goals can be useful not just in a sporting context but in life generally – some will be achieved, others not – but the challenge in trying to achieve them can be a lot of fun and will often produce a more positive outcome. Goals can considered in three different ways:

- ✪ *Outcome goals* **in which the focus is on the result (e.g. winning a race). There is little control in this type of goal, as external factors can dictate the result (e.g. a faster opponent) despite the quality of the performance**
- ✪ *Performance goals* **where the attention is on achieving a standard (e.g. improving on a best time/achieving a qualifying target). Such goals are more flexible and in your control**
- ✪ *Process goals* **where the focus is on the actions of the individual and the quality of the performance (i.e. demonstrating effective technique). This type of goal, when achieved, can improve an individual's self-efficacy and confidence, making you feel good!**

It is common for parents and peers to regard performance goals as the only outcome and to measure success on this basis. A more realistic assessment of individual progress, however, is the achievement of either performance or

David Cave Photography

Figure 11.4 *Discussing and agreeing goals with the performer are essential.*

process goals. In setting goals of this nature, athletes and coaches must apply certain principles for them to be effective. The acronym **S M A R T E R** is a useful way to remember the key principles.

Goals that you set should be:

✪ *Specific*: **State exactly what is being aimed for without being vague, e.g.** *I aim to reduce the number of strides between hurdles*

✪ *Measurable*: **Quantify the goal as precisely as possible, e.g.** *I aim to reduce the number of strides between hurdles by two*

✪ *Agreed*: **Both coach and athlete must be happy with the goal set**

✪ *Realistic*: **The athlete must be capable of achieving the goal and be confident and capable of achieving it. Set moderately difficult but realistic goals**

- ✪ *Time specific*: **The athlete should aim to achieve the goal within a specific time period, e.g.** *I aim to reduce the number of strides between hurdles by two within the next three months*

An effective method of setting long-term goals is to break them down into smaller time periods with a series of stepped objectives to be achieved on the way.

It is important that at the end of each phase goals are:

- ✪ *Evaluated*: **The athlete may have achieved, underachieved or overachieved the goal. Whatever the outcome, it is important that both athlete and coach are aware of the reasons why and use this information to plan for the next goal**

- ✪ *Recorded*: **Writing down the goals will remind the athlete exactly what the objectives are and will also serve as a reminder as to exactly what progress is being made. When an outcome goal is not achieved it will be useful to reflect on improvements that have been made on other aspects of the performance**

Other factors to consider in goal setting are:

- ✪ *Practice goals should be set as well as competition goals*: **Too often, athletes and coaches focus only on competition goals. Setting practice goals is important because of the large amounts of time athletes spend practising and the possibility of becoming bored**

- ✪ *Coaches should help their athletes develop goal achievement strategies*: **This will form part of the training plans. If athletes understand why they are training and are clear about the likely outcomes at the end of it, they are more likely to be motivated to train harder**

- ✪ *Consideration needs to be given to the athlete's personality and motivations when goal setting*: **High achievers will readily seek out and adopt more challenging but realistic goals, whereas low achievers will avoid challenging goals and seek to adopt either very easy or very difficult goals**

- ✪ *There has to be a commitment to achieving a goal from both the coach and the athlete*: **Coaches should promote commitment by encouraging progress and providing consistent feedback. Feedback about performance is essential if goals are going to influence performance**

- ✪ *Group goals should also be considered*: **However, all members of the group should be striving for the same goals and should have had an input into the establishment of the goals**

The strategy will not work, however, if:

- ✪ **Specific goals are not set**
- ✪ **Too many goals are set too soon**
- ✪ **Goals are not adjusted in the event of setbacks (e.g. illness or injury)**
- ✪ **Goals are based only on outcomes**

Used effectively, goals will prove to be a very useful tool in motivation.

Activity 11.12

▶ **TASK 1**

Discuss goal setting with someone who has set themselves a target for achievement in sport.

Write down their short, medium and long-term goals, applying the principles set out above. You should try to make the goals process or performance orientated rather than simply based on outcomes.

Record the goals that were agreed and the strategy being adopted to achieve them.

▶ **TASK 2**

Arrange to meet this same person to discuss progress (or otherwise) towards their first goal.

Evaluate the strategy that was used and review any future strategy and goals accordingly.

▶ **TASK 3**

If possible, repeat Task 2 on several occasions and record your evaluation each time.

In lots of cases, individuals will not fully achieve all their goals. What is important is that the reasons for non-achievement are understood as much as possible – equally, if success has been achieved, it can be helpful to know why, so that a similar strategy can be repeated in the future.

Optimising performance

So much time and attention is paid to improving the physiological state of the body in order to improve performance that little regard is taken of the psychological aspects which can allow the athlete to benefit fully from this. Sports psychology applied effectively will maximise the potential abilities of the athlete, although it will not make them exceed their physiological capability! In this section we will have a look at the different ways in which we can optimise performance – in other words, get the best out of an individual.

Imagery

A proven and extremely effective technique used by many athletes who are competing in particularly stressful situations is a process known as **imagery**. Furthermore, many athletes also use imagery to make their experiences in sport and exercise settings more enjoyable.

Imagery is essentially a way of re-creating previous experiences or picturing new events in order to prepare for performance. Terms such as *visualisation, mental rehearsal* and *mental practice* also describe a similar process. It involves recalling from memory information stored from experience and then shaping these into meaningful images which the athlete would like to re-create. The mind simulates the movement patterns required in advance of carrying out the movements physically.

Golfers, for example, may visualise their swing and feel the sensation of hitting the ball and even 'watch' the ball in trajectory and then landing. Basketball players or footballers may rehearse the technique in their mind's eye and visualise the outcome prior to taking a penalty shot.

It is also possible to re-create movements based on watching successful performers on video in a bid to simulate a similar performance, although it is stressed that the athlete must be capable (i.e. strong enough, sufficient skill, etc.).

Imagery should involve as many senses as possible, particularly those kinaesthetic sensations experienced in the activity being visualised, e.g. the sound of the ball being hit, the sight of the ball, the feeling in the fingertips and muscles of playing the shot. In addition, learning to attach various emotional states or moods to the imagined experiences is also important, e.g. anxiety, anger, joy, pain, etc.

A number of factors will determine the extent to which imagery can improve performance:

David Cave Photography

Figure 11.5 *Imagery: close your eyes and* imagine *the execution of the movement.*

- ✪ *Nature of the task*: **Those tasks which involve mostly cognitive components, such as decision making and perception, show the greatest positive benefits, e.g. a footballer mentally rehearsing the different responses to the ball being crossed from different directions in the goal mouth area, or a tennis player rehearsing how they will react to the different types of shots played by their opponent**

- ✪ *Skill level of the performer*: **Evidence suggests that imagery can help both the beginner and the experienced performer. It may help the beginner learn the cognitive elements which are important to a successful outcome. For example, a coach may demonstrate the correct way to play a backhand shot – and then have the students picture themselves performing the serve. For the more experienced performer, imagery may help refine learned skills and prepare for making decisions and perceptual adjustments quickly**

- *Imaging ability*: **Imagery is a skill which needs to be practised in order to improve its effectiveness**
- *Imagery should be used in addition to physical practice*: **Imagery should be viewed as a way to train the mind in conjunction with physically training the body. Mental practice does, however, improve performance better than no practice at all, and can be useful when an athlete is injured or fatigued**

Activity 11.13

Using imagery in different situations

Imagery should be practised when you are in a relaxed state with no possibility of distraction. As skills develop, you will learn to use imagery in the midst of distractions and in actual competition.

When you practise, consider the visual, auditory, kinaesthetic and mood sensations as realistically as possible.

You can imagine the sensations using **internal imagery**, as if you had a camera on your head and you are visualising the image from your own vantage point, or using **external imagery**, as if viewing from the perspective of an external observer. The former is generally more effective in establishing the kinaesthetic awareness (i.e. the feel of the movement) but using either or both techniques as appropriate to the situation can be just as effective.

What is important is to establish a good clear controlled image. You may use imagery effectively in one or more of the following situations:

- *To improve confidence*: **Imagine yourself in a situation where you often lose your concentration (e.g. after being fouled, or after missing an easy shot in tennis), and then imagine yourself remaining composed and focused immediately afterwards**
- *To build confidence*: **Think of recent performances which have had disappointing outcomes or in which your team mates have turned against you because of your poor performances – all resulting in a drop in confidence. In any of these situations you should imagine yourself taking control and maintaining confidence. Seeing yourself perform well in your mind makes you feel you can perform well under adverse circumstances**

✪ *To control emotional responses*: **Visualise situations which have caused problems in the past, such as choking under pressure or becoming aggressive following a poor result, or after an official's caution. You should picture yourself dealing with these events in a positive way, such as taking a deep breath and focusing on your breathing as you concentrate on the task in hand**

Note: This type of imagery can be useful as an aid to relaxation when stress levels are having an adverse effect on performance; however, imagery can also increase arousal levels which can increase cognitive anxiety which may, in some cases, negatively affect performance (see 'Inverted U hypothesis', which is discussed later in this chapter)

✪ *To acquire and practise sport skills*: **Visualise the execution of a particular skill at which you are reasonably competent (this may be of a performer whose technique you wish to copy, or from video observation of the skill on video or by**

David Cave Photography

Figure 11.6 *Concentrating on the task may improve the final outcome.*

a demonstrator). You can practise skills to fine-tune them or you can focus on weaknesses and try correcting them

Note: This practice can also be used to preview participation either in a forthcoming competition or event, or to review a past performance highlighting skills which were done particularly well

✪ *To acquire and practise strategy*: Useful in team situations. Visualise the different tactical opportunities or responses possible in the area in which you normally play

✪ *To cope with pain or injury*: Instead of feeling sorry for yourself, imagine performing the skills and techniques you once mastered. There is some evidence which suggests this might improve recovery rates

✪ *To solve problems*: If you are not performing up to expectation, use imagery to examine critically all aspects of your performance to find the source of the problem (not always a good idea when you are trying to get to sleep!). You should visually compare what you are doing now and *what you were doing in the past*

Imagery can be practised at almost any time. Ten minutes is recommended as a maximum. Remember that imagery can:

✪ **Improve concentration**
✪ **Develop confidence**
✪ **Improve techniques**

Understanding arousal and perception of stress

Many people confuse the terms of arousal, stress and anxiety. For the purpose of sports psychology, they need to be looked at as three different and distinct entities:

- ✪ **Arousal can be defined as a general physiological and psychological activation of the person that varies on a continuum from deep sleep to intense excitement**
- ✪ **Anxiety is the negative emotional state with feelings of nervousness, worry and apprehension associated with activation or arousal of the body**
- ✪ **Stress is a state of tension that is created when a person responds to the demands and pressures that come from work, family and other external sources, as well as those that are internally generated from self-imposed demands, obligations and self-criticism**

Anxiety has two components: the cognitive anxiety or state anxiety, and the somatic anxiety or trait anxiety.

- ✪ **State anxiety is a temporary and always changing state of subjective, consciously perceived feelings of apprehension and tension, associated with activation of the autonomic nervous system. This is usually brought about as a result of the individual in a particular situation, e.g. prior to a race or a game**
- ✪ **Trait anxiety is behavioural disposition to perceive objectively non-dangerous circumstances as threatening, and respond accordingly. Trait anxiety is directly related to the personality of the individual**

Stress can be extremely advantageous to an athlete in helping them to achieve a better performance. Very often people will actively seek out stressful situations and thrive on the feelings associated with them, e.g. rock climbers. This is called **eustress**.

On the other hand, stress can lead to anxiety resulting in a negative response and a deterioration in performance. This is usually called **distress**.

This section will look at:

- ✪ **The causes of stress and the different ways in which we respond to it**

- ✪ **How it can be used to advantage**
- ✪ **Ways of reducing or coping with stressful situations which lead to anxiety**

The prime objective is to optimise performance. It is a great shame to put in many hours of physical practice and then perform badly because of poor mental preparation. Many elite clubs and national sports teams now employ full-time sports psychologists to accompany them and help prepare the athletes to ensure that they perform to the very best of their ability.

Causes of stress (the stressor)

As we have identified earlier in this chapter, situations can be perceived by different people in different ways, e.g. some will thrive on the challenge of tackling a 16-stone rugby forward thundering towards them, others will seek a hole in the ground! Stress therefore is not an inevitable consequence in all situations. The level of stress will depend on how you perceive any potential threat created by the situation and how you will cope with that threat.

Activity 11.14

Try to identify situations you have been in where you have felt that you have been unable to cope. Do you think that the same stressor will affect someone else in the same way? If not, why not?

The idea of coping is important when we look into the different ways in which we can manage stress.

Common stressors in sport include:

- ✪ *Expectation to do well*: **Very often our perception is that we will disappoint or let others down, particularly if they have invested time and money (or friendship?) in helping you. Media pressures can also be particularly stressful by creating expectation**

- ✪ *Competition*: **This is probably the largest stressor, particularly if the focus is on achieving a result. The (perceived) importance of the event will obviously influence the level of stress. As competition is often perceived as the ultimate assessment of our training, it can create enormous levels of anxiety – especially if we have a *perceived* inability to cope with the level of competition and the consequences of not** achieving the expected outcome. The crowd too can have an effect on stress levels, creating high competitive anxiety – we will look at this later in this section

- ✪ *Uncertainty*: **Uncertainty about the opposition, the venue, the effects of injury or what to do when attending an event for the first time are all stressful situations to many people. Coaches often forget that whilst they may be confident and sure about situations, the athletes in their charge may not be**

- ✪ *Conflict*: **Conflict with the coach, other players, the referee or the opposition can bring about increased stress**

- ✪ *Frustration*: **This often results from aggression when a particular goal is not achieved. This can be caused by a number of factors, such as external influences over which we have no control, e.g. injury, being sent off or substituted, good play by the opposition; or by our inadequacies, which we sometimes have difficulty in explaining: 'I can't understand it, I have been playing well all season!'**

- ✪ *Training difficulties*: **This includes injury, problems with the coach or with the facilities, poor equipment, excessive fatigue or even ill-timed, demanding competitions**

The weather too can create stress, particularly if conditions are in extreme variation to that expected or prepared for.

It is important that we recognise the cause of stress if we are to manage it effectively.

Activity
11.15

From your own experience, list as many stressors as you can think of that have occurred in your sport. Create three columns: the first, which lists the stressors which you believe have assisted in achieving a positive outcome; the second, in which you include stressors which have created unnecessarily high anxiety levels; and the third in which you write your response to the stress.

▼▼▼▼▼▼▼▼▼

Cognitive anxiety
Cognitive anxiety involves mental processes resulting in feelings of uneasiness or worry. Evidence of this is irritability, nail biting, talking a lot, or being unable to keep still

▲▲▲▲▲▲▲▲▲

Responses to stress

If your perception is of a disparity between the demand and feeling threatened by your capability to respond in a particular situation, this will bring about increased worries (cognitive anxiety), heightened physiological activity (somatic anxiety), or both. Stress may also affect concentration and muscle tension.

When creating your list in the last activity, you may have included such effects as worry, a need to withdraw from the situation, irritability (cognitive responses), sweating and feelings of nausea and tension etc. (somatic responses). The chances are that if you have had to perform on the public stage in your life, you will have experienced most of these responses.

In anticipation of a stress, the body will make certain automatic changes to prepare for it – such as increasing the heart and breathing rate, raising blood sugar levels and releasing adrenaline.

There may well be behavioural consequences as a result of stress:

✪ *Improved performance* **as a result of appropriate physical and mental preparation**

✪ *Deterioration in performance,* **where an imbalance between the demand and the ability to cope is perceived – caused by an excessive demand created by the stressors or inappropriate preparation**

✪ *Individual self-esteem and confidence* **can likewise be affected positively or negatively and this may of course affect either of the above. The stress process can therefore become a continuous cycle**

There is a danger that if the stress is not controlled, then, over a period of time, the mind and the body fails to cope, leading to more serious health disorders.

Anxiety

Anxiety is the consequence of excessive stress resulting in worry about the fear of failing in a competitive situation. Arousal levels are high due to the individual's emotional response to the competitive situation – caused by one or more of the stressors identified earlier.

Anxiety is a result of our feelings of being threatened:

✪ **Threat of physical harm**
✪ **Threat to our self-esteem**
✪ **Threat of letting other people down**
✪ **Fear of being punished**

It is important that coaches are aware of how their athletes cope with anxiety – some cope better than others.

Martens developed the Sport Competition Anxiety Test (SCAT) in 1977 in an attempt to identify athletes who were likely to suffer from anxiety in competitive situations.

Martens' theory is based on the principle that athletes will interact differently with competitive situations, resulting in what he termed *competitive trait anxiety*. The competitive process involves the interaction between personality factors, competitive trait anxiety and the situation. This interaction will affect behaviour and may cause *state anxiety*.

Sport Competition Anxiety Test

Competitors were given a self-report questionnaire to assess the anxiety they felt during competition. This test measures *competitive trait anxiety* and is useful in predicting how anxious a performer will be in future competitions – their state anxiety. Both *personality* and *situational factors* can determine anxiety levels.

Assessing your anxiety: Trait anxiety test

Directions: Below are some statements about how people feel when they compete in sports and games. Read each statement and decide if you hardly ever, sometimes, or often feel this way when you compete in sports and games. If your choice is hardly ever, mark 'A', if your choice is sometimes, mark 'B' and if your choice is often, mark 'C'. There are no right or wrong answers. Do not spend too much time on any statement.

1.	Competing against others is socially enjoyable.	A	B	C
2.	Before I compete I feel uneasy.	A	B	C
3.	Before I compete I worry about not performing well.	A	B	C
4.	I am a good sportsman when I compete.	A	B	C
5.	When I compete, I worry about making mistakes.	A	B	C
6.	Before I compete I am calm.	A	B	C
7.	Setting a goal is important when competing.	A	B	C
8.	Before I compete I get a queasy feeling in my stomach.	A	B	C
9.	Just before competing, I notice my heart beats faster than usual.	A	B	C
10.	I like to compete in games that demand considerable physical energy.	A	B	C
11.	Before I compete I feel relaxed.	A	B	C
12.	Before I compete I am nervous.	A	B	C
13.	Team sports are more exciting than individual sports.	A	B	C
14.	I get nervous wanting to start the game.	A	B	C
15.	Before I compete I usually get uptight.	A	B	C

This is the Sport Competition Anxiety Test, a sport-specific measure of trait anxiety developed by Martens *et al.* (R. Martens, R.S. Vealey and

D. Burton (1990) *Competitive Anxiety in Sport*, Champaign, IL: Human Kinetics Books).

Burnout

A continued inability to meet excessive training and competitive demands over a period of time, resulting in ongoing high levels of stress, is highly likely to result in a withdrawal from a previously enjoyable activity.

Burnout can be recognised by the following characteristics:

✪ **Physical and emotional exhaustion – resulting in lack of interest or concern, loss of sleep and lethargy**
✪ **Low self-esteem – resulting in possible failure and depression**
✪ **Impersonal and unfeeling towards others – largely due to exhaustion**

This should not be confused with 'dropping out'. Athletes who burn out will almost certainly adopt characteristics similar to the above. Coaches have to observe their athletes carefully as sometimes athletes can be suffering the effects displayed above and for other reasons (scholarships, parental or coach pressure, for example) remain in the sport.

One has to bring in to question here the longer-term psychological impact that burnout will have on an athlete, perhaps long after they have left the sport.

Activity
11.16

Do you know anyone who once participated in sport regularly and has now given up? If so, ask them why they no longer participate and note down the reasons. Compare the reasons with others. What are the most common responses?

Relationship between performance and anxiety

There are a number of theories which try to explain the relationship between anxiety and performance and you should consider these in terms of how they relate to actual examples of performance.

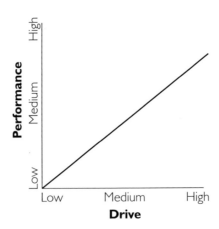

Figure 11.7 *Graph of drive theory*

The **drive theory** (Figure 11.7) suggests that athletes will perform better when arousal levels are higher. For example, players in the school football team are more likely to perform better when their class-mates turn out to watch them. This is perhaps one explanation as to why home performances may be better.

The drive theory, however, does not apply to all individuals, as the increased anxiety levels brought about by increase in arousal may negatively affect performance. This is explained rather well by the **inverted U hypothesis**.

Optimum stress levels

The level of stress under which you operate is important. If you are not under enough stress, then you may find that your performance suffers because you are bored and unmotivated. If you are under too much stress, then you will find that your results suffer as you find it difficult to focus on techniques necessary for a good performance.

Inverted U hypothesis

The graph below shows the relationship between stress and quality of performance:

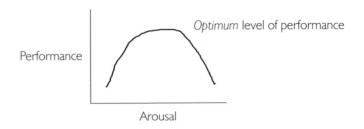

Figure 11.8 *Inverted U graph*

The shape of the graph indicates where the term **inverted U hypothesis** originates from.

- ✪ *Where stress is low,* **you may find that your performance is low because you become bored, lack concentration and lack motivation. If this state persists for a long time, then you may find the sport tedious, and give it up**

- ✪ *Where stress is too high,* **your performance can suffer from all the symptoms of stress. Your flow can be disrupted, you can be distracted, and competition can become threatening and unpleasant**

- ✪ *At a moderate level of stress,* **there is a zone of best performance. If you can keep yourself within this zone, then you will be sufficiently aroused to give a high quality performance, while not being over-stressed and unhappy**

This zone of optimum performance is in a different place and is a different shape for different people. Some people may operate most effectively at a level of stress that would leave other people either bored or in pieces.

It is possible that someone who functions superbly in a low-level competition might experience difficulties in high-level competition. Alternatively, someone who performs only moderately at a low level of competition might give exceptional performances under extreme pressure.

Not only will the zones of optimum performance be in different places for different athletes, they will also be different heights and different widths. This is why you must take responsibility for controlling your own levels of stress, particularly in a team situation: if the team generally needs motivation, but you are in an optimum zone, then paying attention to a motivating team talk may move you to a state of being over-stressed. Similarly, if some team members need to be relaxed, then relaxation techniques applied to an entire team may move you to state of bored demotivation!

You may also find that fine and complex skills are less tolerant to stress than simple skills – your zone of optimum performance may be narrower for very difficult skills than for the basic skills of the sport.

Activity 11.17

Finding your optimum stress level

An effective way of finding the stress level at which you operate best is to keep a training and performance log. In this, record the quality of every training session or performance, along with the level of stress that you felt during that performance.

If you have stress monitoring equipment, and can score your performance, then this gives you hard, objective figures to use in your training log. If you do not have the ability to do this, then record your subjective views of the stress levels you felt and the quality of the session.

After a time, review the training log – this should give you some good information on the way that you respond to stress. This information will help you to decide and implement a stress management programme that is appropriate to the different sporting situations in which you find yourself.

The catastrophe theory

You will note that the graph in the inverted U hypothesis shows a gradual decline in performance as a result of increased levels of anxiety. If the levels of cognitive anxiety are high – you are extremely worried – then, in certain situations, there can be quite a sudden drop in performance. This is known as the **catastrophe theory** – probably because that best describes the outcome!

You may have found yourself in a situation when competing, either as an individual or in a team, when something unexpected happens – the opposition were better than expected and you find yourself losing, or a scout or selector turns up to watch you – and all of a sudden anxiety levels increase to such a level that performance deteriorates quite significantly.

It is very difficult to recover from such a catastrophic drop in performance; however, in situations like this you must try to relax physically, eliminate your worries and regain your confidence. You will then need to control your arousal levels back to an optimum level – no easy task!

Activity 11.18

Note any situations either with yourself or with others which have resulted in sudden over-anxiety and a consequential drop in performance. It would also be useful to record any successful recoveries and note the strategies which were adopted.

Social facilitation theory

The effect of an audience can have a positive or negative effect on performance depending on the ability of the performer to perform a skill confidently. The **social facilitation theory** suggests that the presence of others helps performance on well-learned or simple skills but can inhibit or lessen performance on unlearned or complex tasks.

Perhaps you can remember during PE lessons that when you had learned a skill well and were confident about doing it you would be keen for your class-mates or the teacher to watch you, driving you on perhaps to an even better performance. On the other hand, if the task was difficult and you were not so confident, the presence of others was not at all helpful! The chances were that you would not perform so well.

The type of audience will also influence the anxiety levels of the performer. If you think that your performance is being evaluated (even when it may not be), this too may heighten apprehension and anxiety, leading to an increased probability of error in performance. Such audiences might include parents, coaches, selectors or scouts, or even just friends who may be watching you for the first time.

It may be sensible therefore during important competitions, and if it is possible, for the athlete not to be informed as to who is in the audience and to focus on the forthcoming event.

Aggression

It is likely that you have experienced aggression at some point in your sporting career – either watching others, from an opponent during a game, or perhaps you have even been aggressive yourself in certain situations.

Aggression is normally associated with sports that involve a high degree of physical contact.

It will be helpful to define exactly what we mean by aggression. A number of similar definitions have been put forward, from which four criteria of aggression emerge:

- ✪ **It is physical or verbal behaviour that can be observed by others (e.g. kicking another player deliberately or shouting hurtful abuse at someone). It is not an attitude or an emotion – we cannot 'will' aggression on someone**
- ✪ **Harm or injury is intended**

David Cave Photography

Figure 11.9 *There is no place for aggression in sport.*

- ✪ It is directed towards someone living, e.g. throwing your racket at the umpire. Throwing your racket down on the ground in disgust, however, is *not* an aggressive act as the racket is not living
- ✪ It involves intent. Accidentally kicking someone is not an act of aggression as harm is not intended

Activity 11.19

Using the criteria outlined above, list at least ten possible acts of aggression which you have witnessed in sporting situations. If they do not meet any of the criteria, they cannot be regarded as acts of aggression.

The definition of aggression can be further defined:

- ✪ *Hostile aggression* is regarded as a deliberate act in which the principal aim is to hurt someone and is a clear infringement of the laws, such as stamping on a player in a rugby scrum or deliberately smacking someone across the shins with a hockey stick
- ✪ *Instrumental aggression* is a consequence of reckless play – going in hard to a tackle, for example, or continually mouthing off to a player in order to raise anxiety levels. In either case, the intention is to hurt, although technically they do not deliberately infringe the laws of the game

Neither form of aggression is acceptable and should be discouraged.

Activity 11.20

Consider the acts of aggression listed in the previous activity and determine whether they are *hostile or instrumental acts of aggression.*

What is often difficult to determine is the boundary between instrumental aggression and **assertiveness**. A player who is being assertive, however, has no intention to harm the opponent and is unlikely to be reprimanded by the referee. That said, it is difficult for a referee who has to make a quick decision to decide whether a player is being assertive or aggressive.

There are a number of theories which try to explain the cause of aggression:

- *Instinct theory* suggests that aggression is innate, that it is something we are born with. The theory suggests that sport is a useful vehicle through which people can channel their aggressive instincts through socially acceptable means. (This is often referred to as catharsis.) Many question, however, that this is the case, and certainly aggressive acts in sport should not be an excuse for 'letting off steam' generated elsewhere

- *Frustration–aggression theory* or *drive theory* implies that aggression is the direct result of a frustration that occurs because of failure or if a goal is blocked in some way, e.g. hitting someone who has continually been fouling you and has gone unnoticed by the referee, or someone who has been bad-mouthing you all through a match. Once again, this is a poor excuse for aggression. Many sportsmen and women are able to control their frustration through the adoption of other techniques or simply learn to 'walk away'

- *Social learning theory* explains aggression as behaviour which people learn through watching others display particular types of behaviour and which is reinforced for carrying out similar actions themselves. An example of this would be when a child watches a particular role model on television (a high profile football player, for example) committing acts of aggression time after time and then repeating this same action on the playing field and receiving adulation from his team mates. What is particularly worrying is the number of 'touchline' parents and coaches who apparently condone this kind of behaviour.

  This theory does stress the importance that role models with a high media profile have in influencing many of our young athletes

Activity
11.21

Consider once again the acts of aggression identified earlier. Suggest which of the theories above best explains the reason for this behaviour.

Revision questions

1 Name two possible definitions of personality.

2 What does Cattell's 16PF test attempt to measure?

3 Describe possible characteristics of an introvert.

4 Describe briefly what is meant by the interactional approach to profiling personality.

5 Name four guidelines which should be considered when testing.

6 What can tests tell us about the personalities of top-class sports performers?

7 Name three different forms of motivation.

8 What are the principal differences between 'high achievers' and 'low achievers'?

9 Define the term self-efficacy and how it might affect performance.

10 Describe four ways in which a coach can avoid low self-efficacy in an athlete.

11 What four factors in Bernard Weiner's model suggest possible reasons for attributing reasons for success or failure?

12 Give two examples of extrinsic motivation.

13 Define the term 'social loafing'.

14 Name five important principles which should be remembered when goal setting.

15 What is the difference between a performance goal and an outcome goal?

16 Describe what is meant by the term imagery and how it can benefit athletes in competition.

17 State three factors which can cause stress in sport.

18 Define the term somatic anxiety and give two symptoms which would show evidence of its presence.

19 What is meant by the term 'optimum stress levels'?

20 How does the social facilitation theory suggest performance can be improved?

21 What is the difference between aggression and assertiveness in a sporting context?

22 Name three theories which suggest the causes of aggression.

Assessment activity

> ### TASK 1

Conduct your own research to support or refute a view that personality profiling is a useful tool in predicting sports performance.

> ### TASK 2

Report on your studies into the motivating factors involved in two contrasting sports (team/individual; invasion/racket/field; outdoor/mountaineering/adventure activities; extreme sports).

> ### TASK 3

Conduct your own research, using an original testing procedure to analyse the performance/anxiety relationship, and relate your findings to, and account for, examples of 'choking' in sport.

Sports development

12

Objectives

- **Develop an understanding of what is involved in sports development**

- **Examine how sports development can work in practice**

- **Identify the different agencies involved in sports development, and look at their role in sports development**

- **Analyse the skills needed to be a sports development worker**

- **Examine some of the day-to-day practical considerations involved in sports development**

- **Survey some recent sport development initiatives**

- **Investigate some current sport development initiatives**

This unit is portfolio based. The assessment that you will undertake will probably involve looking at sports development in practice. The aim of this chapter is to try to provide you with background information, and hopefully, point you in the right direction. But a lot of the investigation is down to you. Sports development will be going on in your area – so find out about it!

The sport, leisure and recreation industry continues to grow and prosper. Sports development plays a central role in the expansion of the industry. Employment opportunities are wide and varied. For those interested in sport, there is probably no greater reward than actually to be involved, and play a part, in the development of sport.

This unit has close links with other units on the VCE Leisure and Recreation. These units are: Unit 1 Investigating leisure and recreation, Unit 3 The sports industry, Unit 10 Principles of sports coaching, Unit 13 Running a leisure and recreation facility.

Introduction

It would be nice to start this chapter with a definition of what sports development is. Unfortunately, it is not that easy. One of the problems is that it is very difficult to define what 'sport' is. One of the reasons we have a problem with defining sports development is that sport itself does not stand still and is constantly changing.

Once upon a time, football was a pretty straightforward game without many rules. If I asked someone today to tell me about football, they might well reply: 'Do you mean Association Football, Rugby Football, Rugby League Football, Gaelic Football, American Football, or Australian Rules Football?'

Two of the most important aspects of successful sports development are that we (a) stay, literally, 'ahead of the game', and (b) are able to take a leadership role when necessary. For this to be affective it is important that we:

- **Keep up to date with all aspects of our sport**
- **Keep up to date with what is going on in other sports**
- **Are able to identify any trends in the changes that are occurring**
- **Know in which direction _we_ are going**
- **Know how to take a lead**
- **Are able to work with others**
- **Keep our skills up to date, and are ready to meet change**

Though sports do change, they always seem to retain their popularity, both for people to participate in and to watch. One of the strengths of sport is its ability to adapt and change to new circumstances and the needs of the player and the spectator. The work of the sports development worker is to help maintain and develop this popularity, and be a catalyst in the changes that sport will invariably go through.

Activity 12.1

★ Select two sports. Take your time over this, because you should try and stick to these while you study this unit. Do not choose two popular sports; try to pick one major and one minor sport

★ Begin gathering some information on these sports that you will build into a file of information. You might want to find out if they have a web site, or write to them to see if they could send you some information. And don't forget to look in newspapers and sports magazines

★ With your colleagues, and tutor, agree two target dates on which you will give a short talk. The first talk can be a general one on the sports, but the second one should be on the developments that are occurring in the sports

The elements that make up sports development

How sports development works

Sports development could manifest itself in a number of ways

- ✪ **Creating opportunities for people to take part or progress within sport**
- ✪ **Introducing the sport in new areas**
- ✪ **Trying to get particular groups to participate in the sport**
- ✪ **Ensuring equality of access to the sport**
- ✪ **Building links and partnerships with groups and organisations**
- ✪ **Developing new facilities**
- ✪ **Negotiating access to new resources**

Another way of putting this is to say sports development is about:

- ✓ **Being proactive**
- ✓ **Intervening**
- ✓ **Facilitating**
- ✓ **Targeting**
- ✓ **Enabling**
- ✓ **Differentiating**

Activity 12.2

Have another look at the list above with the check/tick marks. Before you progress, make sure that you know what each word means and how it could be applied to sport and sports development. Why not work with a partner and try to use each of the words to construct a sentence relating it to sport?

The influence of the organisation on sports development

The sports development that is undertaken will be influenced by the aims and objectives of the organisation within which that sports development is initiated. Organisations that operate within the public, private or voluntary sectors often have very different aims and objectives. Also, the sports development may occur across different sectors, with organisations working in partnership. This may mean that the different organisations in the partnership will have different objectives, and may often have to seek some form of compromise on the outcome of any planned sports development.

Activity 12.3

Sponsorship has become an important way in which sporting organisations are able to access finance.

★ Form a small group and select a popular spectator sport

★ Carry out some research on the sport and identify the number and type of sponsors

★ Try to identify the 'business' of the sponsor, e.g. are they an electrical goods manufacturer?

★ Group the sponsors into similar businesses or industries and design a graph that will show how the sponsorship breaks down for your sport

Sports development will also be influenced as to what level that development is being carried out, and how that development fits within the structure of the organisation. Sport is played and sports development occurs at a number of levels: international, national, country (i.e. Scotland, England, Wales and Northern Ireland), county, town, local club and school level. It may be planned or decided by the organisation that development should occur equally at all levels and that the development is interlinked, or it may be that it is decided to carry out development initiatives at a particular level.

The market for sports development

Sport and sports development can benefit all people at all the stages of their lives. The sport that we watch on television tends to be played by men in their late teens to late twenties, but this does not reflect the vast numbers of people who are involved in sport. If an organisation was deciding on which market to operate in, or how best to commit its usually limited resources, it would have to make some stern choices, which would link directly to the aims and objectives of the organisation. The illustration below shows some of the choices that have to be made when deciding.

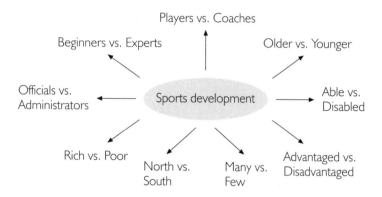

Activity
12.4

'Many people argue that the access to participate in sport and physical activity should be a right rather than a privilege and that the constraints placed on individuals should be related to the boundaries of their ability.'

Have a debate within your group on this statement.

The role of the sports development officer

The sports development officer's first priority will be to follow the aims and objectives of the organisation in which they work. Their work will also be influenced by the internal human resources structure of the organisation. Working practices could range from being under quite strict direction, to having a free hand.

Sports development officers can work in a number of areas:

✪ *Sports specific:* **Developing a particular sport such as tennis, basketball or netball, within an existing structure. Making sure more of the sport is played, and making sure people get better at playing the sport**

- *Targeted*: **Perhaps helping to get more people involved in a sport as coaches or officials. Perhaps making sure that more medals are won in the sport**

- *Facility based*: **This could be general where the development may involve increasing usage, or where the facility is sport specific, such as a national centre, the development could involve co-ordinating groups from all over the country**

- *Project based*: **This could be a one-off project such as organising a competition, or even an international event. It could be a more general project, such as increasing the number of volunteers involved in sport**

Case Study
The English Basketball Associations – Outdoor Basketball Initiative

The development of this project was based around facility development. £10 million had been awarded from the Lottery Fund to supply 10,000 basketball goals free of charge. The initiative involved development work with over 4,000 organisations in installing the goals and in setting up coaching sessions, coach education, fun days and competitions.

So, although at first glance the initiative may appear to be specifically about physical resources, the actual sports development work will go far wider than that. The longer-term objectives of the initiative are:

★ To make basketball available, accessible, and free to all

★ To establish a partnership between the sport of basketball and the community

★ To introduce young people to basketball and provide opportunities for them to develop and progress within the sport

★ To encourage young people in healthy self-development and self-awareness

★ To provide an alternative purposeful activity for young people by keeping them away from damaging activities

1   Find out where the nearest set of basketball goals, set up by the initiative, are to where you live. You could do this by looking at one of the following websites: www.basketballengland.org.uk, www.bballwales.enta.net, www.basketball-scotland.com, www.uba.org.uk (Northern Ireland).

2   If you were working for the Basketball Association and were looking at setting up a new set of goals in your area, (a) decide where you would set them up, (b) list the organisations that you would contact about this.

Though the Outdoor Basketball Initiative did receive a large one-off award, this should be seen as the exception and not the norm. The work of a sports development officer, as with so many other jobs, is usually about achieving or surpassing your aims and objectives through using often limited resources.

How effectively sports development officers use those resources is often down to the drive, determination and personality of the sports development officers themselves. They will need to possess a range of skills to bring together the human, physical and financial resources that will be needed to achieve success. This will be dealt with later in this chapter.

Influences on sports development programmes

Sports development is influenced by trends that are occurring within sport and within wider society. A sport may be increasing or declining in participation levels. More people may be just interested in watching elite sport on television. People under eighteen may become more interested in playing computer games and using their mobile telephone to phone their friends, rather than going with them to play football for a local team or have a swim at the pool.

Sports development may also be influenced by trends that are occurring worldwide. As more people in more countries participate in more sports, this will mean that those involved in sports development will have to work that much harder, and have that many more resources, just to stay in the same place.

Sports developments will also be influenced by initiatives that may come from national or local government, by private companies, or by the sports themselves. These initiatives may be responding to a particular trend. Examples of this may be initiatives that respond to decreasing participation rates, or activity rates in children, or helps their country 'win more medals'.

Some towns and cities, usually in partnership with national government and private industry, have used sports development initiatives to help regenerate their area socially and economically, or have developed initiatives through sports development to enhance the image of their area.

Partnerships, how they are formed and how they operate are a very important influence on sports development.

Case Study
The Youth Sport Trust and TOPS programmes

The Youth Sport Trust was established as a registered charity in 1994. The main aim of the Youth Sport Trust is: 'to develop and implement, in close partnership with other organisations, quality physical education and sports programmes for all young people between the ages of eighteen months and eighteen years'. The Youth Sports Trust is based at Loughborough University, but operates throughout the country. Its headquarters are at: Woburn Buildings, 1/7 Woburn Walk, London WC1H 0JJ.

The TOPS programmes seek to take a multi-agency approach, working in partnership with schools, local authorities, governing bodies of sport, sports clubs and community groups, to provide opportunities for participation and progression in sport. The main features of the TOPS programme include:

★ Training for all those involved in providing sporting opportunities for young people

★ Resource cards and support materials which contain appropriate and progressive activities for young people

★ Child-friendly sports equipment and resources

continued

continued

The TOPS programmes are designed across areas of child development:

★ *Early years*: Early physical activity for children aged from eighteen months to five years

★ *Primary*: Physical education and sport opportunities for children aged between four and eleven years

★ *Secondary*: Physical education and sporting opportunities for young people aged between eleven and eighteen years

★ *Inclusion*: Ensuring all programmes can be accessed by young disabled people. Sportsability creates opportunities for young disabled people to enjoy, participate and perform in PE and sport

They also encourage the participation of parents through Nutella SportS Parent.

Activity 12.6

Try to find out some more about the work of the Youth Sports Trust. You could visit their website at: www.youthsport.net.

Sports development models

The sports development model is based on people's relationship to sport. This is in turn made up of: how much time is committed, what people wish to gain from the sport, what people want to achieve within a sport. The elements of the sports development model can be shown in the following way.

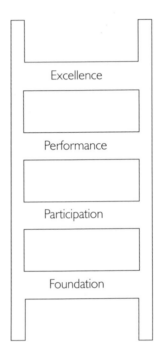

Excellence

Performance

Participation

Foundation

The elements within the model can be categorised in the following ways.

Foundation level

This level relates to people who become involved in a sport for the first time. In most circumstances this will relate to younger children who are beginning to coordinate their mental and physical skills. They will probably be developing basic movement skills, and will not necessarily understand or comprehend all the subtleties of the game, or activity, that they are involved in.

At foundation level it is important that good habits are laid down for later in life; that good basic skills and positive attitudes are developed; that conscious or unconscious learning takes place; that the experience is a rewarding one; and that it is the individual's achievements, not their perceived failures, that are highlighted.

Participation level

Participation level relates to all members of the community who participate in sport for a variety of reasons. Reasons for participation in sport could include enjoyment, socialising, health or fitness related, or 'love of the game'.

Participation level can apply to people of all ages. Again, as with foundation level, it is important that people get something positive from participating and that participation is encouraged and maintained. Participation can be built on and developed, but should never be pushed to such a degree that the person withdraws from participation. Participation at whatever degree this participation involves is always better than non-participation.

Performance level

Performance level is related to all those participating within a sport who wish to improve their skills and abilities. How this improvement in performance is to be measured should be up to the individuals themselves. Again, the important thing is that if individuals are attempting to improve their performance they have a positive experience in doing so. People who are attempting to improve their performance over any length of time will eventually 'run into a wall'. If they overcome that, great, but it is far better that they participate at a lower performance level than withdraw altogether.

It is often thought that performance-level work is what sports development is solely aimed at, but this is not the case. Sports development is concerned with all aspects of 'the model' – remove a rung from the ladder and what happens?

Excellence level

The excellence level relates to those individuals who wish to achieve standards that are pre-set and measurable. These standards are normally set at a consistent level of achievement by country-wide or international bodies.

These standards usually involve some form of grading, or certification, or competition. Activities at excellence level are often used to reward the individual for their effort or performance and used as a way of maintaining motivation or interest. It is very rewarding when we achieve something and this is acknowledged, but it is as important that we all learn how to swim well as it is for one person in ten to achieve 'excellence'.

A very good example of how these stages of sport development can work in practice can be seen in the case study of the Sports Council for Northern Ireland and its 'Strategy for the Development of Sport in Northern Ireland 1997–2005'.

Case Study

The Sports Council for Northern Ireland and its 'Strategy for the Development of Sport in Northern Ireland 1997–2005'

The Mission for the Sports Council for Northern Ireland states:

The Sports Council for Northern Ireland aims to make sport happen for you. As a lead facilitator in the development of sport the Council will work with partners to:

★ Increase and sustain committed participation, especially amongst young people;

★ Raise the standards of sporting excellence; and

★ Promote the good reputation and efficient administration of sport.

The sports development policy of the Sports Council for Northern Ireland contained within the document 'Strategy for the Development of Sport in Northern Ireland 1997–2005' draws together, within one coherent plan, what it sees as the three core areas of the natural stages of sporting life – starting in sport, continuing in sport, and striving for excellence. The Council has laid down objectives under these core areas, which it has titled: 'Starting Well, Staying Involved, and Striving for Excellence'.

Starting Well

'To enable as many people as possible, and especially young people, to take up sport.'

Objective 1 – To create locally available high quality sporting opportunities.

Objective 2 – To equip volunteers, especially those working with young people, for the challenges they face in the development of sport.

continued

continued

Staying Involved

'To enable as many people as possible to remain lifelong active participants in sport.'

Objective 3 – To provide structured opportunities for participants to continue their involvement by fostering co-operation between sports organisations, education services district councils and community groups.

Objective 4 – To train and support volunteers to deliver sport so that as many people as possible are encouraged to participate.

Striving for Excellence

Objective 5 – To establish an organisation focused on the development of excellence.

Objective 6 – To identify talented performers and offer them the support they need.

Objective 7 – To raise the standards of coaching for high level performers.

You may find it helpful to discuss the 'Strategy for Development' with your colleagues, or you may wish to discuss with your tutor how you could base an assignment around the Strategy, perhaps carrying out a comparative study. You can find out more about the Sports Council for Northern Ireland by visiting their website at www.sportni.org/

The sports development model of foundation, participation, performance and excellence was illustrated in the above graphic as a ladder. This does not mean that one level is rather more important than another, but rather it is a continuous, lifelong process/relationship, that is interlinked and bound together. Another way of describing the process/relationship is to think of it as a 'continuum'.

The idea of a 'continuum' is well represented in a model form by the **Sports Development Continuum Model** that was developed by the Sports Council in the early 1990s and is usually illustrated as follows:

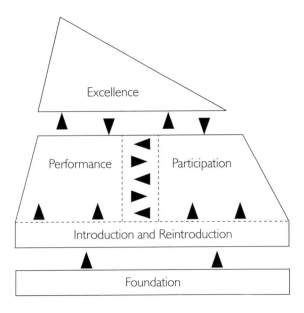

If we study the model we could perhaps draw the following conclusions:

- ✪ **The model is a pyramid rather than a ladder, representing levels of involvement**

- ✪ **The model moves from a strong base of Participation to a 'peak' of Excellence**

- ✪ **There can be movement between each element**

- ✪ **There is movement back and forth within each element except Foundation**

- ✪ **The model not only includes the concept of Introduction at the Participation and Performance level, but also includes the concept of a Reintroduction to each of these levels**

- ✪ **The area of movement between the levels can be seen as a separate area or function within itself and can therefore be studied separately**

The model is a very useful in sports development planning. The model is important in giving an overall view of sports development as well as identifying how resources might be allocated in the shorter and longer term. For example, in the shorter term, we may achieve results if we allocate most resources to excellence, but this cannot be maintained in the longer term unless the levels below it are strengthened.

We will be looking later in this chapter at some of the policies and initiatives that have been developed recently in the UK that seek to strengthen all aspects of the continuum. However, because no development can take place without actual participation, participation feeds all other development. Participation is the keystone to any sports development, and it is some of the efforts to develop participation within the UK that we will first consider.

Participation and sports development – a look at the Sports Council's 'Sport for All' campaigns

The Sports Council (which today comprises the UK Sports Council and the Sports Councils of England, Scotland, Wales and Northern Ireland) was established as an independent body in 1972. The aims of the Sports Council were to encourage wider participation in sport and to help raise the sports performance levels. To achieve these aims, the Sports Council launched a very successful campaign, the title of which has become synonymous with them: 'Sport for All'.

The 'Sport for All' campaign aimed to increase participation in sport and physical activity from all sectors of the community. The campaign involved developing more opportunities for participation, publicising of activities and the development of facilities for participation. The campaign involved the Sports Council in working in a co-ordination role and working in partnership with existing providers such as local authorities and governing bodies of sport as well as private companies.

The campaign was a great success, but it quickly identified that there were a number of groups within society who were not participating in what might be considered large or appropriate numbers. A series of initiatives and campaigns were therefore developed to target and encourage participation of those groups. Examples include:

✪ *Sport for All – Disabled People (1980–81)*: **This campaign, launched as part of the International Year of Disabled People, sought to improve participation by people with disabilities, and to integrate 'able' and 'disabled' athletes and participants. The campaign particularly focused on access to and the usability of facilities for those with disability**

✪ *50+ All to play for (1983–84)*: **As the name suggests, this campaign was aimed at those over fifty years of age. The campaign sought to highlight the beneficial effects as well as the social dimension of participation in sport**

✪ *Ever Thought of Sport? (1985–86)*: **This campaign was aimed at young people who were in their teens or early twenties. It had been established through surveys that although young people while at school are active in sport and physical activity, if they leave school at sixteen it is likely that they will drop sport altogether. However, if they continued their education until their early twenties, they were likely to remain active in sport** and physically active for the rest of their lives. The campaign tried, therefore, to provide opportunities for young people to keep them active and participating in sport, at this critical age band

○ *What's Your Sport? (1987–88):* Following on from the 'Ever Thought of Sport?' campaign, the campaign 'What's Your Sport?' continued to target 13–24-year-olds as well as women, and those in their late forties. Research showed that people, as well as dropping out of sport in their teens, tended to begin returning to some form of physical activity in their mid to late forties. Research also showed that women, as a group, did not participate to the same level as men.

The campaign was aimed at returning people to participating within sports they had once enjoyed and were active in. The campaign used a national advertising campaign to encourage people to get a 'sports pack' from the Sports Council, which helped people to find out more about sports in their area, and gave them contact points for local information.
The campaign also had links to nutrition as the campaign's sponsor was the Milk Marketing Board

○ *What's Your Sport for Women? (1988) and Milk in Action – Women (1989):* These campaigns, targeted particularly at women, sought to emphasise and develop the 'What's Your Sport?' Campaign. Attitudes still prevailed, even in the late 1980s, that because of their 'weaker' physique they could not compete in great physical effort, such as distance events or the 'rougher' sports. By targeting participation of women, these campaigns helped to undermine old attitudes and the level of women's participation in all sports perhaps reflects the success of these campaigns

○ *The Year of Sport (1991):* This campaign sought to develop interest and participation in sport by highlighting the number of national and international competitions being held in Britain that year. The centrepiece of these events was the World Student Games held in Sheffield. The campaign and the Games were particularly influential in the economic regeneration of Sheffield, and in establishing Sheffield as an important centre of sports development

Identify sports development activity in your area that is aimed at increasing participation. Write a brief report about the activity based around the following questions:

★ Which organisation is carrying out the initiative?

★ Does the initiative have a target group that it is aimed at?

★ Are there links to other organisations or do they have partners in the scheme?

★ What are the activities involved in the scheme?

★ How is the participation initiative linked to the other parts of the sports continuum?

If you have any difficulty in identifying participation initiatives in your area, carry out some research on current national initiatives for the sports you have identified in the first activity of this chapter.

Much has been achieved in building levels of participation. To be effective in sports development planning, it is important that we have, at least, a grasp of the factors that might affect participation. It is to the examination to these factors that we now turn.

Factors affecting participation in sport

Activity 12.8

Yes, activities are normally at the end of information, not the beginning. Before you read this section, try to jot down some answers to the questions below and then compare your answers with a colleague, or within your group.

★ What was the first organised physical activity you did and what did this involve?

★ Who organised the activity and where was it held?

★ What is your favourite sport? Why?

★ Is there a sport that you have always wanted to play but never have?

★ What is the furthest you have ever travelled to play sport?

★ Have you ever been upset as a result of being involved in sport? Why?

There are a number of factors that might have an effect on people's participation in sport. These factors include:

✪ **Motivation**

✪ **Social**

✪ **Economic**

✪ **Cultural**

✪ **Geographic**

✪ **Political**

Motivation

A person has to want to play a sport, to become involved. What motivates people often varies from person to person. Motivation may be intrinsic – may come from inside; people may not always be able to put into words why they want to participate in a sport, 'they just do!' Motivation can also be extrinsic – may come from outside; this could include winning medals, or being awarded certificates.

People have different personalities. Some personalities may be suited to the playing and rule subtleties of one sport, while other personalities may be suited to playing another. This will undoubtedly have a direct effect on the person's motivation. It is sometimes easier, rather than analysing motivation, to think about what demotivates people. If someone doesn't enjoy a sport, or is hurt, physically or emotionally, playing it, they are less likely to want to play it again.

Often people are motivated to play a sport for reasons other than the playing of the sport itself. They may want to keep fit, to make friends, or just get out of the house. Sometimes the physical activity is only a by-product. However, if people find the right sport or activity, then in almost every case they will want to enjoy being involved in physical activity.

Social

A person's family background, what sports their family play(ed). The community that the person lives in. What sports their friends play. These are very strong social factors in determining what sport an individual will take up or have a preference for.

The choice of sport a person may make relates to the types or groups of people that they like mixing with and whose company they enjoy, or indeed what is 'expected of them'. This does not necessarily mean that the sport will suit their personality, or that they will be good at it. And this in turn may affect their longer-term participation in the sport.

Economic

Participation in sport can cost money. Equipment can be expensive, facilities may have to be hired, and there may be travelling expenses to train or to participate in competitions. What disposable income a person has, or what money they have to spend on sport, may determine their ability to participate.

If you look across the world at sport, you will see that the most popular sports are the ones that cost very little money to play. So it's not all about money, but it will be a factor affecting the level that those involved can play to, or the type of sport they play.

Cultural

A person's cultural background, their inherited beliefs and values can have an effect on their participation in sport in a number of ways. Firstly, different sports may have been developed, or been adopted, within their culture. We need to look no further than America, Spain or Ireland to see how culture has a direct effect on people's choice of sport.

Secondly, a person's cultural background may affect how they are involved with the sport. Examples could be where a person could not take part in sport on certain days of the week, or at certain times of the year. Or there may be cultural influences on the type of sports clothing that they can wear during participation.

Geographic

Where a person lives, whether it is mountainous or flat, whether it has a cold or hot climate, will influence how sport has developed in that country. Though these factors can be overcome, it is unlikely that Great Britain will ever achieve a large medal count at the Winter Olympics.

Within the area, the facilities, indoor and outdoor, that are available for participating in sport. The level of demand on these facilities and the free time they have available in their programmes.

If there are facilities, how a person gets to those facilities. The time it takes to get to the facilities. Also, whether there is transport, at the appropriate times, to get the person there, and to get them home.

Political

Legislation may be passed at both a local and national level that affects participation. Some of these may not always be obvious. The example of transportation was given in the last section – so, changes in the government's policy on transportation, though not immediately obvious, may have a consequence on improving or reducing a person's ability to participate in sport.

Political intervention also has a direct effect on the availability of many of the leisure facilities we have, or may have. It is also true that a great amount of sports development is initiated and programmed by bodies that have been set up through the political process.

Case Study

Moving through the Sports Development Continuum – The National Coaching Foundation and its Coach Development Programme

The National Coaching Foundation (NCF), originally established in 1983, works to improve the quality of sports coaching at all levels of the sports development continuum.

The NCF motto is: 'Better Coaching . . . Better Sport.'

The NCF supports coaches by providing specialist sports-related products and books through its trading organisation, Coachwise.

The NCF also supports coaches by offering a range of workshops for the different levels of coaching. The workshops are divided into four key areas:

★ *Eight Introductory Workshops*: These are aimed at coaches working towards Level 2 National Standards. Workshops include: Planning and Practice, Improving Techniques, The Body in Action and Safety and Injury.

★ *Twelve Coach Workshops*: These are aimed at coaches working towards Level 3 National Standards. Workshops include: Analysing your Coaching, Goal-setting and Planning, Improving Practices and Skill, and Observation, Analysis and Video.

★ *Performance Coach Workshops*: These are aimed at coaches who are coaching elite and high performance athletes. Workshops include: Field Based Fitness Testing, Performance Profiling and Imagery Training.

★ *Hot Topic Workshops*: These are developed to respond to current topics for coaches working at all levels.

You can get more information about the NCF and details of its workshops by visiting its website at: www.ncf.org.uk.

Building a sports development strategy

A sports development strategy is a plan that draws up priorities and strategies based on the aims and objectives of the organisation. That development strategy is usually designed to be implemented over the longer term. It will normally cover at least twelve months, but more likely will cover several years. A sports development strategy has already been identified in this chapter: the case study on the Sports Council for Northern Ireland.

A sports development strategy identifies key activities and targets, for the short and the long term, that are then included within the strategy. Planning then takes place to decide how these targets and goals will be achieved.

A sports development strategy should include:

- ✪ **Clear and attainable targets and goals**
- ✪ **Suggestions as to how the targets may be met**
- ✪ **Details of any partners who will be worked with**
- ✪ **Details of the resources that will be needed or used**
- ✪ **Details of any training or education which is part of the strategy**
- ✪ **A work programme and timetable**
- ✪ **Key results**
- ✪ **How the strategy will be monitored**
- ✪ **How achievements will be measured.**
- ✪ **A timescale for any revisions of the strategy**

Activity 12.9

★ Obtain a sports development strategy. This could be either one for the area that you live in, or one of the sports that you were asked to choose at the start of this chapter.

★ Go through this document and identify each of the categories of the strategy that are listed in the checklist above.

★ Prepare a short talk to your group about the strategic plan.

The agencies involved in sports development

There are many agencies involved in sports development. Some of these agencies have already been identified within this chapter. How central sports development will be to an agency will be affected by the overall aims and objectives of the organisation, by the internal structure of that organisation, and by the resources that the agency can commit to sports development.

Agencies should not be considered in isolation. Nearly all agencies in sports development are in some way interconnected; if nothing else, they will be interconnected by sport itself. How the strategies of these different agencies are brought together and co-ordinated is one of the most crucial aspects of sports development and of the work of a sports development officer.

The principal agencies involved in sports development are:

✪ **The Sports Councils**
✪ **The governing bodies of sport, county or regional organisations and local clubs**
✪ **The school and education sector**
✪ **Local authorities**

The Sports Councils

The Sports Councils consist of:

✪ **The UK Sports Council**
✪ **The four sports councils based on the countries of the United Kingdom:**
    – **The Sports Council for Wales / Cyngor Chwaraeon Cymru**
    – **Sport Scotland / sport:scc**
    – **The Sports Council for Northern Ireland**
    – **Sport England**

The UK Sports Council focuses directly on high performance sport at a United Kingdom level. It is concerned with supporting world-class athletes and performers. It also works to bring major world sporting events to the United Kingdom.

Each of the four country-based sports councils carries out development work that it believes best fits the people of their area. Each sports council is responsible for sports development within the development continuum and the development of strategies and initiatives based around that. They are also responsible for distributing sports lottery money within their area.

Activity 12.10

Visit the website of the sports council for your area, and spend some time reading though what they do, and what they are up to. Check out any links. Don't forget to bookmark. The web addresses are:

www.sports-council-wales.co.uk
www.ssc.org.uk
www.sportni.org/
www.english.sports.gov.uk

The national governing bodies of sport, county or regional organisations and local clubs

The national governing bodies of sport are independent organisations responsible for the running of their sport. These governing bodies will normally be based on a county or area structure, which in turn will be based on local clubs. The United Kingdom is almost unique in that many of the sports governing bodies within the United Kingdom are organised around the four countries, with each country participating separately in international events.

Most governing bodies will have drawn up a strategy for the development of the sports, with the county associations having a strategy that feeds into the national one. At a local level, clubs will again link into the national and regional strategy, but may also be involved along with other sports in developing an overall sports strategy within their area.

Sports strategies may vary because of the relative popularity of the sports and the amount of resources available. Also, sports may be stronger in some parts of the country, perhaps in numbers participating, qualified coaches, facilities available, or numbers of elite athletes, and the sports development strategy may well reflect these factors.

Because of the advent of the National Lottery, many sports have now been able to access resources they previously could only dream of. This has meant that many sports are now implementing some very ambitious developments. More resources and interest than ever before in sport make it a very exciting time in sports development.

The school and education sector

Most people start their sporting activity at school. There are now, more than ever, opportunities for children and young people to be involved in sport, as part of their studies and as part of extra-curricular activity.

Under 16

The new National Curriculum guidelines for schools, Curriculum 2000, stresses the importance of physical development and physical skilfulness, and seeks to promote knowledge of the body in action. At each stage of the child's development, the curriculum provides that physical education should include:

- ✪ **Acquiring and developing skills**
- ✪ **Selecting and applying skills, tactics and compositional ideas**
- ✪ **Evaluating and improving performance**
- ✪ **Knowledge and understanding of fitness and health**

Additionally, there are opportunities for young people to be involved with school and inter-school sport. Some schools have established links with local clubs and with local authority sports development units. Many schools are involved in the TOPS programmes.

At 16

Many people now have the opportunity to study GCSE Physical Education. The syllabus allows young people to learn about physical education and to improve their skills and performance across a range of sports.

Post 16

The past decade has seen an explosion of opportunities for students to continue their involvement in sport. Sixth Form Colleges and Universities now have a large range of courses available in physical education, sports studies, sports science, sports development, and leisure and recreation management.

Young people also have the opportunity to continue to stay involved through student games up to international level. There are also opportunities for some students to receive sports scholarships.

Local authorities

Local authorities provide many of the sport and recreational facilities, both indoor and outdoor, for sport to be played and sports development carried out.

Most local authorities have a sports development unit, whose primary function will be the development of sport in their area. Local authorities form a focal point for sport and sports development in their area. They provide a convenient forum for all those interested in different sports to work together. Many local authorities now have a comprehensive sports development strategy that they have drawn up in partnership with local sports organisations.

Activity 12.12

★ If you haven't already done so, check whether your local authority has a sports development officer. Discuss with your tutor the possibility of inviting them along to give a talk.

★ Identify a sports development unit of a local authority outside your area. Try to assemble some information on the work that they do to include within your portfolio. Here is a start:

www.swansea.gov.uk/Leisure
www.nottscc.gov.uk/sport
www.surreycc.gov.uk/sportsdev

Current initiatives in sports development

As you will have no doubt have found out through your research, and by reading this chapter, there are a great many sports development projects and initiatives going on.

Here are examples of some that you may or may not have identified already:

The sports development project	Who runs it?	Details of the project
Sport Action Zones	Sport England	This is an initiative with communities in areas of social and economic deprivation. The aim of the projects that are spread across the country is to help build a sporting infrastructure within the local community.
Coaching Scotland	sportscotland	The strategy aims to improve the standards and performances of sportsmen and sportswomen through the development of their coaches.
The Sports Colleges Initiative	The Department for Education and Employment	This is an initiative where schools can apply for sports college status. The sports colleges are intended to play an important role in their area, raising the standard of physical education as well as helping to develop and meet the needs of talented youngsters.

The skills of a sports development officer

A sports development officer, though they often work as part of a team, will in nearly all circumstances be required to take individual initiatives. They must be proactive and be a 'self-starter'. If things are to change, then they must be a catalyst for that change.

The sports development officer may have to work between different organisations that have different objectives. They will need to manage finance, manage paid and unpaid staff, and know how to purchase and manage physical resources.

It is important that the sports development officer has a range of skills that they are able to apply to a range of circumstances.

They need to know:

- ✪ *How to lead*: **Know when to lead from the front, when to lead from behind, and when to take a step back**
- ✪ *How to communicate*: **Know when to talk and when to listen. Know how to present information in a clear and positive way**
- ✪ *How to plan*: **Know how and when to check the detail. Know how to prepare for every possibility and always have a backup plan ready**
- ✪ *How to organise*: **Know how to set up events and adapt them to the needs of participants. Have a place for everything, and everything in its place**
- ✪ *How to market events and activities*: **Know how to spend the minimum amount of money in the most effective way to achieve the greatest success for the event or activity. Always archive the best type of publicity for the activity**
- ✪ *How to manage resources*: **Know how to account for and control money and finance. Know how to write a job description and how to hire the most appropriate person. Know the best time to buy equipment and how to keep it in good condition**
- ✪ *How to monitor and evaluate*: **Know what indicators are. Know what the measures of success and achievement are. Know how to assess success and failure**

Oh! And don't forget, they will need to know something about the sport!

Revision questions

1 Explain the different ways in which sports development could be categorised.

2 Why doesn't the UK compete in the Association Football or Rugby Union World Cups?

3 How could the market for sports development be divided into different segments?

4 'Children under the age of 12 benefit most from sport, therefore most sports development is undertaken for under 12s.' Is this a true statement? If not, why not?

5 Give three ways in which targeting sports development might be put into practice.

6 What is the main aim of the Youth Sports Trust?

7 What are the main features of the TOPS programme?

8 What are the components of the sports development model?

9 Explain the term 'continuum' within the context of sports development.

10 'Sports development is about winning more trophies!' Explain the validity of this statement.

11 What is the significance of the gaps in the sports development pyramid?

12 Give two examples of the 'Sport for All' campaigns.

13 State three factors that may affect an individual's participation in sport.

14 State five elements that should be included in a sports development strategy.

15 What is the role of the UK Sports Council?

16 What does 'NCF' stand for?

17 Identify a sports development initiative currently being undertaken by the Sports Council for your country.

18 How might a sports development officer evaluate success?

Assessment activity

> **TASK 1**

The first activity of this chapter asked you to select two sports and then start gathering information on them. If you have not done so, do this NOW!

Identify an agency involved in sports development and collect information on it.

> **TASK 2**

Your group as a whole should organise a sports development information day. Each person within the group should be responsible for a display/stall during the information day. The display/stall should be based on the sport/agency that you have identified. You should prepare your own information, examples of which could include participation rates, comparisons with other countries, or comparisons with other sports. Remember to include information on local initiatives.

> **TASK 3**

Publicise the information day and encourage people to come along and ask questions.

> **TASK 4**

After the information day, construct a file of the information that you have put together. Include an introduction and contents page in the file.

Running a leisure and recreation facility

13

Objectives

- **Describe and understand the aims and objectives of a leisure and recreation facility**

- **Identify how a facility is programmed to meet the needs of its customers**

- **Investigate the products and services that a facility may provide**

- **Identify different booking systems and pricing structures**

- **Survey some of the possible physical resources of a facility**

- **Examine the operational procedures practised within a facility**

Because this unit is externally assessed, it is important that you do attempt to become familiar and commit to memory some of the terms that are used. It is also important that you understand how to apply much of the knowledge you will gain while studying this unit. Examples, questions and tests are given in order to help you, but try, wherever possible, as a customer or visitor, to gain more information about leisure and recreation facilities, particularly those in your area.

This unit has close links with other units of the VCE in Leisure and Recreation. These are: Unit 1 Investigating leisure and recreation, Unit 2 Safe working practices and optional Unit 22 Human resources in the leisure and recreation industry. In order to cover all the aspects of your external assessment you will need to have an understanding of these as well.

Introduction

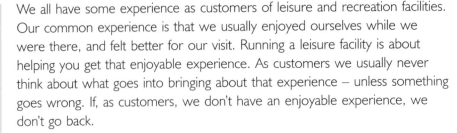

▼ ▼ ▼ ▼ ▼ ▼ ▼ ▼ ▼

Facility
The means or materials that allows us to carry out an activity that we wish to do

▲ ▲ ▲ ▲ ▲ ▲ ▲ ▲ ▲

We all have some experience as customers of leisure and recreation facilities. Our common experience is that we usually enjoyed ourselves while we were there, and felt better for our visit. Running a leisure facility is about helping you get that enjoyable experience. As customers we usually never think about what goes into bringing about that experience – unless something goes wrong. If, as customers, we don't have an enjoyable experience, we don't go back.

At first glance, running a leisure and recreation facility may appear pretty straightforward. But, think about it, some leisure and recreation centres are open seven days a week, sixteen hours a day, and every customer has to have an enjoyable time – NOT SO EASY!

Background

If we consider the term 'leisure facility' we could include the following:

- **Sports centres**
- **Swimming pools and leisure pools**
- **Theme parks**
- **Sports stadia**
- **Bowling alleys**
- **Cinemas**
- **Theatres and arts centres**
- **Community centres**
- **Outdoor activity centres**

There is a wide variety of what we might call leisure facilities. The leisure facilities that are available will vary from one part of the country to another. People want to spend their leisure time in different ways, and this may be reflected in the facilities available.

In some parts of the country we may have a large number of leisure activities and facilities under one roof. Here the facility may include a sports hall, swimming pools, health facilities, theatre, arts centre and shopping area. In other parts of the country there may be a number of smaller centres spread throughout an area. This may be with school-based sports facilities that are used outside school hours in a dual-use capacity, or small community centres or village halls.

Some leisure facilities may be so specialised, such as theme parks, that there may be only a few in the whole country, while others such as cinemas will be spread throughout the whole country and be very similar in actual design and operation, no matter where you go.

Individually, study the list of leisure facilities given above and identify facilities in your area that could be put under one of these headings. If you can't identify a local facility, e.g. a bowling alley, don't worry, just do the ones you can. Once you have listed some of the facilities in your area, write a brief description about them.

With a partner, or in a small group, identify a facility outside of your area that you may have visited, or may wish to visit. It may be that you wish to look at a facility under a heading that you have not been able to identify in your area. Try to get some more information about the facility – you may be able to do this by telephone or by writing to them, or perhaps they have a web page.

Some hints and tips for using Web pages

You may find that many of the leisure facilities in an area are listed in the web pages of a local Council. Some details of the facilities may be found here. These may cover a district or rural area, or a city, or a large county. Some examples of these types of websites include:

www.charnwoodbc.gov.uk
www.derbycity.com
www.caerphilly.gov.uk

You may also find details of facilities within large leisure companies. For example, you may find information about leisure pools at:

www.centerparcs.com

Some of the larger theme parks or sports stadia will also have sites. Try:

www.alton-towers.co.uk
www.wembleynationalstadium.co.uk

Also, looking at what is provided at a facility will give you a lot of information about the facility. Sites such as these include:

www.uci-cinemas.co.uk
www.superbowl.co.uk

The aims and objectives of running a leisure and recreation facility

The way in which a leisure facility is run, why it does particular things in a particular way, why it puts on one sort of an event and not another, will often be dependent on what the facility wishes to achieve. In other words, what the aims and objectives of the facility are.

The aims and objectives of facilities may vary, and will often be dependent on such factors as whether it is in the private, public or voluntary sector. It is now common for facilities to state in reports, or even in signs in the reception areas of facilities, exactly what their aims and objectives are.

These aims and objectives of a facility can be broken down under a number of headings:

✪ **Social**

✪ **Financial**

✪ **Organisational**

✪ **Equal opportunities**

✪ **Health**

✪ **Educational**

✪ **Developmental**

Social objectives

These are objectives that meet the need of a community, a group, or an individual that the facility serves. A social objective may be to improve the quality of people's lives, by giving greater opportunity of access to leisure activities. The facilities may want to give people the opportunity to meet friends, neighbours and others within their community, and for the community to influence, and even design, the leisure activities at the facility.

Alternatively, an objective of a facility may be the improvement in the quality of life through the reduction of crime. Many studies have shown that leisure programming can have a direct result on the behaviour of an individual and in the reduction of crime.

Financial objectives

All organisations will have financial targets and objectives. Wages have to be paid, and all facilities have running costs. The financial objectives may vary depending on the type of organisation; some organisations may wish to make a certain percentage profit, while others may wish to stay within any spending budgets that they have received, with the target that income is always greater than expenditure. Other financial objectives may be subtler, for example generating a certain amount of income from the ticket sales of a new activity at the facility.

Organisational objectives

People run organisations and facilities. When people are brought together and work together, even if it is only for the local Sunday league football team, they will have objectives. Within a leisure facility an objective may be to provide high levels of customer service, or to exceed standards set for safety – to be twice as quick at clearing the building in the event of a fire alarm than they are required to do.

Equal opportunities objectives

These are objectives about inclusion: about giving opportunity of access to the facility to all members of the community. Activities may be organised to tackle sections of society that may be excluded from particular leisure activities. As well as actual participation, the facility may wish to promote equality of opportunity to those who want to participate in higher levels, for example those wishing to develop higher levels of skill in a sport.

Health objectives

Access to enjoyable leisure can not only make us mentally healthier and happier, but we can also become physically healthier. Leisure facilities may have objectives to maintain or improve health within their area by providing access to sports, fitness and health facilities. Leisure facilities can also develop and promote health and fitness-related programmes. Also, leisure facilities may operate GP referral schemes with local doctors, where patients of the doctor visit the centre and participate in activities as part of their treatment in recovery from an illness.

Educational objectives

Many organisations have as one of their objectives the education of the public. They wish to make the public aware of what they do and why they do it. They wish to raise awareness amongst us of the importance of their facility. Many facilities provide education packs for students in schools and colleges, and it will be worthwhile investigating these. The educational objectives of facilities can range from helping us to improve our performance in a specific sport, to raising our general level of health, to ensuring that we have an enjoyable and fulfilling leisure experience when we visit the facility.

Developmental objectives

These, as the name suggests, are objectives that deal with new developments. This could include the promotion of a new activity or initiative, or promoting access to the facility to sections of the community who have not been participating in activities at the facility. It could involve helping to develop a new sport, or enabling and encouraging different levels of leadership training, coaching and training for a sport. It could also include developing outreach activities in order to encourage participation.

So to recap, we could give examples of the various objectives as:

- ✪ *Social objective*: **Improving the quality of life through leisure**
- ✪ *Financial objective*: **Making a profit/making a surplus**
- ✪ *Organisational objective*: **To provide quality customer service**
- ✪ *Equal opportunities objective*: **Sport for all**
- ✪ *Health objective*: **A reduction of heart disease within the community**
- ✪ *Educational objective*: **Ten qualified coaches in the most popular sports in the area**
- ✪ *Developmental objective*: **Launch a new multi-sport playscheme during the Easter holiday**

Case Study

In order to better understand how the aims and objectives for leisure, recreation or sport might be quantified, it may be useful if we look at a recent document produced by Sport England – the organisation that now carries out many of the duties for which the Sports Council had previously been responsible. Once you have read through the extracts, it may be helpful to you if you organise a discussion within a small group, and then organise a short presentation based on the conclusions that you reach in your discussion.

continued

continued

▶ A LOOK AT A RECENT SPORT ENGLAND PUBLICATION – *THE VALUE OF SPORT*

In a foreword to the publication, Trevor Brooking, the Chair of Sport England, states:

> *Sport is an integral part of British life. It provides enjoyment for millions of spectators, and it can unite the whole country behind our top competitors and teams.*

> *But sport isn't simply entertaining. It is hugely important, too. It can play a key role in tackling social exclusion, stimulating economic regeneration and giving young people the best possible start in life.*

The document itself lists the value of sport as:

> *Tackling social exclusion. Evidence suggests that participating in sporting activities increases people's sense of integration in their local community.*

> *Community safety. Evidence from across the country shows that sport reduces the chances of young people slipping into lives of crime.*

> *Increasing employment. Sport is already a major employer, providing 400,000 full-time jobs. It is also a growth industry.*

> *Enhancing the environment. Sports fields provide the green 'lungs' for our towns and cities.*

> *Promoting health. Cars, computer games and laboursaving devices have their attractions, but they mean too many people are leading comparatively sedentary lives.*

> *Urban regeneration. Improving sports facilities, and hosting major sporting events, can modernise an area's image and improve local self-esteem.*

You may wish to study this document in greater depth. *The Value of Sport* (reference number 887) can be obtained from: Sport England Publications, PO Box 255, Wetherby LS23 7LZ. Tel. 0990 210255. Or you can visit the website at www.sports.england.gov.uk.

Meeting objectives – Compulsory Competitive Tendering and Best Value

Compulsory Competitive Tendering was first introduced in 1988, having particular effect on leisure facilities operated by local councils. It meant that the running of all council leisure facilities (in England and Wales) had to be put out to competitive bidding. In other words, though the council retained the ownership of the facility, a contractor would carry out the day-to-day operation of the facility, working to guidelines drawn up by the council. The idea behind Compulsory Competitive Tendering was that it would provide better facilities and services because of the competition to gain the contract for the running of the facility, and by increasing competition between facilities. The result of Compulsory Competitive Tendering was that there were changes in the aims and objectives in the running of facilities. Because facilities were more competitive and accountable for financial dealings, there was a great emphasis on cost effectiveness, and on the efficiency of the facility.

Best Value is a concept that was introduced recently by the government and was defined in the Local Government Bill in 1998 as:

> *A Best Value (local) authority must make arrangements to secure continuous improvement in the way in which its functions are exercised, having regard to a combination of economy, efficiency and effectiveness.*

Best Value has attempted to broaden out the objectives of Compulsory Competitive Tendering, which were seen as being overly financially driven. Efficient management of leisure facilities is still important, but there is now great emphasis on the relationship between the leisure experience of the users of the facility and the cost of its provision. Best Value is seen as a total concept, looking at all inputs and outputs of the provision of the leisure experience and the consequences of that experience – the effect on the community and the differences it makes to people's lives.

The characteristics of Best Value could be listed as:

- **Providing services that the local community want in consultation with the local community**
- **The removal of barriers to participation**
- **Performance measurements and monitoring**
- **High quality and continuous improvement**
- **The development of partnerships with the private or voluntary sector, to improve and add value to the service provided**
- **Integrated and joined-up provision of services**

★ Form a small group and discuss how the characteristics of Best Value, listed above, could be applied to leisure and recreation

★ Provide a short presentation on how *one* of the characteristics of Best Value might work to the benefit of your town's or area's provision of leisure and recreation. Make sure you include one word-processed OHT

The programming and services of a leisure and recreation facility

What is programming?

Once a facility has decided on what its aims and objectives are, the management of that facility will begin to plan a programme. Programming is about putting the aims and objectives of the facility into practice. Leisure programming is about achieving a balance between finite resources. It is about providing individuals and groups – customers – with the activities that they want, while making best use of the resources available to meet the needs of those customers.

A programme is made up of:

- *Activities*: **What is available 'to do'. What activities are planned, or what activities different customers demand, at different times of the day, week or year, will affect how the overall programme of the facility is put together. Time available, and the demands of different groups on that time, and the activities, will mean that a system for giving priority within the programme will need to be established**

- *Facilities*: **This includes the areas of the building, areas where the activities take place, such as a sports hall or a viewing room at a cinema, and areas that support this, such as eating areas. Within the category of 'facilities' should also be included any equipment that is used**

- *Services*: **The help, advice and assistance that is provided to a customer. These services may include things like reception work, or coaching and induction/introduction to the facilities and activities**

Designing a programme

In designing a programme, a leisure facility will attempt to meet the needs of its customer. Though at first glance this may seem relatively simple – what's on when – a number of factors have to be taken into account:

- *Catchment area*: **How far people will travel, or the time they are willing to spend travelling, to the facility. This will be primarily influenced by the uniqueness of the facility**

✪ *Population factors*: **The facility may be providing for a population that is increasing or decreasing in overall size. Another population factor that needs to be considered is the age range of the population. For example, are there disproportionate numbers in certain population bands such as those under 20, or between 50 and 60 years of age?**

✪ *The design of the facility*: **The design of a facility, what areas are available and how they interlock will often determine what can be programmed. This can limit changes, or expansion of the programme available**

Activity 13.3

USER PROFILES

One of the ways in which a facility can identify the needs and wants of their existing and potential future customers is to carry out a 'User profile'.

Design a questionnaire that would enable you, firstly, to identify the characteristics of the individual customers of a facility, and secondly, to decide how you may be able to categorise their reasons for using a facility.

When designing a programme, a facility will normally include within the activities it provides opportunities for different forms of participation. Examples of these could be:

✪ **Family activities**

✪ **Casual use**

✪ **Club activities, held on a regular basis**

✪ **Coaching or education**

✪ **Competitions, leagues and knockout cups**

✪ **One-off events, special events or annual activities**

Once a facility has enough information to analyse the characteristics of its users and the form of participation they prefer, they will be able to design a programme that could provide for different user needs at different times. It would also mean that the facility could target different groups to ensure that the facility was used to its maximal capacity.

Target groups

Target groups can be thought of in a number of ways.

In terms of 'marketing', we could try to identify and define a particular part of the overall market to target. Say, for example, we were about to launch a new film. Our research would tell us that the main group of visitors to nearly every cinema consisted of young people. It would seem obvious, then, that this would be our 'target' group.

Alternatively, we may try to build a programme of activities for as many people as possible, in other words, the whole market. For example, it is sometimes found that though people often travel some distance to visit a facility, people who live in the immediate area have never visited. It may therefore be a logical conclusion to target activities, or publicity, at this target group.

Finally, for social reasons, we may wish to target a particular group, perhaps people who are less well off financially, or those who do not have regular opportunities to participate in leisure.

Booking and pricing

Though many aspects of booking and pricing will be dealt with later as part as operational procedures, it is important to mention it at this point because of the link to programming. The philosophy of booking that we wish to develop for a facility involves decisions about the different groups that we would like to use the facility, the days and times when we would like them to use it, and the price that we wish to charge them, will in turn influence our overall programme. Many facilities encourage different groups to use facilities at different times and often have cheaper pricing to encourage them to do so. This may help the facility generate revenue, or encourage use, at an otherwise quiet time. It may also mean that if the facility is trying to target a particular group, priority of booking is given to that group at a particular time irrespective of price or revenue.

Evaluating a programme

A great deal of time goes into planning programmes based on the aims and objectives of the organisation, but we often only judge the success of an activity by how many people turn up. However, the evaluation of the programme must be a dynamic ongoing process, part of the programming itself, so that we can ensure that the programme is an ongoing success. This cycle can be illustrated as shown in Figure 13.1.

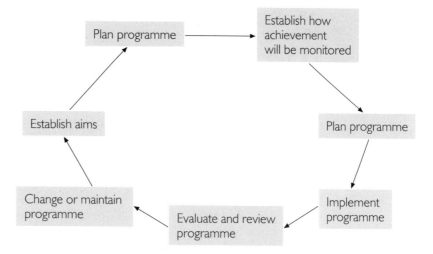

Figure 13.1 *The programme cycle*

The evaluation of a programme will of course depend on the aims and objectives that have been set for the programme. Some of the ways that might be considered to evaluate the success of a programme could include some or all of the following criteria:

- ✪ **Have people enjoyed themselves and will they visit again?**
- ✪ **Are there external statistics, for example a decrease in the crime rate, or an increase in economic prosperity within the community, that are attributable to the programme?**
- ✪ **An increase in numbers of people visiting the facility and participating in the programme**
- ✪ **Exceeding financial targets set**

Activity 13.4

Evaluating a programme

Prepare a short presentation on a leisure facility with which you are familiar. You should organise your presentation under the following headings:

★ *Your* analysis of what the aims and objectives of the programme are

★ How you could quantify or qualify these aims and objectives in a measurable form

Finally, present your analysis of the success of the programme together with recommendations for changes in the programme.

Before you begin work on your presentation, make sure you know the difference between a quantitative and qualitative measure within the context of leisure.

The physical resources of a leisure and recreation facility

The physical resources of a facility can be broken down into three broad categories:

- *Core facilities*: **The core facilities are those parts of the building where the activities take place. So, in a sports centre this may include sports halls or a swimming pool, whereas within a theme park this would mean the rides themselves**

- *Ancillary or peripheral facilities and resources*: **These are areas of the facility that relate to the core facilities and allow their day-to-day running. These include areas where machinery or plant may be held, where the public will not be allowed access, or areas that will aid the core business such as shops selling equipment, food or souvenirs, or toilets and changing facilities**

- *Equipment*: **This can be categorised as either specialist or general. Specialist equipment includes equipment that is needed to participate in an activity, such as posts, rackets, nets, whereas general equipment can include office equipment, stationery or vending machines**

The aspects of the design and dimensions of a facility

The activity for which a facility is designed often determines the dimensions of that facility. If we designed an area such as a sports hall in which we could play badminton, basketball or tennis, then the floor dimensions needed to play the games would determine space. Additionally, if we wished to play volleyball or practise trampolining within the sports hall, the height of the hall would need to be sufficient to allow clearance for the ball or trampolinist.

At the highest level, for example national or international competitions, the design of a facility for a particular activity, or for a particular sport, may be so specific that it prevents, or makes it unsuitable for, other activities.

Activity 13.5

★ In a group, identify two or three sporting activities – try to choose contrasting sports

★ Decide how you are going to investigate the recommendations or rules on the playing dimensions for these sports, and the type of surface the sports should be played on

★ Prepare a short presentation, or an information pack for your portfolio, on the information you have gathered

You will find that many facilities, which are designed to serve local communities, are designed in such a way as to accommodate a number of activities. Figure 13.2 shows the layout of a typical community recreation centre.

The illustration of the facility shows 'wet' as well as 'dry' activity areas. How these areas interact with each other and with any outdoor area is an important aspect of design as well as having an influence on how the different areas are managed.

In the design of a facility, not only do we have to consider the actual dimensions of the area, we need to think about other factors of design that may have an impact on the use to which a facility is put. As well as the dimensions of a facility, other factors such as the type of flooring/surfaces, intensity of lighting or the temperature of the area are often predetermined by the activity that is taking place.

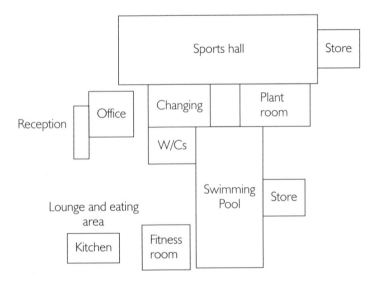

Figure 13.2 *The layout of a typical community recreation centre*

If we were to examine the different qualities that sports surfaces had for the playing of sport, we would take into account:

- **Grip and the need for specialist footwear**
- **Rebound for ball and/or participant**
- **How the surface affects the 'roll' of a ball**
- **How the flooring responds to usage, or how long it will last before it needs to be replaced**
- **How flexible the flooring is in allowing a range of activities to be undertaken**

When considering lighting we would need to think about:

- **The brightness of the light**
- **The type of lighting**
- **Any patches of shadow or poorly lit areas**
- **The height of the lighting**
- **The protection against damage**
- **How, and how often, the lighting is replaced**
- **The use, or elimination, of natural light**

When considering temperature we would need to think about:

- **The level of temperature appropriate for the activity**
- **Cooling the area down as well as warming it up**
- **Where hot and cold spots may occur**
- **The circulation of the air, and how often new, fresh, air is introduced**
- **Levels of humidity**

The approach to the design of the wet areas of a sports facility shows how the approach to design has changed, as people's demand for the type of recreation within a pool area has also changed. When thinking about the design of a pool area, some considerations may be:

- **The shape of the pool – traditional rectangular or a free-form leisure pool, perhaps with islands and beach areas**
- **The depth of the pool in different areas**
- **Additional training or paddling pools**
- **The use of inflatable features**
- **The use of water slides**
- **The use of water features such as wave machines or water jets**
- **Diving areas**

Design and dimensions

 TASK 1

Form a small group and talk about what you would like in your ideal leisure centre. Give it a name, and together draw up a floor plan for the facility showing all the different areas. You may also wish to draw an illustration showing how you would want either the front of the building or the reception area to look. Don't forget to include actual measurements in your proposal.

► **TASK 2**

Arrange a visit to a local sports centre. Make notes on the following:

★ The dimensions of the areas where activities take place

★ The type of surfaces in the playing and non-playing areas

★ The type and colours of marking used in the playing areas

★ If there is a pool area, make notes on the design of the area for both leisure and sport activities

Access to a facility

It is important that both customers and equipment are able to enter and exit a facility. It is important that customers are able to gain access to participate in activities and that if a safety risk occurs, such as a potential fire, they are able to exit quickly. Also, within leisure, large equipment is often used and it is important that the dimensions for access to the building take this into account.

Within any facility there will be only one or two entrances as it is important that the flow of people into the facility is controlled, usually through reception. However, there will be a greater number of exits from the building, usually to be used in case of an emergency. These exits are normally alarmed or controlled in some other way.

Once people are within the facility, they must be able to move between the areas they need to visit, and be able to find their way around the facility easily. Within any facility there will be areas that are restricted to the public at all times, such as offices and male/female changing areas. There are also areas where restricted access may be imposed at different times, either as a health and safety consideration, or because an activity requires quiet or privacy.

Additionally, it is important that there is access to all our customers, and it should be remembered that some of our customers may have 'special needs' as regards gaining access and using the facility.

What might be included as a 'special need'?

- ✪ **Children**
- ✪ **People who walk with difficulty**
- ✪ **Wheelchair users**
- ✪ **People with hearing problems**
- ✪ **Blind or partially sighted people**
- ✪ **People with learning difficulties**

What areas do we need to consider as regards access to the facility?

- ✪ **Parking**
- ✪ **Footpaths**
- ✪ **Doorways**
- ✪ **Steps**
- ✪ **Access to different floors of the building**
- ✪ **Signposting**
- ✪ **Public announcement systems**
- ✪ **Circulation in the building**
- ✪ **Toilets**
- ✪ **Changing and showers**

If you wish to research the issue of access and the control of the public within a facility, you could look at the *Guide to Safety at Sports Grounds*.

Equipment used in a facility

The equipment used within a facility falls within a number of categories: general equipment used and managed by staff in the running of a facility; equipment hired or sold to customers; and larger equipment used in activities.

General equipment could include:

- ✪ **Computers**
- ✪ **Vending machines**
- ✪ **Tills and cash machines**
- ✪ **Scanners, e.g. for membership cards**
- ✪ **Equipment to prepare surfaces such as grass, Astroturf or ice for activities**
- ✪ **Stationery**

Special equipment used to participate in an activity could include:

- **Specialist safety equipment such as helmets, padding or guards**
- **Specialist footwear**
- **Balls, shuttles, goggles, floats**
- **Rackets, bats, sticks**
- **Clothing**

Special larger equipment could include:

- **Posts or nets**
- **Inflatables**
- **Mats**
- **Fitness equipment**
- **Rides and slides**
- **Sound and lighting equipment**
- **Play structures**

The list for the specialist equipment could be very long, and is usually quite specific to the pursuit or sport.

As with the dimensions that an activity is played within, or the surface that the activity is played on, the activity itself, and the level at which it is played, usually predetermines the equipment used. It is important that you familiarise yourself with the equipment used in a range of activities. You may wish to carry on your study from the activity on dimensions. Why not try to build up a resource base for your group, giving individual members of the group responsibility for collecting information? **BUT** don't forget to read the information you gather!

Ancillary areas and their influence on a facility

Customers visit a facility primarily to participate in the core activity of the facility. Within any facility there are areas that support the core activity, usually called ancillary or peripheral areas. The majority of complaints relate directly to the ancillary areas rather than the core activities themselves. The positioning of ancillary areas in relation to core activities, their design, and the management of the areas is important if the customer is to gain a quality experience from their visit to the facilities. Management of ancillary areas will be dealt with in greater detail under operational practices.

Ancillary areas can be broken down into:

- ✪ *Areas used directly by staff/employees:* **offices, staff rest room, meeting room, plant and machinery rooms, kitchens, storage rooms**
- ✪ *Areas that are used and accessed by the public:* **car parks, toilets, changing rooms and shower areas, crèches, eating areas and refreshment areas, locker and clothes storage areas, meeting and rest areas, shops, first aid rooms, spectator areas**

The design of ancillary areas has to take into account the number of people, both employees and customers, using the areas, and the variations in this number at different times. Design also needs to take into account the characteristics of the users. Ancillary areas should be designed to be functional – that is, practical and serviceable, and that they perform to meet the function for which they are designed. Also, the design should be one that is as attractive and appealing as possible, to add to the comfort and overall experience of the user.

Where the ancillary facilities are situated in relation to the core facilities is important, for the ease of flow of people (staff and customers) between the core and ancillary areas. The flow of people between different areas of the facility will also have an influence on the design of pathways and corridors, and crush and waiting areas. The relationship between areas, or the movement of people between them, is often a very direct one; for example, it may be essential to visit one area before another, or there may be direct links in terms of the technical operation of a facility, for example between a swimming pool and the filtration room.

Activity 13.7

 Task 1

Get some coloured card and a larger piece of white paper. Cut up the card and write on the cards as many ancillary areas as you can think of. Draw a circle in the middle of the paper and label it 'core area', then place your set of cards around this.

▶ **Task 2**

Using two different-coloured pens, draw a flow line, one for customers, and one for staff, between the core and ancillary areas.

▶ **Task 3**

Below the diagram, or on a separate piece of paper, list the direct and indirect relationships between core/ancillary and between ancillary/ancillary areas.

Operational procedures

Operational procedures are 'how things are done' within a leisure facility on a day-by-day basis. Often, operational procedures are written down, so that employees can easily follow them and put them into practice. Sometimes these procedures might have to be followed quite strictly, for example how to introduce chemicals into a swimming pool, other times they may be guidelines, for example how to deal with customers.

The role of the receptionist and customer induction

The customer will normally gain an impression of a facility through the outer design, signposting and approach to a facility, but the first person they normally encounter is the person, or persons, working in the reception area. The receptionist should act towards the customer, as should *all* members of staff, by:

- **Being polite, smiling and being welcoming**
- **Being of a neat and tidy appearance, possibly wearing the facility uniform**
- **Being attentive and establishing the customer's needs**
- **Communicating effectively**
- **Recording information accurately**

Staff working in the reception area may also have specific responsibilities, such as:

- **Taking and recording bookings, or dealing with enquiries from customers in person or by telephone**
- **Handling payment by cash, cheque, credit card or debit card**
- **Controlling entry to the building and issuing tickets for the appropriate activities**
- **Coordinating evacuation from the building and liaising with the emergency services**
- **Communicating instructions to staff through the communication system**
- **Directing the customer to the appropriate area or activity**

Where a facility or activity is new, or where there is a new visitor, it is usually necessary to follow an induction procedure. Staff working in a reception capacity, or other staff who have been allocated this responsibility, may sometimes carry this out. A typical induction would seek to:

- ✪ **Familiarise the customer with the layout of the facility and emergency signage and procedures**
- ✪ **Introduce the customer to the activity they wish to participate in and explain safety measures**
- ✪ **Provide information on other activities at the facility**
- ✪ **Arrange future visits of the customer, or explain and enrol them into any membership schemes**

Booking systems

With so much demand from often large numbers of customers who wish to use a leisure facility, it is usually necessary to operate some form of booking system. A booking system within a leisure facility is the link between the programme of the facility and the customer. A booking system should be as simple to use as possible. Most facilities have procedures in place stating how bookings are to be taken, and whose responsibility it is to take bookings. These procedures must be followed if the booking system is to operate efficiently. An efficient booking system:

- ✪ **Allows a facility to plan ahead in order to prepare areas for activities**
- ✪ **Allows the scheduling and prioritising of different activities within the programme**
- ✪ **Enables a facility to manage its staff resources against the timing of the activities**
- ✪ **Enables a facility to coordinate the different spaces and areas within the facility**

Booking systems can be paper based, normally with the use of pre-printed forms, but more usually today booking forms are computer based. Both systems have their advantages and disadvantages.

Advantages of a paper-based system

- ✓ **Low cost**
- ✓ **Easy to use**
- ✓ **Little training needed**
- ✓ **Format can be updated easily**

Disadvantages of a paper-based system

✗ **Difficult to correct errors**

✗ **Can become damaged or look scrappy**

✗ **Difficult for more than one person to use at a time**

✗ **Extracting information from it can be laborious**

Advantages of computer-based systems

✓ **Fast**

✓ **Prevents double booking**

✓ **A centralised system can take bookings for a large number of venues**

✓ **Information easily accessed to help improve management planning**

Disadvantages of a computer-based system

✗ **High initial cost**

✗ **Needs specialist training**

✗ **May be difficult to update**

✗ **Can crash**

Membership schemes and pricing policies

Many leisure facilities operate membership schemes. Though some do operate a 'members only' policy, more often the schemes are operated to allow the facility to plan programming of the facility for greater utilisation.

Some of the reasons for operating a membership scheme include:

✪ **Generates regular income through membership fees, which allows better financial planning**

✪ **Enables the facility to target particular 'customer groups' as part of the membership schemes**

✪ **Creates a database of members, allowing more focused customer service and marketing of the facilities and related products**

✪ **Encourages loyalty and commitment of the members**

✪ **Allows different categories of membership and graduated pricing, to promote non-peak usage, and greater control of peak-time usage**

Many facilities also operate a type of membership scheme that is aimed at encouraging participation by as many groups as possible. These schemes' aims are to be inclusive rather than exclusive. They can give priority of booking facilities and/or enable a policy of concessionary pricing – these are sometimes known as 'Passport to Leisure' or 'Leisure Card' schemes.

Some of the reasons for operating a Leisure Card scheme include:

✪ **Encourages greater usage of facilities**
✪ **Allows the facility to monitor usage of target groups of customers or individual customers**
✪ **Can be used to discriminate in favour of the people in the local geographical area/community**
✪ **Enables the facility to encourage participation in particular activities or events**
✪ **Allows the facility to offer concessionary pricing to groups such as school children or young people, students, the unemployed and people on low incomes, those who are registered as disabled, people of pensionable age**

As well as, or instead of, operating membership schemes or Leisure Card schemes, facilities may operate price discrimination, through offering different price rates. This could be in order to offer cheaper prices at different times of the day. Or it could be one that offers different pricing for different groups, e.g. family/adults/children. Or the pricing scheme could be one that is priced in favour of educational/coaching/club usage as opposed to recreational or casual use.

Licensing

Because leisure facilities are open to the public, have a large flow of people through the facility and usually charge a fee for admission, it is important that the public know that they are safe and secure and that the management of the facility is reputable. One of the ways in which this is ensured is by the 'licensing' of premises to allow them to carry out different activities.

Though licences are usually linked in the public's mind to the pub/public house 'licensed premises' or the television licence, they have a far wider-ranging application that goes back many centuries and has particular reference to leisure facilities. The type of licences that a leisure facility may have to obtain include:

- ✪ **Liquor**
- ✪ **Restaurant**
- ✪ **Entertainment**
- ✪ **Indoor sporting events**
- ✪ **Theatre and cinemas**

A licence usually only has to be applied for if a business is being carried out, and where an event is a public event. Public events do not include bazaars, fetes or local sports events. If you are organising an event and have any doubt, contact the police or the local council.

Liquor licences – To obtain a licence to sell intoxicating liquor, it is necessary to make an application to the local Licensing Justices. If the person applying for the licence and the premises in which the alcohol is to be sold are deemed suitable, the licence will normally be issued for a period of twelve months. The licence must be renewed and if the premises have become unsuitable or if objections have been made for any reason, the licence may be withdrawn. A licence that allows alcohol to be sold within a leisure facility is known as an **on-licence**. Another type of liquor licence that has relevance to a leisure facility is an **occasional licence**. This is a licence that can be applied for when there is a need for special activities, such as a special function or event, to sell alcohol.

Restaurant licences – In most instances, there is normally an eating or drinking area within a leisure facility and if meals are served, it will be necessary for the premises to obtain a restaurant licence, and show that the premises are suitable. They will also have to follow the Food Hygiene Regulations as laid out in the Food Safety Act 1990. If the facility wishes to serve alcohol with meals, they will have to apply, and follow the procedure, in the same way as liquor licences are granted.

Entertainment licences – A Public Entertainment Licence must be obtained if a facility intends to provide 'public entertainment' such as music or dancing, or where there are public displays. Again, with such activities, the safety of the public is paramount, and to obtain a licence it is necessary to convince the police, the fire service and the local council that the facility is a safe place in which to carry out the activity, and that the correct safety and emergency procedures are in place.

Indoor sporting events – Where a sporting activity takes place and it is open to the public as spectators, this can be seen as part of 'an entertainment'. Some events often attract large numbers of people, so licences have to be applied for in the same way as Public Entertainment Licences.

Theatre and cinema licences – These are very similar to Public Entertainment Licences, and can of course apply to leisure facilities that are exclusively theatres or cinemas. They also apply where cinemas or theatres are incorporated within a multicomplex facility. These types of licences also cover the showing of videos or the playing of recorded music as public entertainment, and will have particular relevance where the public is attracted into a facility to watch, for example, live sporting events on satellite or digital television.

Equipment

One of the most important areas of responsibility of staff within a leisure centre is the supervision and control of equipment. Areas of responsibility include:

- ✪ **Checking the equipment is suitable for the user**
- ✪ **Checking the equipment is safe for use**
- ✪ **Moving equipment**
- ✪ **Assembling equipment**
- ✪ **Storing equipment**
- ✪ **Maintaining equipment/reporting damage**
- ✪ **Recording the use of equipment and maintaining appropriate levels of stock of equipment**
- ✪ **Supervising the use of equipment**

The use of equipment is often central to leisure activities, and it is therefore central to the daily operational procedures of those working in leisure. Equipment needs to be ready when the customer wishes to use it, and if a number of activities are going on, one after the other, this may mean that different equipment is required. It is important that those working in a leisure facility examine their programme of activities regularly to ensure that the equipment is set up/available on time, and that suitably trained members of staff are available to set up the equipment and, if necessary, supervise the activity.

Activity 13.8

1 Using the programme of a leisure facility, list the different types of equipment that may be used for the activities

2 Using badminton as an example, list the actions you would take, in the appropriate order, when preparing an area that had just been used for five-a-side football for use by the badminton club

A leisure facility has a legal obligation (under The Occupiers' Liability Act of 1957 and 1984) to ensure that the facility is safe for use. This is known as 'a duty of care'. So, if a person is injured because of faulty or badly maintained equipment, the facility may be open to legal prosecution.

Because of the risk to the public when using equipment, any staff that have responsibility for equipment should always follow approved safety procedures. Within any facility there will normally be guidelines, in a published format, to cover the procedures a member of staff should follow in each of these areas. With some specialist equipment, the manufacturer of the equipment will give guidelines as to its use and maintenance.

Organisations such as the Institute of Leisure and Amenity Management and the Institute of Sport and Recreation Management publish guidelines relating to equipment. The following example shows just how detailed some of these guidelines can be.

An example of guidelines for the safe use of equipment – 'The Use of Play Equipment and Water Features in Swimming Pools – A Recommended Code of Practice'

This guide, produced by The Institute of Sport and Recreation Management, deals with the large number of features and equipment that can be found in a pools area. The guide covers:

- ✪ **Small inflatable toys (e.g. inflatable animals and balls)**
- ✪ **Non-inflatable play structures (e.g. floats)**
- ✪ **Large/small inflatable play structures (e.g. a bouncy castle/animal in the water)**
- ✪ **Large inflatable structures (e.g. plastic islands that need a constant air flow to keep afloat)**
- ✪ **Inflatable water slides**
- ✪ **Wave machines**
- ✪ **Water cannons**
- ✪ **Jet streams, or rapids**
- ✪ **Geysers**
- ✪ **Waterfalls**
- ✪ **Masks, snorkels and fins**

The guide gives a series of safety recommendations in relation to this equipment, including:

✪ **Risk assessment**

✪ **Manual handling/transportation of equipment**

✪ **Hazards**

✪ **Control measures**

✪ **British Standards**

✪ **Pool operating procedures**

✪ **Use of electric blowers**

✪ **Installation of equipment**

✪ **Deflation of equipment**

✪ **Storage**

✪ **Maintenance**

✪ **Supervision requirements**

✪ **Instruction for use**

✪ **Emergency action plan**

This guide can be obtained from The Institute of Sport and Recreation Management, Giffard House, 36/38 Sherrard Street, Melton Mowbray LE13 1XJ.

Maintenance and cleaning

Maintenance keeps facilities and equipment in a usable and safe condition. Cleaning is part of that maintenance; if facilities and equipment are kept clean, they are more likely to last longer, they are safer, and this is what the public expects. A clean and well-maintained facility will present the right image to customers, it will save money on repairs, and it will ensure that staff are set a standard for their everyday work within the facility.

The amount of maintenance and cleaning carried out will depend on the level of use of facilities and equipment; this may very through different times of the day, month or year in line with the programme of the facility. For the operation of a facility, this cleaning and maintenance is either planned in and around a programme, or it is responding to unforeseen circumstances.

✪ *Planned cleaning and maintenance*: **Specific tasks are timetabled, detailing the frequency with which they should be done. There are normally written procedures for carrying these out. Within these procedures will also be guidelines on who should carry out the cleaning and maintenance, and, where appropriate, the training they should have before carrying out the tasks**

✪ *Unforeseen cleaning and maintenance*: **Staff need to respond to unforeseen spillages and breakages, or an area being used with greater intensity or by a more 'untidy' group than has been anticipated. Additionally, even where maintenance or cleaning is planned, e.g. the replacement of lighting or the replacement of a drain, the facilities and equipment often have a habit of not sticking to the plan**

Activity 13.9

Select one of the following areas of a leisure facility:

★ Sports hall

★ Pool area

★ Reception

★ Car park

★ Eating area

Draw up a cleaning and maintenance schedule appropriate to:

★ A daily and weekly plan

or

★ A monthly and yearly plan

Staffing

Leisure and recreation is a very 'labour intensive' activity. In other words, when customers participate in leisure activities, a proportionally high number of staff, sometimes even on a one-to-one basis, are required. Also, the peak time for participation in leisure activities normally occurs outside of the 'normal' working day, so leisure and recreational facility staff have to have the aptitude and attitude to work, and give of their best, at these times.

The programme of activities is the normal starting point for determining and planning staffing of those activities. To ensure the smooth running of a facility and facility programme, the correct number of staff who are suitably trained and qualified have to be in place, at the required time, for the activity to take place. Factors that could influence staffing levels include:

✪ **Numbers using the facility and/or participating**

✪ **Age of participants**

- ✪ **Intensity of activity**
- ✪ **Level of experience or skill of participants**
- ✪ **Number of existing supervisors, e.g. for some club activities, the club may provide their own coaches/supervisors. Also, for some activities, children may be under the supervision of their parents, or parents may be present as helpers**
- ✪ **Legal responsibilities**

It is normally the job of the manager, or duty manager, within a leisure and recreation facility to plan staffing requirements, making sure that staff are fully aware of:

- ✪ **What their job role is for the different activities**
- ✪ **What is expected of them**
- ✪ **With whom they are to work**
- ✪ **For whom they are responsible**
- ✪ **To whom they are responsible**

It is also the job of the manager/duty manager to ensure that staff have the appropriate level of experience or training to carry out the tasks they are asked to do.

Training for staff at a leisure and recreation facility can be:

- ✪ *Specific to the task*: **Here, training is normally carried out at the facility, to enable people to reach the required level of competence. This may be a task such as how to handle cash, or how to replace markings in a sports hall. These types of activities are sometimes brought together systematically as part of a National Vocational Qualification (NVQ)**
- ✪ *General training*: **This could be where staff receive training either on a short course such as a first aid qualification or a National Coaching Foundation Course such as 'Working with Children'. Or, longer-term training, such as a Leisure Management course, or a VCE**
- ✪ *Specific to the job*: **Examples of this could include a Governing Body Coaching Award that may be required to lead a particular activity, or a Lifeguard Award that is required to work poolside**

Using the programme of a leisure facility, select two hours and list the activities going on at the facility. Once you have done this, try to identify for those two hours the following:

★ The number of staff required

★ How this is broken down into staff leading or supervising the activities and other support staff

★ The training and qualifications it is advisable for (all) staff to have to ensure the safe operation of activities

Revision questions

1 Name three types of leisure facility.

2 What is a 'dual-use' facility?

3 What does 'gov' mean in a web address?

4 What is the difference between an aim and an objective?

5 Give an example of a social objective that a leisure facility might have.

6 Give an example of how a financial objective of a facility in the private sector may differ from one in the public sector.

7 Write a definition of 'Best Value'.

8 State the three components of a leisure and recreation programme.

9 Briefly explain the difference between 'core' and 'ancillary' facilities.

10 What design factors might be taken into account for a new pool area?

11 Give three examples of groups of people who might be considered to have a 'special need'.

12 Give five examples of larger specialist equipment used in a leisure facility.

13 Give two advantages and two disadvantages of a computerised booking system.

14 Briefly explain why a leisure facility might run a Leisure Card scheme.

15 Give three types of licence that a leisure facility might need to apply for.

16 Give three examples of *general* training that could be undertaken by a person working in a leisure facility.

Assessment activity

TASK 1

Individually prepare a presentation, with OHTs and handouts, on a leisure facility that you have investigated. The presentation should cover the following areas:

- ★ The aims and objectives of the facility
- ★ The facility's programme
- ★ The facility's uses of information technology
- ★ The physical resources of the facility
- ★ Examples of operating procedure
- ★ Any of your own ideas for improvements that could be made

TASK 2

When the other people in your group make their presentations, make sure you make comprehensive notes. You may even wish to ask them if you could photocopy some of the material.

TASK 3

Write a report comparing the two facilities based on the guidelines given for your presentation.

Financial planning and control

21

Objectives

- **Understand accounts**
- **Understand how to price leisure and recreation products and services**
- **Understand how to produce budgets**

In the highly competitive leisure and recreation industry, planning and controlling finances is essential for survival and the long-term growth of enterprises. In this unit you will investigate how organisations control their flow of money in order to make sure that they are as profitable as possible, that bills are paid when they are due and that management can plan for the future with confidence. You will develop the skills and understanding that are necessary for dealing with basic financial matters in a leisure and recreation organisation. In particular, you will learn about the importance of accounts in measuring the profitability of an organisation. You will also investigate how leisure and recreation products and services are priced. The final part of the unit looks at the procedures used in producing budgets, including a cash flow forecast and a profit and loss account.

Understanding accounts

Key topics in this section

- **The importance of understanding accounts**
- **Understanding cash flow, the profit and loss account and balance sheets**
- **Factors affecting the financial performance of a leisure and recreation organisation**
- **Extracting information from the balance sheet and profit and loss account**
- **Interpreting accounts**

The importance of understanding accounts

Accurate and easily accessible accounts are the cornerstone of successful financial planning and control. Every leisure and recreation enterprise, no matter how big or small, needs to keep careful accounts or 'books' in order to:

1 **Keep track of how well the organisation is performing in terms of generating revenue and controlling costs**

2 **Meet the legal requirements to present audited accounts at the end of each trading year**

3 **Make sure that its selling, purchasing and payments transactions are free from error**

4 **Provide continuous feedback to management to help decision making**

5 **Form the source data from which the year end or final accounts are produced**

In leisure and recreation organisations, even employees who are not directly concerned with financial planning and control need to understand the type of information provided by accounts, such as sales volumes, pricing, cash flow and profitability. The long-term success of any organisation relies on keeping control of money within the organisation and all employees contribute to this by making effective use of resources, maximising customer spending and encouraging new business.

Accounting methods used in the leisure and recreation industry mirror closely those used by organisations in many other sectors of the UK economy. Financial accountants are bound by legislation contained in the various Companies Acts concerning the method of presentation of financial data and the disclosure of certain information. As well as meeting the needs of shareholders, financial accounts include information required by the Inland Revenue and the Registrar of Companies. The accounts of all leisure and recreation companies are subject to auditing, a technique that attempts to ensure that the financial information disclosed to shareholders and other interested parties is objective and fair.

Leisure and recreation organisations in the public sector are also required by law to produce annual accounts. Under the Local Government Finance Act 1982, local authorities are required to produce Statements of Accounts, which include income and expenditure, summaries of capital expenditure, the consolidated balance sheet and the statement of sources of funds. With the development of 'contracted out' services, individual business units within local authorities, including leisure and recreation facilities, are required to produce a separate annual report, prepared along the lines of commercial sector accounts. Many voluntary sector organisations also have to produce accounts to satisfy the requirements of the Charity Commission or the providers of National Lottery funding.

Understanding cash flow, the profit and loss account and balance sheets

All public limited companies (plcs) produce annual reports, which provide interested parties with details about business performance and company activities. Publicly funded and voluntary bodies also produce financial reports so that anybody with an interest can investigate how effectively public money is being spent.

Financial accounting is concerned with the preparation of the financial information an organisation is required by law to produce. In the private sector, these statutory accounts comprise:

- ✪ **The cash flow statement**
- ✪ **The profit and loss account**
- ✪ **The balance sheet**

We will now look at each of these in greater detail.

The cash flow statement

The cash flow statement is a detailed record of cash flowing into and out of an organisation, usually on an annual basis. From this can be derived the monthly cash flow and, by adding together each month's figures, the organisation's cumulative cash position. Detailed cash flow management is critical to any leisure and recreation organisation, in order to:

- **Be in a position to meet cash demands**
- **Ensure that maximum credit is being obtained**
- **Make sure that debtors are kept under tight control**
- **Determine when extra borrowing is needed**

The cash flow statement identifies:

- *Cash inflows*: **This will include revenue from the sale of products or services, the start-up capital, loans obtained and income from other sources, such as rent from property and dividends received from shares**
- *Cash outflows*: **These include all the expenses incurred in making the sales of products and services. These will include running costs such as wages, rent, postage, telephone, advertising and stationery, as well as interest and loan repayments**
- *Net cash flow*: **By deducting total cash outflows from total cash inflows, the balance arrived at will show, on a monthly basis, the amount of cash forecast to be in the bank. For new businesses in leisure and recreation, the operators can see immediately whether their efforts are likely to pay dividends**

An organisation's cash flow statement provides a link between its profit and loss account and balance sheet. It forms part of the audited accounts and shows the funds that have entered the company, how they have been used and how any net surplus or deficiency in short- and long-term funds have been applied.

The cash flow statement will indicate the periods in the year when extra financing, in the form of an overdraft or loan, is required.

The profit and loss account

The information contained in the profit and loss account is probably the most important in managing and controlling the finances of a leisure and recreation organisation. The profit and loss account, more precisely called the trading and profit and loss account, is a summary of all the income and expenditure of an organisation, over a given period of time, sometimes quarterly, half yearly or annually, depending on custom and practice. However, by law, companies must produce their final accounts at least once per year.

All profit and loss accounts will show whether the organisation is carrying forward either a surplus or deficit into the next accounting period, and are useful for comparing financial performance over different periods of time.

The purposes of a profit and loss account can be summarised as follows:

- ✪ **To indicate the success or failure of management policies in deploying available resources to generate profits. To achieve this, the profit and loss account should be read in conjunction with the balance sheet**
- ✪ **To show the extent to which an organisation can cover its debt servicing costs, e.g. bank and loan interest, from the profits earned in the course of its day-to-day activities**
- ✪ **To determine whether an organisation's goods and services are sufficiently popular to cover its necessary expenses, such as staff costs, rates, insurance and administration costs**
- ✪ **To illustrate how an organisation's profits have been divided among claimants, such as external lenders, the Inland Revenue and the owners**
- ✪ **To determine the extent to which profits are susceptible to erosion by rising costs**
- ✪ **To give an impression of whether an organisation seeks a high turnover with low percentage profit margins, or a lower turnover with higher margins**

Profitability is the ultimate objective of commercial leisure and recreation enterprises. It is the management's responsibility to maximise profitability, which is usually the prime concern of the owners of the business and any shareholders it has. They will be particularly concerned that the return on their investment should be more than that available elsewhere, given the same or lower level of risk.

Activity
21.1

Research a range of annual reports of leisure and recreation organisations and compare the financial data given in their profit and loss accounts. Compile a chart showing which have the highest turnover and calculate the increases or decreases in turnover between current and past years.

Interpreting the profit and loss account

The results shown in an organisation's profit and loss account can be interpreted as follows:

- ✪ **By comparing the results against budgeted figures and analysing any variances (differences)**
- ✪ **By comparing the results against previous years' results and analysing differences**
- ✪ **By comparing the results against the performance of competitors**
- ✪ **By comparing the results with 'industry norms', i.e. how an organisation in the same sector would normally be expected to perform**

The balance sheet

The balance sheet of a leisure and recreation enterprise is a very important document. It is a statement of the assets, liabilities and capital of the organisation and summarises its financial position at a specified date, in other words a 'snapshot' of the financial health of the business on a particular day. Balance sheets are drawn up at least on an annual basis and often more frequently than this, depending on the financial systems of the organisation.

The balance sheet revolves around an organisation's assets and liabilities, the difference between the two being the working capital that it has available to use for day-to-day operations.

We will now explain some terminology:

- ✪ *Fixed assets*: **These are items of a monetary value that have a long-term function and can be used repeatedly. Examples include land, buildings, vehicles, equipment and machinery. Fixed assets are not only useful in the running of an organisation, but can also be used as security for additional loans**
- ✪ *Current assets*: **These are items owned by an organisation, where the value is constantly changing, for example stock, debtors (those who owe you money) and cash. The balance of current assets over current liabilities is called the working capital**
- ✪ *Current liabilities*: **These are amounts owed to other businesses, where the amounts are constantly changing. Typical current liabilities are creditors (those to whom you owe money), overdrafts and dividends**
- ✪ *Net current assets (working capital)*: **This is the difference between the current assets and the current liabilities**

✪ *Owner's capital employed*: **This represents the money that the owner has put into the business either directly or indirectly by trading, making a profit and leaving some of the profit in the business**

The main purposes of a balance sheet can be summarised as follows:

✪ **The organisation's ability to pay off outstanding debts can be assessed by comparing current assets with current liabilities**

✪ **It gives an opportunity to determine the extent to which an organisation is able to borrow further funds from external sources, without straining its capability to service its debts**

✪ **It illustrates the division of capital employed among outsiders, owners, proprietors and shareholders**

✪ **It allows an examination and analysis of the organisation's fixed assets to reveal whether assets are underutilised**

✪ **It provides evidence of management policies on subjective issues, such as the writing off of goodwill, the treatment of development costs and the expiry of fixed assets through depreciation**

Who uses financial accounts?

Various people, both inside and outside the organisation, will use accounting information to help determine how a leisure and recreation enterprise is performing, including:

✪ *Owners*: **All those who have invested, or are considering investing, capital into a leisure and recreation business will be keen to assess profitability, liquidity and activity, in the past, present and future. How the organisation is performing is the responsibility of management and is, therefore, an assessment of how well they deploy their resources**

✪ *Shareholders and investment brokers*: **Individuals and organisations that own shares in companies, as well as their advisers and brokers, will need access to accounts to check financial performance**

✪ *Managers*: **All managers have a duty of stewardship, i.e. to report to the shareholders and to operate the organisation in their best interests. Effective managers in leisure and recreation will monitor progress throughout the year, by comparing actual with budgeted results and taking steps to correct any problem areas**

✪ *Providers of finance*: **Whether a banking institution in the private sector or 'the public purse' in the public sector,** providers of finance will be interested in how well an organisation can repay its debts, now and in the future

○ *Tax authorities*: **The Inland Revenue and HM Customs and Excise will need to see accurate records for correct assessment of income tax and VAT**

Activity 21.2

Taking the examples of a voluntary sector organisation, such as a local swimming club, and a private sector leisure and recreation company, such as David Lloyd Leisure, compile a chart to show who would be likely to need to use the financial accounts of each organisation and for what purpose.

Factors affecting the financial performance of a leisure and recreation organisation

The wide-ranging nature of the leisure and recreation industry means that there will be many reasons why the financial performance of an organisation changes, for the better or the worse. External factors, outside the immediate control of the organisation, may include:

○ *Seasonality*: **Although a great deal of effort is channelled into extending the tourist season, some sectors of the UK leisure and recreation industry operate on a seasonal basis only, rather than throughout the year. This will mean that there will be wide variations in cash flow over a 12-month period**

○ *State of the economy*: **In times of recession, levels of disposable income (the amount left over when essential expenses have been met) will be depressed, leading to reduced demand for some leisure and recreation products and services. The reverse will be the case in boom times, with demand sometimes outstripping supply, thus forcing prices up**

○ *Competitor activity*: **A change in demand for a competitor's product or service, or an alteration in prices, may have an effect on the profitability of a leisure and recreation organisation. For example, a 50 per cent reduction in the** admission price for a major theme park is likely to reduce attendances at competitor attractions in the same locality

✪ *Changes in tastes and fashions*: **A particular tourist destination or resort can quickly come into, or go out of, fashion, making it difficult for some operators to forecast revenue. Organisations must be flexible enough to respond to sudden changes in demand**

✪ *Government legislation*: **Unexpected changes in legislation, for example health and safety measures or changes in travel taxes, can have serious implications for an organisation's costs and revenues**

✪ *Industrial disputes*: **Strikes, and other industrial action, can bring leisure and recreation facilities to a halt, e.g. airports, ferries and rail services**

✪ *The weather*: **A wet British summer can affect the attendances at outdoor events and attractions**

Internal factors that may affect financial performance include:

✪ **Low sales volume**

✪ **Poor quality products**

✪ **Poor customer service**

✪ **Inappropriate pricing for products and services**

✪ **High levels of credit**

✪ **High levels of debt**

✪ **High fixed costs**

✪ **High variable costs**

✪ **Poor stock control**

The measures discussed later in this unit concerning the techniques to monitor an organisation's profitability and liquidity are designed to provide an early warning of any problems with these internal factors.

Extracting information from the balance sheet and profit and loss account

In today's highly competitive leisure and recreation industry it is not enough merely to be able to understand a set of accounts. It is also necessary to be able to extract information from them to be able to answer such questions as:

- ✪ **How well is the business performing in terms of generating revenue and controlling costs?**
- ✪ **Has the business performed better than last year?**
- ✪ **Is the organisation as profitable as its competitors?**
- ✪ **Will the Inland Revenue be happy with the information supplied on the financial statements?**

Potential investors in a leisure and recreation company will want to examine the annual report and accounts to decide whether or not the enterprise is a good investment. In particular, they will study the financial information contained in the annual accounts to examine:

- ✪ *Turnover*: **total revenue earned by the organisation**
- ✪ *Gross profit*: **turnover less direct costs**
- ✪ *Net profit*: **gross profit less indirect costs**
- ✪ *Direct costs*: **cost of sales or costs that can be directly attributed to the sales, e.g. stock or labour**
- ✪ *Indirect costs*: **overheads such as management salaries**
- ✪ *Fixed assets*: **items owned by the business and not intended to be sold on, e.g. vehicles**
- ✪ *Current assets*: **items that can be easily turned into cash, e.g. stock and debtors**
- ✪ *Current liabilities*: **debts that are due imminently**
- ✪ *Long-term liabilities*: **debts to be repaid over a longer time period**
- ✪ *Capital*: **original investment in the organisation**

Investors may well be deciding between two or more leisure and recreation companies as potential investments and will compare these measures to gauge the companies' prospects.

Study the financial information in the annual report of a public limited company (plc) in the leisure and recreation industry. You could choose from David Lloyd Leisure, Virgin, Manchester United Football Club, Fitness First, Holmes Place, etc. From the information given in the annual report, extract the following information (refer to the above explanations of these terms to help you in this task):

Turnover, gross profit, operating profit (net profit), cost of sales, fixed assets, long-term liabilities, and capital and reserves

You may find the information you need on a company's Internet website.

Interpreting accounts

The accounts of an organisation are an important source of information that enable the managers/owners and interested parties to examine and evaluate its financial performance. All leisure and recreation organisations, regardless of which sector they operate in, are striving towards effective management and control, which should lead to a healthy profit and loss account and balance sheet. These statements, together with other performance indicators, should be used by managers to assess efficiency and indicate areas that may need adjustment to improve the overall outcome. It is common practice for organisations to develop ratios from the accounts, which can be used for performance appraisal.

Accounting ratios

Ratios tend to be the most common method by which financial information is interpreted, offering an easy way of comparing performance both within and between organisations. Comparisons between one year and another, between similar organisations in the same sector or comparisons with budgeted targets are much more useful than actual figures. It is important not to consider a single ratio in isolation or make decisions based on a single set of figures. It is much better to study a number of ratios in order to assess the state of health of the organisation. Also the ratios themselves can only be as good as the financial information from which they are compiled;

inaccuracies in the original data will result in ratios that give a false picture of performance.

It is possible to calculate many ratios from financial accounts. We will look at the most important under two main headings:

✪ *Profitability*: **A measure of the size of profit an organisation has made compared with previous years or throughout the year when comparing actual with budgeted results**

✪ *Liquidity*: **Sometimes called solvency, this is a measure of whether the organisation has sufficient funds to pay its debts when they fall due. Comparisons can be made between years to see whether liquidity is improving or declining, or whether the organisation is remaining in a solvent state when comparing actual with forecast**

We will now look at the ratios used to investigate profitability and liquidity in more detail.

Profitability

The most widely used indicator of the profitability of an organisation is based on the return on capital employed (ROCE), since it is meaningless to look at profitability without also analysing the resources that have been used to generate the profit. In simple terms, the ROCE is calculated as follows:

$$\text{Return on capital employed (\%)} = \frac{\text{Net profit}}{\text{Capital employed}} \times 100$$

This is known as the primary ratio. It has many variations, which can sometimes lead to a lack of consistency and distortion. In particular, there are a number of interpretations of resources or capital employed in a business. The ratio can be used to compare the amount of profit made per £100 invested in the organisation. This could be useful to both investors and business operators, for example:

✪ **Investors could compare the ROCE figure for a particular organisation with the return given by another company, or even a bank or building society investment account**

✪ **Sole traders and partnerships could compare the return with the amount they might get if they invested in a bank or building society. In comparing the two percentages, they may ask themselves whether the return from the business is good enough, taking into account the extra risk and work involved in running an enterprise**

Other important profitability ratios used by leisure and recreation organisations include:

- *Gross profit percentage*: **Sometimes referred to as the gross profit : sales ratio percentage, this will show how much profit the organisation is making as a percentage of sales. A fall in this ratio may be the result of increased competition, forcing a reduction in prices for facilities and services. The calculation is as follows:**

$$\text{Gross profit \%} = \frac{\text{Gross profit}}{\text{Sales}} \times 100$$

- *Net profit percentage*: **Sometimes called the net profit : sales ratio, this will give a figure for profit (or loss) made per £ of income. The percentage profit on sales varies between different sectors, so it is essential to compare the ratio with similar businesses and also to make allowance for the prevailing economic conditions. It is calculated as follows:**

$$\text{Net profit \%} = \frac{\text{Net profit (before tax)}}{\text{Sales}} \times 100$$

Liquidity

Liquidity is a measure of whether an organisation has sufficient funds to pay its debts when they fall due. In established leisure and recreation companies, comparisons can be made between years to see whether liquidity is improving or declining, or whether the organisation is remaining in a solvent state when comparing actual with forecast results.

Two of the most important liquidity ratios are the current ratio and the acid test:

- *Current (or working capital) ratio*: **This tells us the ratio between a company's readily available cash or near cash assets and its current liabilities. It is calculated as follows:**

$$\text{Current ratio} = \frac{\text{Current assets}}{\text{Curent liabilities}}$$

There is no ideal current ratio, but any figure in excess of 2 : 1 is considered healthy, although many companies will survive on a lesser figure than this. Just as important as the actual ratio figure is the consistency of ratios over time; any sudden change in a ratio gives cause for concern and should be investigated immediately

- *Acid test (or liquid ratio)*: **This is the relationship between what is owned by an organisation, where the value is constantly changing, and what it owes its creditors, where the amount is constantly changing. It is calculated as follows:**

$$\text{Acid test} = \frac{\text{Current assets excluding stock}}{\text{Current liabilities}}$$

As a general rule, the acid test ratio should be in the region of 1 : 1. A figure much lower than this may indicate that the business will struggle to pay its debts on time. If it is very much higher than 1 : 1, the business may not be making best use of its funds

Financial ratios in the public sector

Most public sector leisure and recreation organisations, facilities and activities, such as your local sports development unit and your local authority leisure centre, are subsidised from either central or local government funds and are not normally expected to make a profit. However, it is still important to measure the ratio of income to expenditure in order to calculate to what extent the income from such items as ticket sales and admission charges can be offset against operating costs. The ratio, usually expressed as a percentage, is calculated as follows:

$$\frac{\text{Income}}{\text{Operating expenditure}} \times 100\%$$

Another useful ratio for public sector organisations is the level of subsidy per visitor or user, which is calculated as follows:

$$\frac{\text{Net operating expenditure}}{\text{Number of admissions}} : 1$$

This ratio can be applied to a whole range of leisure, recreation, leisure and recreation facilities provided by local councils, including leisure centres, swimming pools, theatres, museums and entertainment venues.

A number of other primary ratios can be applied to public sector provision, including:

- ✪ **Staff costs : operating expenditure**
- ✪ **Bar gross profit : bar revenue**
- ✪ **Catering gross profit : catering revenue**
- ✪ **Income : number of admissions (to give spend per head)**
- ✪ **Bar income : number of admissions**
- ✪ **Catering income : number of admissions**

The number and range of secondary ratios that can be developed for public sector leisure and recreation organisations is vast. It is important to calculate only those ratios that will contribute to the manager's decision-making process. From the expenditure point of view, common ratios that could prove useful include:

- ✪ **Energy costs : operating expenditure**
- ✪ **Marketing expenditure : total operating expenditure**
- ✪ **Cleaning costs : operating expenditure**

Ratios related to revenue include:

- ✪ **Bar income : total income**
- ✪ **Shop income : total income**
- ✪ **Catering income : total income**

It must be remembered that whether financial ratios are being applied in the private, public or voluntary sector, they are just one of the methods by which financial performance can be measured. Decisions taken on the basis of financial ratios alone will not produce the desired satisfactory outcome.

Activity 21.4

With the help of your tutor, arrange an interview with the manager of a local public sector leisure and recreation facility to find out what financial and operational ratios are used by management.

Pricing leisure and recreation products and services

Key topics in this section

- **Introduction**
- **Types of costs in leisure and recreation**
- **Fixed costs**
- **Variable costs**
- **Methods used to calculate prices for leisure and recreation products and services**
- **Pricing strategies in leisure and recreation**

Introduction

You will have learned in Unit 4, Marketing leisure and recreation, that calculating prices for leisure and recreation products and services is a very complex task, involving a multitude of factors, including levels of demand, time of year, quality of facilities and, perhaps most important of all, the costs of providing the product or service.

The competitive nature of the leisure and recreation industry means that companies often operate a market-based pricing policy, adjusting their prices according to what their competitors are charging. In order to fully appreciate how leisure and recreation products and services are priced you need to understand a little more about how costs are calculated, the subject of the next section of this unit.

Types of costs in leisure and recreation

It is essential for managers in leisure and recreation to have accurate, relevant and up-to-date information on the costs of running their organisation. Without this detailed information, they will not be in a position to appraise past performance and control future developments. The organisation's management information system (MIS) should be designed in such a way as to provide data on costs at regular intervals and in an appropriate format.

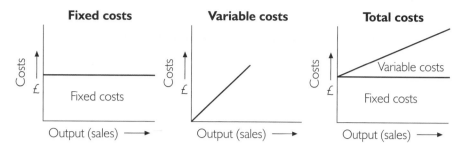

Figure 21.1 *The relationship of fixed, variable and total costs to output*

As well as having detailed cost data on which to base their management decisions, organisations and their personnel need to understand the different types of costs that they will encounter and their likely impact on organisational performance. Costs may be classified according to:

✪ **The nature of the costs (fixed and variable costs)**
✪ **The type of costs**
✪ **Function within the organisation**

Classification by nature (fixed and variable costs)

The nature of costs varies between those that remain constant despite changes in the level of activity (fixed costs) and those that alter in direct proportion to the volume of business generated (variable costs). Fixed costs for a cinema, for example, would include rent, rates, insurance, interest charges and permanent staff costs, all of which stay the same regardless of how many people visit. The same cinema variable costs could include casual labour, telephone charges, postage, advertising and stationery, all of which will vary, depending on the level of use. Figure 21.1 shows the relationship of fixed, variable and total costs to output.

A third category of costs is semi-variable costs, which are made up of both a fixed and a variable element. Energy costs, telephone, Internet, telex and fax costs fall within this category, since there is usually a fixed charge for rental, with added usage charged thereafter.

The costs incurred by the majority of leisure and recreation organisations tend to be fixed rather than variable, given the high levels of overheads associated with many sectors of the industry, such as swimming pools and theme parks.

Classification by type

Costs can be classified into two types, direct and indirect. Direct costs are those that can be directly identified with the service or facility, for example the costs of hiring equipment and employing an extra instructor to run a series of health and fitness courses at a hotel's leisure facility. Indirect costs, also known as overheads, are those costs within an organisation that cannot be readily allocated to a specific function. Taking the example of the hotel's leisure facility organising the health and fitness courses, indirect costs would include the rent and rates for the centre, insurance and energy costs. In this example, it would not be easy to calculate an exact proportion of the overhead costs that should be allocated to the running of the courses.

Classification by function

This method groups costs on the basis of the functional department that incurs them, such as administration, sales, marketing and personnel. Each of these departments would have several cost centres, which are readily identifiable locations or functions against which costs can be charged. If we take the example of a large health and fitness centre, the expenditure incurred by its marketing department may be divided into the following cost centres:

- **Product development**
- **Customer services**
- **Brochure production**
- **Brochure distribution**
- **Photographic costs**
- **Market research**
- **Above-the-line activity (e.g. consumer and trade advertising)**
- **Below-the-line activity (e.g. sales promotions, PR, direct marketing)**
- **Agency sales support**
- **Agency marketing and merchandising**

Each cost centre will be allocated a cost code to ensure that all the costs it incurs are easily identifiable. In a local authority leisure centre, each of the main facilities and services, including the leisure pool, sports hall, outside pitches, health and fitness suite, restaurant/cafe, squash courts, vending and courses, will be an independent cost centre, with its own cost code.

Activity 21.5

While you are on work experience, find out if the organisation you are working for operates a system of cost centres. If so, make a list of the main cost centres identified.

Methods used to calculate prices for leisure and recreation products and services

Organisations such as health and fitness clubs and local authority leisure facilities have a complex pricing system for all their products and services based on how much it costs to run them (known as unit costs) and the level of demand.

Once the unit costs of a product or service are known, it is then possible to begin to calculate a final selling price. The difference between the cost of supplying a product or service and its selling price is known as the profit margin or 'mark up'. There are three main methods of calculating prices, known as:

✪ **Absorption costing**
✪ **Marginal costing**
✪ **Activity-based costing**

We will now examine each of these in a little more detail.

Absorption costing

Absorption (or cost-plus) pricing is a pricing method that identifies all the *direct* costs of producing a product or service and adds to this an appropriate proportion of the overheads (*indirect*) costs of the organisation to arrive at the final price to charge, i.e.:

Price = Direct Costs + Proportion of Indirect Costs + Profit Margin

Absorption costing assumes that an organisation can calculate its indirect costs accurately, something that a large leisure and recreation organisation may find difficult to do. Also, it does not allow for flexibility, and any discounts or concessionary prices will directly affect the profit margin.

Marginal costing

Marginal costing (or contribution pricing) is a technique for setting prices for products and services on the basis that as long as the prices set cover the variable costs, then the product or service is making a contribution to the overheads (fixed costs) of the business.

Activity-based costing

This is a very flexible method of pricing. It looks at all costs, fixed and variable, and focuses on what drives them in order to arrive at a final price to charge.

With activity-based costing, the prices charged more accurately reflect the true costs of the activity.

Pricing strategies in leisure and recreation

From the many different pricing policies in use in leisure and recreation, the following are some of the most common:

- ✪ *Skimming*: **This is when a high price is charged initially for a new product that is unique and that attracts people who are willing to pay the high price for status reasons**

- ✪ *Penetration pricing*: **This is used by organisations wanting to get into a new market where there are existing suppliers of the same product or service. The price will be set sufficiently low to persuade customers to switch their allegiance (sometimes known as a 'loss leader'). It is important that this pricing method is seen as a long-term strategy since customers will resent an early rise in price**

- ✪ *Competitive pricing*: **Sometimes referred to as 'the going rate', competitive pricing assumes that where products or services are similar, the organisation will charge the going rate, i.e. will match the price of competitors. This method often leads to very low margins and, in the long run, the collapse of some organisations**

- ✪ *Concessionary pricing*: **The pricing strategies in many public sector organisations within the leisure and recreation industry can be relatively complex. This is due to the corporate aims of the public sector. These can include encouraging socially and financially excluded people to take part in sport and physical activity, or encouraging the elderly and children to take part. Subsequently discounts, through subsidies, are offered to relevant target groups. This pricing policy is known as concessionary pricing**

Activity 21.6

Examine the pricing structure of a local leisure and recreation facility with which you are familiar. Analyse the factors that have influenced the prices charged and whether there is any evidence of skimming, penetration, concessionary or competitive pricing.

Producing budgets

Key topics in this section

- **Introduction to budgeting**
- **What is a budget?**
- **Limitations on budgets**
- **Sales and expenditure budgets**
- **Producing a profit and loss forecast**
- **Producing a cash flow forecast**
- **Monitoring and controlling budgets**

Introduction to budgeting

Good management in leisure and recreation involves not only reviewing past performance and the progress of current work, but also looking ahead to the future development of the organisation and the products and services it offers to its customers. The leisure and recreation industry is constantly evolving, new technology is being introduced, customers are demanding better quality, and tastes and fashions are changing. To be successful in such a diverse and dynamic industry, private, public and voluntary sector organisations must identify and anticipate market changes and plan accordingly, both in the long term and short term. Budgeting helps them to do this by establishing future objectives and helping to manage cash flow. All leisure and recreation organisations, however large or small, use budgets to ensure that there is enough money in the business to meet bills and other payments when they become due. Budgets can be set for a large facility such as sports halls and swimming pools or a one-off activity such as The Millennium Youth Games or an international athletics meeting.

What is a budget?

In simple terms, a budget is a forecast of likely income and outgoings over a given period of time. We all have to budget in our everyday lives, trying to balance our income, in the form of wages, salary or government benefits, against our living expenses, including rent, energy costs, taxation and costs for food and clothing. Another type of budget is the one presented by the Chancellor of the Exchequer every year to Parliament, setting out the income and expenditure plans of the government for the next 12-month period.

At the organisation level, a budget can be defined as:

⊘ **A plan, quantified in financial terms, prepared and agreed in advance, showing the anticipated revenue and expenditure over a given time period**

The budget is the action plan for the coming financial period, which can be used to delegate responsibility to departmental managers or supervisors, leaving senior management to concentrate on investigating any major deviations from the plan. This delegation will mean that, in practice, a large leisure and recreation organisation will have many different budget heads, i.e. a range of budgets that set out the financial responsibilities of each manager or supervisor. These detailed budgets will be consolidated into one master budget for the organisation, which will detail its overall short-term financial plan. The budget is the principal tool for allowing managers to coordinate and control the activities of their organisation. Performance is constantly monitored against the budget plans and feedback is an important part of the budgetary process.

Activity 21.7

With the help of your tutor, organise and carry out an interview with the manager or owner of a local leisure and recreation facility and find out what budgets are used.

Limitations on budgets

Senior management teams in leisure and recreation organisations are regularly faced with conflicting demands on the use of resources. The demand to improve or maintain services often conflicts with the need to minimise costs and keep within financial limits. Decisions on the use of resources have to be made at the time of preparing annual budgets. There are a number of questions that an organisation will need to consider when determining its budgets and allocating its limited resources, including:

⊘ **Is the information on which the budget decisions are made accurate?**

⊘ **Is the information valid and reliable?**

⊘ **How can the information be easily collected?**

⊘ **Has the information been interpreted correctly?**

⊘ **Does the organisation have the necessary staffing resources to be able to carry out the budgeting process effectively?**

- ✪ **Is there sufficient information on the external environment in which the organisation operates?**
- ✪ **Are the cost and revenue targets achievable and realistic?**
- ✪ **Are there sufficient staff benefits in place to reward achievement?**

The process of setting budgets needs to take place with the best information available at the time, but with built-in flexibility to allow for changes in circumstances.

Preparing a sales budget

This is normally the starting point for all budgets, since demand for leisure and recreation products and services is often the overriding factor in determining success or failure of a business. In attempting to forecast its future sales pattern and volume, a leisure and recreation organisation will need to take a number of important matters into account, including:

- ✪ **Past levels of sales, unless it is a new business just starting**
- ✪ **Market research**
- ✪ **The state of the economy**
- ✪ **Trend analysis, i.e. performance over past years**
- ✪ **Existing and potential competition**
- ✪ **The state of the market in which it is operating**

A health and fitness club, for example, will be concerned with a number of factors when producing its sales budget, for example:

- ✪ **Last year's sales figures**
- ✪ **Local competition from other facilities**
- ✪ **Inflationary effects on its principal suppliers' product prices (e.g. the cost of equipment, maintenance and repair costs)**
- ✪ **Results of marketing and promotional activity**
- ✪ **The resources of its own staff, including training**
- ✪ **National trends in leisure activities**
- ✪ **The state of the local economy**

The expenditure budget

The expenditure budget shows the spending limits that must be adhered to so that an organisation as a whole, or an individual department, achieves its

Item	Current month			Cumulative totals		
	Budget	Actual	Variance	Budget	Actual	Variance
Sales – product 1 – product 2 – product 3						
Total sales						
Expenditure – item 1 – item 2 – item 3 – item 4						
Total expenditure						
Gross profit (loss)						

Figure 21.2   *The structure of a combined sales and expenditure budget*

financial targets. It will include all the fixed and variable costs that are attributable over a given period of time, which could be annual or monthly.

The expenditure budget shows the spending limits that must be adhered to so that an organisation as a whole, or an individual department, achieves its financial targets. It will include all the fixed and variable costs that are attributable over a given period of time, which could be annual or monthly. Showing monthly expenditure will allow management to rectify any variances in the budgeted and actual expenditure by taking the appropriate action.

The performance of the expenditure budget cannot be divorced from the figures contained in the sales budget and it is a matter of preference whether the two budgets are kept separate. Many organisations choose to operate a combined sales and expenditure budget. (See Figure 21.2.)

The combined budget allows for monthly figures and a cumulative total combining data from previous months. Any variations from the budgeted figures are included in the variance columns, which may contain actual figures or a percentage difference.

Producing a profit and loss forecast

We saw earlier in this unit that the profit and loss statement is perhaps the most important item of financial information for managing and controlling a leisure and recreation organisation (page 270). You will remember that the profit and loss account is a summary of all the income and expenditure of an organisation, over a given period of time, sometimes quarterly, half yearly or annually, depending on custom and practice.

As its name implies, a profit and loss *forecast* is an estimate, based on all available data, of the expected profit (or loss) of an organisation over a given future time period. Anybody who is needing finance to start a leisure and recreation business will need to draw up a profit and loss forecast to convince a bank manager that the project is viable in the short and long term. Leisure and recreation businesses that are already in operation will also construct a profit and loss forecast to gauge their future financial performance. Of course, they have an advantage over a new business since they can look back at actual figures when calculating their forecast.

Figure 21.3 gives an example of a profit and loss forecast schedule.

The profit and loss forecast schedule in Figure 21.3 shows that the figure for cost of goods sold (B) is deducted from total sales (A) to give the gross profit (C). From this figure, total overhead costs (E) are deducted to give the net profit before tax (F).

Activity 21.8

Working as a member of a group, complete the profit and loss forecast schedule shown in Figure 21.3 for your chosen business.

Producing a cash flow forecast

An essential financial item needed by any new leisure and recreation business, and indeed one that is up and running, is the cash flow forecast. This is usually set down in a planning schedule that totals each month's projected flow of money into and out of the business. Put simply, a cash flow forecast is:

✪ **An estimate of an organisation's anticipated future cash inflows and outflows presented on a monthly basis**

In leisure and recreation organisations, cash *inflows* will include:

✪ **Payments received from customers using facilities**
✪ **Injections of capital or personal investment into the business**
✪ **Money received from selling assets, e.g. surplus equipment, unwanted stock, etc.**

Enter month					
Figures rounded to £s		**Budget**	**Actual**	**Budget**	**Actual**
	Sales				
1	Home				
2	Export				
A	**Total Sales**				
	Direct Costs				
3	Materials – purchases				
4	Wages and Salaries				
5	Stock changes (Increase/Decrease)				
B	**Cost of Goods Sold**				
C	**Gross Profit (A – B = C)**				
D	**Gross Profit as % of Sales (C ÷ A × 100 = D)**				
	Overheads				
6	Production				
7					
8					
9					
10					
11					
12	Selling and Distribution				
13					
14					
15					
16					
17					
18	Administration				
19					
20					
21					
22					
23					
24	Other Expenses				
25					
26					
27					
28					
29					
30	Finance Changes				
31	Depreciation				
E	**Total Overheads**				
F	**Net Profit Before Tax (C – E + F)**				
G	**Sales required to break even (E ÷ D × 100 = G)**				

Note: The schedule normally spans twelve months.

Figure 21.3 *A profit and loss forecast*

UNIT 21 FINANCIAL PLANNING AND CONTROL

Cash *outflows* will be made up of:

- **Payments to principals, e.g. leisure centre operators**
- **Salaries and wages for staff**
- **Rent, rates and associated premises/transport costs**
- **Money paid for advertising**
- **Legal and finance charges**
- **Tax payments**

Figure 21.4 shows an example of a cash flow forecast schedule.

The cash flow forecast schedule in Figure 21.4 indicates that figures for receipts and payments are the two main items that go to make up the forecast. From these, net cash flow and the closing bank balance can be calculated.

A cash flow forecast is essential to the smooth operation of a business since it:

- **Convinces potential lenders of finance (banks, friends, shareholders, etc.) that the business is viable**
- **Allows the management of an organisation to track actual against forecast cash inflows and outflows**
- **Enables an organisation to schedule its payments to creditors**
- **Makes it easier to plan for large items of expenditure**
- **Allows management to monitor sales on a monthly basis**

Activity 21.9

Continuing to work in a group, complete the monthly cash flow forecast schedule shown in Figure 21.4 for your chosen business over a full season of operation.

Monitoring and controlling budgets

Once budgets have been agreed and the mechanisms for recording the financial data are in place, it is necessary to introduce a monitoring and control process. Control is based on the concept of management by exception, i.e. the investigation of any items that deviate from the agreed budget. This is done by comparing the actual costs with the budgeted costs to identify any over- or under-expenditure. The differences are known as variances and their

Enter month		Budget	Actual	Budget	Actual
Figures rounded to £s		**Budget**	**Actual**	**Budget**	**Actual**
	Receipts				
1	Sales (including VAT)–Cash				
2	–Debtors				
3	Other trading income				
4	Loans you have received				
5	New capital				
6	Selling of assets				
7	Other receipts				
A	**Total Receipts**				
	Payments				
8	Cash for goods you have bought				
9	Payments to creditors				
10	Owner or directors' withdrawals				
11	Wages and Salaries (net)				
12	PAYE/NI				
13	Capital items (for example equipment and vehicles)				
14	Transport and packaging				
15	Rent or rates				
16	Services				
17	Loan repayments				
18	Hire or leasing repayments				
19	Interest				
20	Bank or finance charges				
21	Professional fees				
22	Advertising				
23	Insurance				
24					
25					
26	VAT				
27	Corporation Tax and so on				
28	Dividends				
B	**Total Payments**				
C	**Net Cashflow (A – B)**				
29	**Opening Bank Balance**				
D	**Closing Bank Balance (C ± Line 29)**				

Note: The schedule normally spans twelve months.

Figure 21.4   *A cash flow forecast schedule*

investigation is known as variance analysis. Variances may arise in any items of revenue or expenditure, including labour costs, sales figures and energy costs. Where actual costs are greater than budgeted costs, the term unfavourable or adverse is applied and where actual costs are below budget, the variance is favourable. The opposite is true of revenue variances, where favourable variances occur when the actual sales are above budget.

The aim of variance analysis is to highlight areas needing immediate attention. Minor variances from budget are common and are unlikely to require detailed analysis, but when the variance is large, either in percentage or monetary terms, the situation will need reviewing. Once a variance has been investigated and a cause identified, remedial action can be taken. For example, a visitor attraction, such as Alton Towers or Legoland, that experiences a 10 per cent adverse variance in its admission income for a particular month, will need to investigate the cause and put matters right immediately, if it is to achieve its annual budget targets. However, not all causes of variances from budget are capable of immediate solution. A permanent change in market demand, perhaps away from an existing type of home entertainment product that loses its appeal with the buying public, will force an organisation to feed the information back into its planning stage for alteration to projected sales figures. There must be a degree of flexibility in any budgetary planning system, which takes account of the fact that leisure and recreation is a very dynamic industry.

A budget is generally broken down into shorter periods for control purposes. These are normally monthly but can be shorter or longer as the case demands. As well as a comparison of actual with budgeted figures, budgetary control often involves a comparison with data from the same period in the previous year. Whatever time period is agreed, managers will need a constant flow of financial information that they can use for control purposes. The sales budget shown in Figure 21.5 includes budgeted and actual sales. Presenting

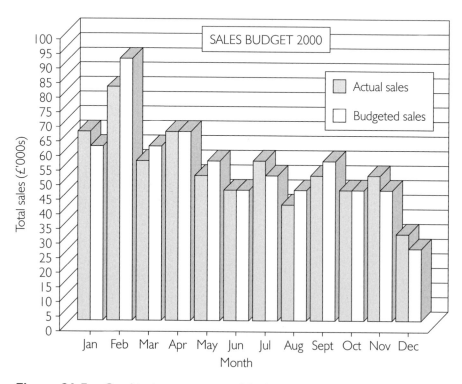

Figure 21.5 *Graphical presentation of budget data*

information in this graphical form has now been made much easier with the use of graphics software which is part of spreadsheet packages.

The presentation of information in this form provides a quick and easy way of identifying problem areas and is often an easier means of identifying budget variances. Graphical presentation should also be considered for comparing current year data with that from past years.

As well as comparing actual with budgeted results, the budget information can be used to measure performance of individual cost centres within the organisation.

Human resources in the leisure and recreation industry

22

Objectives

- Define and give examples of the factors that influence Human Resource Management (HRM)

- Understand the effects of external and internal influences on people working in the leisure and recreation industry

- Give reasons for using various recruitment and selection methods in leisure and recreation organisations

- Understand the recruitment and selections processes and procedures carried out in the leisure and recreation industry

- Summarise the legal requirements, practical and ethical requirements involved in employment

- Evaluate techniques and approaches used to motivate staff in the leisure and recreation industry

This unit will explore one of the most important resources in a leisure and recreation organisation – people or human resources.

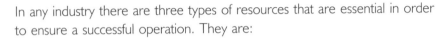

Introduction

In any industry there are three types of resources that are essential in order to ensure a successful operation. They are:

Human resources
People at work

1   **Physical resources such as buildings and equipment**

2   **Financial resources – money is essential**

3   **Human resources – we need people at work too**

In this unit you will explore the important role people play. People can be the difference between success and failure. At work we all need to be understood and motivated. Generally, the happier we are, the more productive we are and this can lead to increased profits and so is beneficial for the organisation.

The leisure and recreation industry is predominantly a service industry. This means customers spend their money on something they cannot pick up, see or touch. As a consequence, if the service is to be sold successfully, the person selling it has to be trustworthy, informative and accurate. In other words, the member of staff is the key to a successful sale.

It follows therefore that in the leisure and recreation industry, staff should be well trained, know what they are doing and be well suited to their jobs. The amount of money that is spent on staffing is massive. In most organisations people are the most expensive resource; in a service industry, such as leisure and recreation, this is even more the case. It seems to make sense, therefore, that if people are so costly, they are worth thinking about, treating well and developing.

As human beings we all deserve respect and courtesy!

Human resource planning

We have already decided that people are worth looking after; planning the people that will be, and are, employed is part of this. This planning process is important for the following reasons:

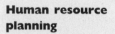

Human resource planning
The matching of skills and qualities of people at work with the jobs needed to be completed now and in the foreseeable future

- ✪ **For an organisation to remain competitive**
- ✪ **So an organisation can attract the right staff**
- ✪ **So pay is at a fair and reasonable rate**
- ✪ **To plan for retirement by looking at the age structure of employees in an organisation**
- ✪ **So an organisation can supply the demand from customers**
- ✪ **To avoid problems that could have been avoided**
- ✪ **To avoid redundancies**
- ✪ **Because people deserve to be looked after**

There are many aspects to consider closely before a successful team of people can be put together. These considerations can be out of the control of the organisation, and are known as **external influences**, or they can be controlled by the organisation, and are known as **internal influences**. Whichever is the case, they are important factors in creating a successful business.

External influences

Factors to consider are:

The national and local economic climate

This refers to how rich or how poor the country is as a whole and also in a particular area. In other words, the financial state of the country or a locality. This can be affected by interest rates. The higher the interest rate, the more costly a mortgage is. This can affect how much money people have to spend on anything that is not classed as a necessity, such as leisure.

World economics can affect the performance of an organisation for example, if a foreign currency collapses it can greatly affect the stock exchange, which can devalue an organisation. This is a complicated subject. As a leisure and recreation student it is necessary to understand that the willingness of people to spend money, the number of people employed by an organisation and how much they are paid can be affected by what is happening on the other side of the world.

It is easier to understand that when a locality is enjoying high employment and plenty of customers, working conditions can be good and the number of people employed can rise. However, if there are high levels of unemployment and the number of customers is dropping, the organisation may need to look at cutting its workforce, perhaps by reducing the working conditions. This is a much more difficult situation to handle and one that needs to be planned for.

Employment trends

Sometimes money is invested in a locality for a particular purpose, such as to regenerate derelict land. This money can come from the National Lottery or other government grants, or may be invested by a private company. This can create jobs.

Jobs can also be created by fashion trends. In the 1990s there was a growing number of private health facilities and so this is an area where jobs are available and people are seeking employment. Sometimes these trends for career choice can come from the media, particularly television. In the late 1990s, there were many television programmes on the travel and tourism industry and the number of people seeking employment in this area grew. Within this decade we will probably see an increasing number of jobs for people in information technology, particularly with the increasing popularity of the Internet and mobile communications.

Skills shortage

Sometimes there are jobs to be done, a person in mind to do the job but no one in reality who is able to do it. This is called a skills shortage. It may be because there is no one suitable living in the location or there is a shortage of qualified people throughout the entire country, for example staff who can speak a foreign language. It may be that the person an organisation is looking for just does not exist. There are a number of things that can be done to ease the situation, such as training, a compromise on the skills required, offering flexible employment conditions or even relocation.

Location

People tend to like to go to work not far from home. More and more people are becoming frustrated at the length of their journey to work, not to mention the costs of travelling to work, and sitting in a car doing nothing can be boring. This can be enough to make someone look for another job. The location of an organisation has to be good for the customers and the staff too. For example, if an organisation relocates to the other side of town it may struggle to retain its original staff.

Factors that can affect staffing include:

- ✪ **Ease of parking**
- ✪ **Being on a local bus or train route**
- ✪ **The availability of nurseries**
- ✪ **The social side of the location, such as being close to shops, gyms and restaurants**

Competition

It is essential that organisations are aware of what their competitors are doing. To attract the best staff you have got to offer more than your competitors; this does not just mean paying more but offering superior working conditions too.

Internal influences

The aim of an organisation is to have a stable, happy and effective workforce. The way an organisation is managed can help achieve this.

Factors to consider are:

1   *Staff turnover*: **This is a measure of the frequency with which staff join and leave an organisation. This can be calculated as**

$$\frac{\textbf{Number joining or leaving}}{\textbf{Average number of employees}} \times \textbf{100}$$

The aim is to keep this as low as possible. However, you could come across a situation where the staff turnover is zero because the pay is well above any competitors; this is clearly not desirable. Other influences that need to be considered are the number of unavoidable separations from the organisation, such as to move closer to a poorly relative or the number of people internally promoted and so creating vacancies

2   *Sickness rate*: **How many days are taken off during a year due to sickness. If this rate is above the national average and there is a high frequency of days taken off in one- or two-day blocks, alarm bells should start to ring. This could be measured as absenteeism**

3   *Absenteeism*: **The number of days taken off work that are not genuine, perhaps days where staff just cannot 'face it'. This can be used as a guide to the morale of an organisation**

Any organisation needs to create a workplace where staff can be happy and develop. There needs to be a career and pay structure in place to allow staff to progress. A valued member of staff should not have to move out of an organisation in order to move up.

4 *Organisational structures*: **This is how the organisation is planned and is often illustrated by an organisational chart. This is a picture showing a plan of the organisation. There are a number of commonly used charts. These include:**

✪ **Hierarchical**

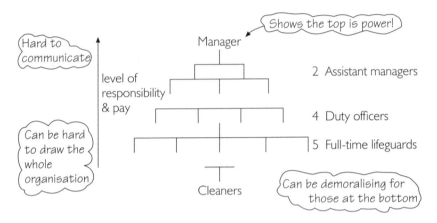

✪ **Flat**

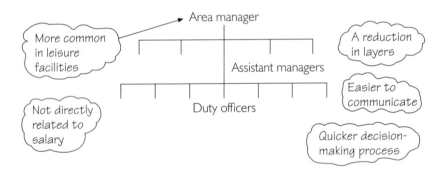

✪ **Simple**

✪ Functional

Organisation divided into areas of work

Manager

Often used in conjunction with another chart

Restaurants & Bars Swimming Pools Dry Facilities Personnel Marketing & Sales

✪ Centralised

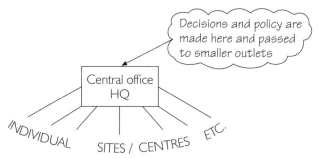

Decisions and policy are made here and passed to smaller outlets

Central office HQ

INDIVIDUAL SITES / CENTRES ETC.

+ The whole organisation operates in the same way, giving **corporate identity**; generally cheaper in terms of wages
− Lose sight of the customers: customers are numbers, not faces. Individual outlets can lose their creativity

✪ Decentralised

Leisure facilities

| 1 | 2 | 3 | 4 | 5 | 6 | 7 | 8 |

+ Independent outlets that can develop their own ideas and creativity; adds the personal touch; can react to the customers; are trusted and given the opportunity to be the best they can
− Can be costly, difficult for the larger organisation to control

The aim is to find a structure that will help aid communication, allow quick decision making, provide a career structure and help motivate everyone

5 *The roles and responsibilities of the employer*: **As you will see later in this chapter, there are certain responsibilities that the employer must provide. Most organisations want to treat people fairly**

Things employees can expect from their employer

- ✪ Pay at a reasonable rate, at or above the minimum wage, on a specified date and paid in a specified way
- ✪ An itemised pay slip
- ✪ An employment contract
- ✪ A safe environment to work in
- ✪ Fair and equal treatment
- ✪ A reasonable workload
- ✪ Clear guidelines
- ✪ Wash and rest facilities

The employer has to be fair but the employee does too. We do not live in an ideal world but there are basic rights that everyone should enjoy.

Activity 22.1

It can be difficult to find out what goes on within an organisation, particularly where money is concerned. Consider a locality (20-mile radius).
On a map identify:

1 All the family pubs with soft play areas
2 All the leisure centres with swimming clubs
3 All private health facilities
4 Football stadia

If you can, choose a job for each of the four venues and find out how the rate of pay and working conditions differ. If you could choose, where would you work and why?

Recruitment and selection in the leisure and recreation industry

The aim of the recruitment and selection process is simple: to get the right person in the right job. This may seem an easy thing to say but in practice it is much more difficult to achieve. A new member of staff can be appointed after only a brief meeting with their future colleagues and a quick tour around their new place of work. This can be a precarious position for both the new employee and the employer and the consequences of employing the wrong person in the wrong job can be costly for both parties.

There are a series of procedures that can be followed to try to prevent this happening. They are time consuming and initially costly but in the long term they illustrate that planning and making a decision for the right reasons are worthwhile.

The recruitment and selection process (see Figure 22.1) is made up a series of linking steps. These steps cannot be viewed on their own and have to be followed in order. Once one stage has been completed, the next one can be tackled but with reference to what has gone before!

Figure 22.1 *The recruitment and selection process*

When do we need to use the recruitment process?

The simple answer is all the time, as the latter stages are relevant to everyone. There is not one person who does not need training or refreshing or who cannot improve at all. Some stages are reviewed annually, such as job analysis, whereas some are only completed when necessary, such as recruitment advertising.

Who needs to be aware of the recruitment and selection process?

Everyone. Every member of staff will receive an induction and every member of staff will be appraised. This process will directly affect all of us as everyone is appointed in a particular role at some point in their lives. Also, most people will influence the appointment of a new recruit.

Stage one: Job analysis

▼ ▼ ▼ ▼ ▼ ▼ ▼ ▼ ▼

Job analysis
The study of a job and what it will achieve in relation to the organisation

▲ ▲ ▲ ▲ ▲ ▲ ▲ ▲ ▲

A position can become vacant by someone leaving to start a new job, sometimes at a different company or sometimes within the same organisation On the other hand, sometimes there is a need for a new person to be appointed because there are new jobs to be done. Whatever the reason, it is always useful to examine the reasons for a particular role and relate them to the organisation as a whole.

There is a series of questions that need to be clearly answered before it is possible to move on to the next stage of the recruitment and selection process.

Consider:

- ✪ **Is the job necessary?**
- ✪ **Is the pay in line with what is offered by competitors?**
- ✪ **Can the position be improved? For example, by installing a new desktop publishing package on a computer, could the standard of promotional material be improved?**
- ✪ **Is someone else already doing the job?**
- ✪ **What is the financial state of the organisation? Can the organisation afford it?**
- ✪ **Can internal members of staff fill the vacancy?**
- ✪ **What are the main duties of the job and do they match with the objectives of the organisation?**

It may be that not all of these questions are relevant but once those that are relevant have been answered, the actual framework for the job starts to take shape.

Stage two: Job descriptions

▼ ▼ ▼ ▼ ▼ ▼ ▼ ▼ ▼

Job description
A statement of the tasks, duties and standards attached to a particular job

▲ ▲ ▲ ▲ ▲ ▲ ▲ ▲ ▲

Once it has been decided that a position is both necessary and viable within an organisation it is possible to progress to the next stage of the recruitment process, which is to detail what the position will involve.

So the job description will carefully state not only what you are expected to do but also how often you are supposed to do it and to what level. The job description helps motivate people at work. It can be very frustrating not to know what you are supposed to be doing and then as a consequence of this, not know if you are doing your job well. It helps us to see where it is possible to improve; this is often linked to the appraisal (see page 334). It is also used when producing the recruitment advert.

The prospective candidate will first see the job description in a recruitment pack. In order to attract the best candidate to a particular role the candidate must be clear what the job involves. It is of little use to both candidate and the organisation to find that the job the candidate finds themselves in is very different from the one they were expecting.

As with all documentation used in recruitment and selection, the job description needs to be objective, accurate and relevant. It will also change frequently and so should be regularly updated. The process of monitoring and evaluating should occur at least every year. This is generally linked to the yearly appraisal or when the position becomes vacant.

It should never be the responsibility of just one person to produce, update or change a job description. A variety of relevant employees should help bring about changes. These could include:

✪ *The line manager*: **This person will provide direction and a focus to the role**

✪ *The person already in the position*: **This person can accurately assess the specific requirements of the job; after all, they know it best**

✪ *A representative from human resources*: **This person is the expert at recruitment and selection procedures and should act in an advisory capacity, particularly in legal matters. They also will ensure that recruitment and selection follows a corporate strategy, for example all leisure centres within a national chain of hotels use the same logo on the job description**

Contents of a job description

- ✪ **Name of the organisation**
- ✪ **Location of the organisation**
- ✪ **Title of the job**
- ✪ **Section that the job falls within**
- ✪ **Salary**
- ✪ **Who the line manager is**
- ✪ **Who the position is responsible for**
- ✪ **Purpose of the post**
- ✪ **The main duties of the job, including a flexibility clause**
- ✪ **A brief summary of working conditions**
- ✪ **Annual leave entitlement**
- ✪ **Hours of work**
- ✪ **Any other major benefits**
- ✪ **A reference that will identify when the job description was written and who wrote it**

Hints and tips

The salary helps quantify the position. In many instances a different title can be used to describe a similar role in different organisations; for example, in a leisure centre a duty officer often means the same as duty supervisor. However, without the salary it can be difficult to assess the level of responsibility.

Do not assume the candidate has a detailed geographical knowledge of the area; include a reference to the nearest well-known town or city.

Choose the title of the job carefully. Don't say technical supervisor when you mean head cleaner!

Avoid the use of names, because they change. Job titles are more appropriate.

Start each main duty with *To*, for example:

- ✪ **To assist**
- ✪ **To prepare**
- ✪ **To liaise**
- ✪ **To monitor**

Avoid the use of jargon and ambiguous terms; for example, the hours of work for this role are office hours. Instead, state that the hours are Monday to Friday 8 a.m. until 5 p.m. with one hour for lunch.

It is recommended that a flexibility clause is included. This is usually a final statement that notes that other duties may be required within the role, BUT add that they will be appropriate to the general level of the role. It is both a poor use of resources and frustrating for a stadium manager paid £32,000 per year to be emptying vending machines and counting change for two hours each evening. I am sure this person will have successfully completed these types of tasks in the earlier part of their career.

Let's have a look at a very ordinary job description and see how to improve it (Figure 22.2).

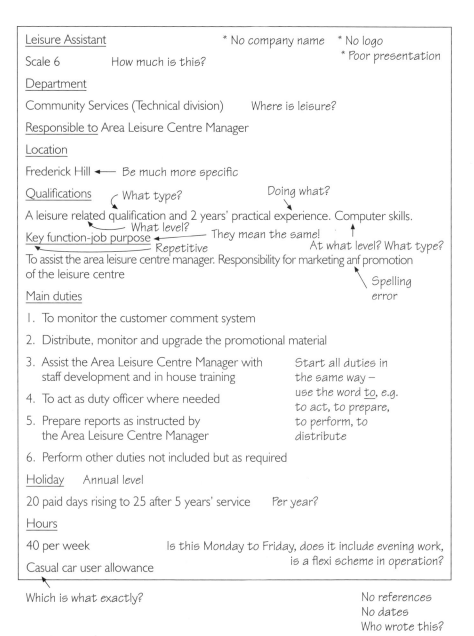

Figure 22.2 *Job description*

The job description was not really very impressive. Now it's your turn to put it all together. Transform this less than perfect job description to a professional and impressive document, ready to attract the best leisure assistant!

Stage three: Person specifications

▼ ▼ ▼ ▼ ▼ ▼ ▼ ▼ ▼

Person specification
A description of the ideal candidate for a particular job

▲ ▲ ▲ ▲ ▲ ▲ ▲ ▲ ▲

Now stage two is complete it is possible to move on to person specifications, the next stage of the recruitment process.

The job description concentrates on the tasks, duties and standards of a job and the person specification concentrates on describing the person that would complete these tasks, duties and standards the best. Unfortunately, many employees can identify a colleague that is not suitably qualified or experienced to complete a task and often it is the other employees who complete the unfinished tasks for them. This can create a poor atmosphere in a place of work and often builds resentment and ill feeling.

The person specification should be introduced, along with the job description, in the recruitment pack. The recruitment pack should help the prospective candidate decide if the job is one they would like to do. As a consequence, it is useful for both the organisation and the candidate if the candidate can match their qualities and attributes with the specification generated by the organisation. If they just don't match up, the candidate is unlikely to apply. The person specification is also useful later on in the recruitment process. At the point of shortlisting and at interview it is essential that the shortlister or interviewer knows what characteristics to look for. The person specification is the ideal reminder (see page 321). It is also needed when producing the recruitment advert (see page 312).

The same three people who produce the person specification should also produce the job description. The two documents are so closely linked. Ideally they should be produced together. Beware though! It is difficult to describe the ideal candidate for a job if you are the person doing it! The person specification can easily become subjective. It is essential that the focus of the person specification is on the characteristics of a person that will complete the job as successfully as possible, NOT irrelevant attributes that will be insignificant to the job.

Content of a person specification

The characteristics can be divided into two:

- ✪ *Essential criteria*: **Without these are qualities, it would be impossible to carry out the job successfully. For example, you must hold a current National Pool Lifeguard Award to be a pool lifeguard**
- ✪ *Desirable criteria*: **If a candidate possessed these qualities it would be preferable, BUT these qualities could be developed later, perhaps through staff development plans. It may be useful for a Recreation Marketing Officer to have the ability to produce and present IT-based presentations but the core job could be carried out without this**

The criteria could fall into the following headings:

- ✪ **Qualifications, for example a sport-related degree**
- ✪ **Skills and abilities, for example the ability to use spreadsheets**
- ✪ **Experience, for example two years' supervisory experience in wet-side facility**
- ✪ **Attitudes, for example an understanding and commitment to equal opportunities**
- ✪ **Other requirements, for example the ability to work and meet deadlines**

Hints and tips

It would be great to live in an ideal world! If we could all produce the perfect person specification for our partners for life and find the person to match it, there would be no marriages ending in divorce. The person specification has to be flexible. The ideal candidate may simply not exist so it may be necessary to compromise.

Activity 22.3

Think about your perfect job: after all your training and experience, the job you would choose to do for the rest of your life. Produce a person specification for this role and compare it with a description of yourself. Include essential and desirable criteria.

For a bit of fun, devise a person specification for an ideal husband or wife! Your could even think about an ideal description for your perfect lecturer. Remember, make sure the description is relevant to the job only.

Stage four: Recruitment advertising

Once the person specification and the job description have been produced it is time to move on to recruitment advertising. After all, it would be extremely difficult to produce an advert not knowing what the job involved and what the characteristics of the person are. Too many organisations find that when an employee leaves a job they just put an advert in the local newspaper without once thinking if the position has changed.

The advert is probably the most important part of the selling process within recruitment and selection. It is the first contact the candidate is likely to have with the organisation and so it needs to be perfect. First impressions last for ever; the advert can create a perception of the organisation that will always remain and can decide whether a candidate applies for a job or not.

The aim of the recruitment advert is simple: to attract the best candidate to apply for a particular vacancy. Anyone who is looking at vacancies will have some interest in new opportunities, otherwise they would not be looking in the first place. The chances are that one of these candidates is just right for the vacancy. The way the advert is produced and the impression it creates have to ensure that this candidate, who is just right for the job, actually notices the advert, realises what the role is about and then APPLIES.

During the production of the advertisement two documents are needed at all times. These are the person specification and the job description. Having them open and available should ensure that the advert is focused and relevant and therefore does not drift off the point.

The same three people who have already had an involvement in the recruitment process for the same three reasons (see page 307), will produce the advert. The line manager, the person in the role and a representative from human resources will all help to produce the ideal advert.

Contents of a recruitment advert

- ✪ **Name of the organisation**
- ✪ **Location of the organisation**
- ✪ **Telephone/e-mail contact for the organisation, including a contact that is available outside of normal working hours (this helps candidates request information when they are not at work)**
- ✪ **Job title**
- ✪ **Salary and other benefits of the job**
- ✪ **Summary of the main duties of the job**
- ✪ **Summary of the person specification**
- ✪ **Conditions of work such as hours of work and annual leave**

- ✪ **A summary of the organisation, including brief aims and possible career development**
- ✪ **A closing date for the vacancy**

Hints and tips

Remember that the advert is part of the selling process of recruitment and selection. It has to be attractive, eye catching and create a positive image. It is useful to use a company logo that can help develop an instantly recognisable identity, such as the Derby Ram or indeed any of the Premiership football club logos.

The advert, however, does need to be balanced and realistic. There is little benefit in making a menial position sound glamorous, for example titling the pool plant operator a technical supervisor.

The language chosen for the advert needs to be appropriate; ideally, it should be clear, relevant and precise. The use of jargon should be minimised and only used perhaps as a method of attracting suitable candidates. Sometimes the advert can be written in a different language to the native tongue; for example, if the person specification states that the ability to speak Welsh fluently is essential, the advert could be produced in Welsh.

The advert may include any certification or policies that will prove attractive to the target audience, such as a statement relating to equal opportunities or provision for the disabled. The Investors in People award is another example that should be included.

It is beneficial to include the word YOU where possible. This helps the candidate feel that the advert is aimed at them only. It helps personalise the advert and emphasise the fact the advert is part of selling the organisation to the candidate. For example, instead of stating 'We are looking for someone who has a VCE in Leisure and Recreation', replace this with 'Have YOU achieved a VCE in Leisure and Recreation?'

Above all, consider the target audience at all times. It is essential that the staff contributing to the advert can remain objective, take a step back and be sure that if they were the ideal candidate they would want to apply.

Once the advert is produced it is time to consider where it is going to be placed. This clearly must be through a method that the target audience is likely to see.

Methods of recruitment advertising

- ✪ **Local and national newspapers**
- ✪ **Local or national radio**
- ✪ **Local or national TV**

- The Internet – some organisations promote themselves and any vacancies they may have by a website, for example the BBC (www.bbc.co.uk), and there are also websites dedicated purely to recruitment, for example www.jobhunter.co.uk
- Teletext
- Professional journals
- Direct mailing, for example through The Institute of Leisure and Amenity Management (ILAM)
- Magazines
- The cinema
- Through colleges and universities
- Recruitment agencies, including the Job Centre – these agencies match the candidate to the vacancy, sometimes at a charge. There are a small number in the leisure and recreation industry
- Internal and external noticeboards – at Christmas it is common to see posters displaying vacancies for the seasonal period
- Newsletters or job sheets
- Careers fairs
- Shop windows – sometimes the best way to attract a candidate to a casual and often low-paid role is through a local post office window, particularly if the location is remote

It is likely that a combination of methods of advertising will be used; the key again is what are the most appropriate methods and what are the cost implications. To advertise on national television can cost thousands of pounds; however, a lineage advert in a local newspaper can cost £15. Factors that will affect the method chosen can be the local and national labour supply, the location of the job, and the level of the job.

Activity 22.4

Find a selection of recruitment advertisements from a variety of sources. Ensure there are local and national adverts, and adverts for part-time and full-time roles. Include a junior and a senior job. Look for two adverts off the Internet, one from a recruitment website and one from a company website. Ensure they all are from the leisure and recreation industry.

Now devise a checklist of aspects you would expect to be included and score the adverts. Justify your decisions.

Application form

A description of the candidate by the candidate but in a structure that the organisation has chosen

Curriculum vitae

Also a description of the candidate by the candidate but the candidate structures this. A letter of application often accompanies it

Stage five: Method of application

The recruitment and selection process continues to flow. The right candidates are now interested in the vacancy but how will you ask them to register their interest? There are two standard methods of application, through an application form or through a curriculum vitae and letter of application.

Both methods are, in the main, the same thing, that is, a description of the candidate, but there are a variety of reasons why an organisation may choose to receive this information in one format or another.

There is information that would be collected in both an application form and a CV. This includes:

- **Name**
- **Address**
- **Contact numbers**
- **Education and qualifications**
- **Employment history including salary**
- **References**
- **Personal statement**

However, the following information would generally only appear on an application form:

- **National Insurance number**
- **Reason for leaving a position of employment**
- **Notice required from current position**
- **Equal opportunities details such as date of birth, nationality and a question asking if the candidate has any relationship to any existing member of the organisation**
- **A specific question asking the candidate to detail why they are suitable for the particular vacancy**
- **Days lost through sickness over a period of time and the reasons why**
- **A disability declaration**
- **A criminal convictions declaration**
- **Advertising monitoring; for example, in order to assess our advertising please specify where you learnt of this vacancy**
- **A declaration of truth**
- **The signature of the candidate**
- **The date**

The application form is specific to an organisation and the aim of it is to ensure the organisation attains as much relevant information prior to shortlisting as possible. The time spent interviewing candidates can prove costly, so those interviewed need to be worth spending money on. The more relevant information the organisation has, the better the chance of eliminating unsuitable candidates.

The CV is specific to the candidate and aims to describe the candidate in the best possible manner. There are some aspects that a candidate may not put in a CV that would be asked in an application form. Examples of this can be the declaration of criminal convictions or the fact that a candidate has had 15 days off sick in one- and two-day blocks. This information can be vital in successful recruitment, particularly when working with children or when working shifts may be involved, as is common in the leisure and recreation industry.

Probably the most important addition that the application form has over the CV is the declaration of truth coupled with the candidate's signature. This is an important safety net for the organisation. If recruitment is based purely on a CV with no signature (which it never should be) and the candidate is not being truthful, the company could recruit a candidate who is a liability. This can be compounded if the candidate has a motive for lying, for example a convicted paedophile working on a playscheme during school holidays.

As the candidate compiles the CV it can be easier to omit details or stretch the truth a little. It is easier to cover gaps in employment in a CV. There are many genuine reasons for periods of unemployment, such as having a baby, but there are also reasons that the organisation may want to know about, such as time spent in prison.

Although not sufficient on its own, the declaration does protect the organisation. Many declarations actually state that employment would be terminated if this situation did prove to be the case.

An example of a declaration could be:

> I certify that, to the best of my ability, the information that I have provided is true. If this information is found to be false or I fail to declare any criminal convictions, my employment with New Town Rugby Club may be terminated.
>
> Signed _____ Date _____

In the selection process it is easier to assess the suitability of candidates from an application form. All candidates are described in the same order and they are all asked the same questions so they are all given the same opportunity to sell themselves. Therefore decisions can be made objectively.

Speculative use of a CV is certainly useful. The CV can be distributed where there is not a specific position to apply for but the candidate or the

Mary Freds

93 West Road
Weston
Birmingham, BE72 2AS
Phone Work: 01635 963242 Mobile: 0907 341792 Home: 01672 124682 E-mail:freds@perinet.co.uk

EXPERIENCE

(Pleasant to look at)

September 1993–present
Chedling Borough Council
Recreation Client Officer / Assistant Leisure Centre Manager
£18,000
Core duties include:
• Sport development
• Customer liaison through corporate systems and administration
• Project management
• Monitoring of CCT contracts
• Staff recruitment, selection and training
• Duty officer relief
Project managed a £1.5 million refurbishment package on budget and on time.

(All structured in the same way)

August 1990–September 1993
Renbridge District Council
Recreation and Tourism Officer
£12,000
Core duties include:
• Marketing and promotion of leisure centre
• Timetabling and monitoring of the fitness suite
• Deputising for the assistant manager where necessary
• Duty officer role including safety and security of centre
Produced a successful marketing campaign which increased attendance by 10%.

(Includes dates, place of work, salary, main duties)

EDUCATION

Loughborough University (1989)
BSc (Honours) Recreation Management, Sport Science and Physical Education
Upper second class

(Give any key achievements of the job)

John Port School Derby (1986)
• General Studies A level   D
• Advanced VCE in Leisure and Recreation

(Includes qualification, dates, grade)

GCSEs (1984)
• Maths   C
• English   B
• Double Science   D
• French   C

Figure 22.3 *An example CV, with comments*

PERSONAL PROFILE

> Shows what Mary does other than work & education

I am an ambitious lively person who enjoys a busy professional and private life. In my leisure time I enjoy running and completed the London Marathon in 1997, raising £1,500 for diabetes. I swam competitively for 12 years, representing and captaining national, regional and local teams. I have won seven national titles, including some at masters level.
I enjoy listening to music and travelling abroad, particularly to Florida.
I am seeking a rewarding and challenging role.

> Doesn't sound arrogant

> We've seen what she's done – now where she wants to go

ADDITIONAL SKILLS

- Full clean driving licence
- Good working knowledge of packages such as MS Office.

> No longer than 2 sides – 1 side and you're not interesting, more than 2 sides and you're boring

Figure 22.3   *(cont'd)*

organisation may feel it is useful to look at the candidate's details. The same can be true if qualifications for a position are standard, such as a National Pool Lifeguard Qualification for employment as a lifeguard. If a candidate offers a CV the organisation has hard evidence of information about the candidate and is more likely to confirm their interest at a later date.

Figure 22.3 shows an example of a CV, with comments.

The application form or the CV?

Although both offer information about a candidate, from the point of view of the organisation the application form is more specific and thorough. The CV offers the candidate much greater flexibility. The CV could be used to assess initial interest and then followed up with a more detailed application process.

It will depend on the organisation, the position and other parts of the recruitment and selection process as to which method the organisation will choose to use.

Activity 22.5

This is difficult!

Ask your local authority if you may have a copy of their application form (or go on the Internet and print a copy of an application form from one of the websites).

In a group (the larger the better), each fill in the application form, making comments about what you found easy, hard and the suitability of the form. Choose the position you are applying for. It could be a professional footballer, a lifeguard or an athletics development officer.

If you can, copy the form for each member of the group.

Then all produce a CV and ask two of your friends to assess it. Ask your friends to list the good parts and the areas that could be improved and then do this yourself.

Keep this information. You will need it when we get to the next stage.

Letters of application

▼▼▼▼▼▼▼▼▼▼

Letter of application

A covering letter, briefly introducing the candidate and the CV, which will be attached

▲▲▲▲▲▲▲▲▲▲

If the chosen method of application is by a CV, the statement often used to identify this is 'Please send a letter of application to . . .' or 'Please apply in writing to . . .'.

Figure 22.4 shows an example of a letter of application, with comments.

All the usual rules of how to write a business letter apply. It should be professional in its appearance, and the language should be clear, simple and to the point. There should be a date and signature and it should end on a high point and create the best first impression possible.

Activity 22.6

It is difficult to write about ourselves and not sound arrogant. Using a letter of application and the CV you have already produced, apply for your 'perfect' job.

Using the same method as previously, ask two friends to evaluate your letter. What do you think of their comments? What do you think would now happen to the information that you have provided to the organisation?

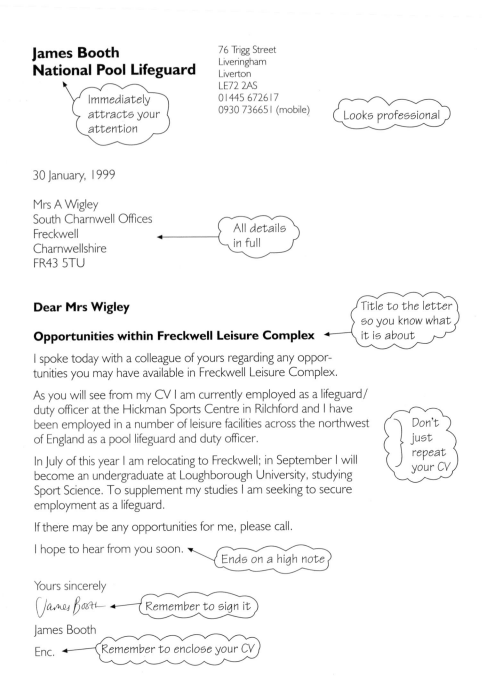

James Booth
National Pool Lifeguard

76 Trigg Street
Liveringham
Liverton
LE72 2AS
01445 672617
0930 736651 (mobile)

Immediately attracts your attention

Looks professional

30 January, 1999

Mrs A Wigley
South Charnwell Offices
Freckwell
Charnwellshire
FR43 5TU

All details in full

Dear Mrs Wigley

Opportunities within Freckwell Leisure Complex

Title to the letter so you know what it is about

I spoke today with a colleague of yours regarding any opportunities you may have available in Freckwell Leisure Complex.

As you will see from my CV I am currently employed as a lifeguard/duty officer at the Hickman Sports Centre in Rilchford and I have been employed in a number of leisure facilities across the northwest of England as a pool lifeguard and duty officer.

Don't just repeat your CV

In July of this year I am relocating to Freckwell; in September I will become an undergraduate at Loughborough University, studying Sport Science. To supplement my studies I am seeking to secure employment as a lifeguard.

If there may be any opportunities for me, please call.

I hope to hear from you soon.

Ends on a high note

Yours sincerely

James Booth

Remember to sign it

James Booth

Enc.

Remember to enclose your CV

Figure 22.4 *An example letter of application, with comments*

Stage six: Decision making

Probably the most difficult aspect of the recruitment process is actually having to make a decision. It may be the decision to interview a candidate or whom to appoint or whether to recruit in the first instance. Whatever the decision, it has to be the right one at that particular time.

Aim

Within recruitment and selection, the aim is to make a decision that is good for both the organisation and also good for the individuals concerned.

There can be situations where the decision a manager takes is good for the organisation but terrible for the individual and vice versa; this can often be true of a redundancy or a sacking. These types of situation require even more careful thought. The organisation needs to develop a list of criteria that can be used in making a decision. The criteria also need to be placed in order of importance and later scored. Most of all, the decision needs to be made objectively, that is, by considering the facts and not with emotion and bias. A new national sports development officer must be appointed because they are the best candidate, not because they enjoy a drink on a Saturday night with the Chief Executive.

A guide to making a successful decision

1   **List the criteria for making a decision. For example, what qualifications do you need to do the job?**

2   **Put all the criteria in order of importance; for example, the ability to use Microsoft Word is less important than holding a variety of coaching qualifications or the ability to handle change**

3   **Give each criteria a value or a score out of ten. Criteria can be given the same score**

4   **Score each option or, in the recruitment process, score each candidate**

5   **Add up the scores**

6   **Discuss the scores – remember that in the recruitment and selection process more than one person is involved and the individual scores may be different and so need discussing**

7   **Make an objective decision; for example, any candidate who scores over 55 will be interviewed**

It may be necessary to justify a decision so it is useful to make a note of how a decision was made. Often within the recruitment and selection process, a candidate is more likely to request reasons for non-selection. This decision-making process can demonstrate that a decision was made objectively and therefore allowing equality of opportunity. It can also provide useful and constructive feedback to an unsuccessful candidate.

Activity 22.7

Have a go at this case study.

Make a Choice

The following case study puts you in the position of line manager. You need to select the right candidate for the role of area leisure club manager, a new and demanding position.

You are Sarah Gilson, the manager of a highly successful chain of hotel leisure clubs. The department you manage has consistently won internal awards for performance, innovation and customer service. You pride yourself on the fact that you are proactive and have boundless enthusiasm that filters through your team. As a consequence, you are often asked for help and advice from other departments and many members of your team have progressed within the company and in turn, become well respected and sought after.

However, you find yourself in a flattering but difficult situation. A vacancy has arisen in a leisure club within the same chain, fifty miles north of yours. This area has been blighted by a lack of natural tourist attractions and high unemployment levels. It has always had a reputation for being a department with a problem. Sickness levels in this department are the highest throughout the entire organisation. Staff morale is considered to be poor and there is a tradition of industrial unrest. The department has slightly fewer employees than yours does. It has benefited from a substantial cash injection to refurbish some older facilities and bring the club up to date and this has meant considerable change and expansion.

Your line manager has asked you to recommend a member of your department to fill a position the same as

continued

continued

yours in this troublesome department. This is a huge compliment for you and your team and whilst you were flattered at first you now are having some doubts about this task you are being asked to complete. You are keen to impress your boss as you would like to move on and up in your career, but your department has become settled and effective in the past two years and the morale and general working atmosphere is efficient but jovial. Your department is a nice place to work!

You know from your role what the position will entail. There will be large amounts of data and preparation of detailed reports, which will be used throughout the organisation. Much of the work involves technical expertise and budgetary control. In your role you need excellent interpersonal and communication skills and the ability to build a team, handle conflict and provide a first-class service for the customer. In this troublesome department this role will be twice as hard (you do wonder why you weren't asked to fill this role!).

Two candidates come to mind immediately.

Laura is 31 years old. She gained a first-class degree in leisure management at Sheffield Hallam University. She also has a Masters degree in IT. She may be considered young for this new role. She certainly has progressed rapidly within the organisation to date. She has taken her area of responsibility to new heights and has worked tirelessly to achieve excellent results. Her interpersonal skills are fine. She is flexible, considerate and can empathise. You really enjoy working with Laura as she has the same boundless energy as you do and seems to fit so much into her days. You find Laura refreshing and sometimes hard to keep up with; she has plenty of new and bright ideas, and some are very ambitious. She has recently got married though, and you wonder whether she may be thinking of having children soon. She also goes to the gym with you three times a week and you enjoy her company.

You also remember recently at directors meetings being asked to encourage the promotion of women, as 82 per cent of managers in this organisation were male.

continued

continued

There is also Jack. He is much older than Laura, at 47. He has also achieved outstanding results in the department over the past eight years. He is a long-standing member of the organisation, having joined straight after his A levels. In fact, Jack is one of your most loyal team members. He is married with three children, ranging from three years old to fourteen years old, and has recently asked you in his annual appraisal if you considered he was ready for promotion. You answered yes!

He also works tirelessly and you often arrive in work on a Monday morning to find he has been in during the weekend. You have some reservations about his communication skills; he can appear abrupt but your team all respect Jack and know not to be offended. At the end of the day he certainly gets a job done.

Jack has an NVQ Level 3 in Management which he completed three years ago. Jack has devised a number of very effective procedures that, although simple, have saved significant amounts of time and money. He expects everyone to work the same way as he does . . . hard all the time. He does not suffer fools lightly and will not listen to excuses.

This decision is difficult. Not only are you thinking of the two members of your team but also the effect a promotion would have on the rest of your team. You also are unsure how the unsuccessful candidate would feel.

So you now try and compile some criteria. You jot down some of your main points:

★ How will Laura or Jack react to the situation?

★ Which one can handle change the best?

★ What would be the effect on the loser?

★ What would be the overall effect on the organisation?

★ What are the main requirements of the new position and how do the two candidates match up to this?

You feel it is a pity that both cannot be offered a position but you know this is not possible. What do you do?

1 Compile a list of criteria that you feel are essential for the position

2 Compile a list of criteria you feel are desirable for the position

3 Prioritise and score these lists; for example, management skills may be essential and rated at 10, technical expertise may also be essential but rated at 7

4 Assess Laura and Jack against the criteria; for example, Jack may score 8 out of 10 for management skills and 4 out of 7 for technical expertise

5 Add up the scores

6 Make a decision

Remember you must justify your decisions. This includes your choice of criteria and the candidate you choose. Compare your results with others in your group.

Stage seven: Interviewing

The process of successful interviewing can be a tricky one. Recruitment interviewing should be as relaxed as possible; it should help the candidate and the organisation decide if the vacant position will be mutually beneficial. It should not be full of nasty surprises and certainly not an interrogation.

Aims

✪ **To meet the candidate in person**
✪ **To gather as much relevant information as possible**
✪ **To ensure the decision-making process is successful**

The interviewing process requires a great deal of planning in order to run smoothly. There are many different aspects within this process. It can be broken down into three stages:

1 **Planning before an interview**

2 **The interview**

3 **After the interview**

Planning before the interview

Consider:

- ✪ **Where should the interview take place?**
- ✪ **When should the interview take place?**
- ✪ **Who should take the interview?**
- ✪ **What format should the interview take?**

Hints and tips

At least two weeks prior to the interview:

- ✪ **Decide who is to take the interview and check their availability on a number of days. Ensure that the interviewers are appropriate and not too overpowering; remember that the candidate needs to be relaxed to perform at their best**
- ✪ **Choose a suitable venue for the interview and ensure that it is booked – a double booking on the day is a nightmare!**
- ✪ **Ensure that the venue is the appropriate size and has suitable furniture**
- ✪ **Ensure the venue is realistic. If possible, interviews should take place in the working environment. It can be demoralising to find you work in a bleak, lonely office when the interview took place in plush new offices down the road**
- ✪ **Decide on the seating arrangements for the interview and forward a request for this. Try to minimise any physical barriers between the interviewer and the interviewee, for example avoid large desks and rows of interviewers**
- ✪ **Arrange for all interviewers to meet at least one week prior to interview to discuss the format of the interview**
- ✪ **Invite the candidates for interview, and remember to tell them when, where, with whom and the format of the interview; they need to be relaxed to perform at their best**

One week prior to interview:

- ✪ **Confirm attendance with the interviewers**
- ✪ **Ensure all relevant staff are aware that interviews are taking place. It can be embarrassing to both parties if a receptionist is told a candidate has arrived for interview, and is unaware that interviews are even taking place**

- ✪ Ensure that a request is made for the interview to progress without interruption; for example, ensure that phones will be redirected and a sign is placed on the door
- ✪ Agree a realistic dress code. This does not have to be formal business dress. It is perfectly acceptable for a duty officer at a leisure centre to interview in a clean, smart tracksuit with the company logo on it
- ✪ Distribute the necessary documentation. This should include the job description, the person specification, the recruitment advert, the criteria to be assessed during the interview and the candidate's application form or CV. Ensure all interviewers are familiar with these documents
- ✪ Agree on the format of the interview and the questions to be asked (see Table 22.1).

Some interviews can run over a number of days and comprise a variety of tests, placing the candidate in the workplace and a more formal traditional interview; on the other hand, some are scheduled to last 20 minutes and involve a formal

Types of questions	Worth using for . . .	But be careful!
Open Starting with how, tell me about, what do you think, why	Encourage the candidate to talk. Great for finding out as much as possible. A good starting point in an interview	Sometimes they allow the candidate to talk and talk and talk. This type of question needs to be controlled.
Closed Encourage a one-word answer, such as are you 28? Do you think this is the best way?	For clarifying a fact	These questions are not good if you are seeking lots of information. Reword them to become open questions
Leading Encourage the candidate to answer in a particular way, such as I suppose you are angry now?	Not of much use as often the candidate answers in a way they think the interviewer wants them to answer	You want the views of the candidate so AVOID these types of questions
Hypothetical Such as what if situations, what would you do if?	Puts the candidate in a situation and allows both the candidate and interviewer to see how the situation would be handled	These types of questions can only be used as a guide as they are not entirely accurate. They also do not allow time for consideration and reason
Multiple A series of questions asked together	Worth very little. Always focus on one question	AVOID

Table 22.1 *Interview questions*

interview only. **The aim is to obtain as much relevant information as possible and the format of the interview should help to achieve this aim**

Immediately prior to interview:

- ✪ **Check that all requests have been actioned, so check that the phone is diverted, remind the front-line staff that interviews are taking place, check the room is set out as needed and so on**
- ✪ **The interviewers should familiarise themselves with the documentation again and the format of the interview**

During the interview:

- ✪ **Greet the candidate with a welcoming smile**
- ✪ **Explain to the candidate what is going to happen during the interview**
- ✪ **Explain to the candidate what will happen after the interview and how a decision will be reached and communicated**
- ✪ **Remember to score the candidates against the agreed criteria – it is very easy to become confused about who said what or simply to forget**
- ✪ **Listen to the candidate**
- ✪ **Allow the candidate time to respond and ask any questions they may have**
- ✪ **Clarify the conditions of the post to the interviewee**
- ✪ **Ensure the interviews are running to time (within reason)**
- ✪ **At the end of the interview, the interviewer should ask if the interviewee is still interested in the vacancy**
- ✪ **Say goodbye and shake the hand of the candidate, thank them for their time and effort – even if they are unsuccessful the organisation still want the interviewee to have a positive impression of the company. They could take up another position in the future**

After the interview:

- ✪ **All the interviewers should discuss their observations and their scores against the agreed criteria**
- ✪ **Make a decision based on the information gathered so far**
- ✪ **Take up references**
- ✪ **Tell the successful candidate and confirm acceptance of the position**

- ✪ **Tell the unsuccessful applicants as soon as possible. Be honest and objective. This will help the candidates in the future; they may be disappointed with the decision but at least will feel the decision was reached fairly**
- ✪ **Discuss start dates with the successful candidate**

Hints and tips for the interviewee

- ✪ **Find out prior to the interview exactly where it is. The last thing the interviewee wants to happen is that they get lost or they are late**
- ✪ **Research the company prior to interview; it essential that the company is worth working for. Check how long the company has been established, what their growth is and any good or bad publicity they may have had**
- ✪ **Consider the dress code for the interview**

Activity 22.8

Prepare a checklist for an interview for your 'perfect' job. Ensure you cover all the aspects that will lead to the interview running smoothly.

Now complete the checklist for the interview, for example identify where the interview should take place and who the interview panel should be.

Using the decision-making process (page 321), prepare a criteria score sheet for your 'perfect' job.

Get together with a friend and let them conduct the interview, assessing your performance. Change places, this time with you interviewing your friend for their 'perfect job'.

If you can, video the interviews and then analyse them. What were your strengths and your areas for improvement?

Stage eight: Induction, including probationary periods

Once the candidate has accepted the offer of the vacancy a start date will be decided. Once the start date arrives, the candidate does not just start the job and suddenly know exactly what they are doing. It is fair to say that most employees feel nervous on their first day at work. The induction process should help ease the new employee into a new position and into a new environment. It should help calm those nerves.

The aim is to help this transition from new employee to experienced member of staff.

Everyone needs a formal induction. Even if the new employee has been doing a very similar job in another organisation or the same job for the same organisation but at a different location, there will be different practices and procedures that are specific to one place of work only. Examples of these are completing a time sheet, the emergency evacuation procedures or even where the kettle is.

Reasons for planning an induction

First impressions are exceptionally powerful; the induction process can help create a positive first impression, and if successfully completed, the organisation will look planned and efficient.

The organisation should ensure that the new employee is accurately introduced to as many aspects of the company as possible. This can have legal implications, such as the employer has a duty of care to the employee with respect to the emergency procedures on poolside. If the employee is not introduced formally to these procedures, they can argue they are put at personal risk in relation to the Health and Safety at Work Act 1974.

The efficiency and effectiveness of a member of staff will be improved through the induction process, as hopefully it will prevent mistakes.

The induction process allows both the new employee and existing employees the chance to assess each other. Any problems can then be resolved early.

Hints and tips

The induction process should be completed by a variety of colleagues who will represent the different areas that the position involves. There is one rule when selecting who should complete the induction process; they must know how to complete the job correctly. It is no good passing on bad habits.

A centre attendant can expect an induction process to include:

- ✪ **A member of personnel to introduce payment procedures and pension contributions**
- ✪ **The technical supervisor to introduce the pool testing equipment and the emergency poolside alarm**
- ✪ **The duty officer to introduce the shift rotas and other lifeguards on duty**

This process is a great opportunity to 'break the ice' between existing employees and the new member of staff. It gets people talking. However, the process does need to be monitored by one person. It is essential that all areas of the induction process are covered. A lead named person should ensure this. This task would normally fall to the line manager; for example, the area controller will lead the induction process for the team leader at a theme park.

The length of the induction process will vary, depending on the place of work, the size of the organisation, the level of the candidate and the complexity of the task. Most new employees will take an entire year to settle down fully into a new job. This is because over the course of a year certain processes will only occur once, such as the Christmas party rush in a restaurant in a leisure complex or an Easter playscheme or the end of a financial year. Therefore the induction process continues for up to a year. The method of introduction may alter though; this type of induction may be on the job and informal.

The formal recorded induction process generally occurs over a 2–4 week intensive period. As a result of this intensity many aspects will be forgotten. To counteract this, a staff handbook can act as a useful reference. The staff handbook explains the main practices and the expectation of the place of work.

In some organisations, the induction process is linked to a probationary period or a trial period of employment. During a set and agreed time, the employer will assess the employee. If the employee is not performing as the employer would expect at the end of this time, the employer can terminate the employee's contract. It would be unfair to assess a new member of staff without allowing them to settle in and introducing them properly. As a consequence, the end of the induction process is often linked to a probationary period.

Any shortfall on either side should be discussed in regular structured meetings during the induction process. The organisation is responsible for ensuring the employee is aware of the probationary period and how they will be assessed. The probationary period can last over one, three, six or twelve months.

In order to complete the induction process correctly, documentation needs to be produced stating the various aspects of the process. This also acts as a record of the process.

Figure 22.5 shows an example of an induction form, with comments.

Newtown Leisure Club

Induction for new leisure assistants

Name _____ Date _____

Aspects to be introduced during the first hour
Tour of the leisure club ☐
Line manager ☐
Colleagues on duty   Names 1 ☐ _____
                             2 ☐ _____   *(Main aspects)*
                             3 ☐ _____

Location of staff room
Personal locker with key
Toilet and staff washing facilities
Kitchen facilities

Aspects to be introduced during the first day
Staff handbook issued ◄——— *(Given for references)*
Emergency evacuation procedures
Poolside alarm
Time sheet and method of payment
Uniform issued
Name badge issued

Aspects to be introduced during the first week
Staff rota
Sickness procedures
Annual leave procedure
Pool testing procedure

Aspects to be introduced during the first month
Pension scheme
Career structure
Organisational structure
Other local/sister facilities
Competitors

To be completed after one month
The induction process has now been completed as listed above

Signature Leisure assistant ___ *(Only sign when fully completed)* ___ Date _____
Signature Line manager _____ Date _____

Figure 22.5 *An example induction form, with comments*

Staff development and training

Once the recruitment and selection process has been completed and the candidate is in position, the next move is consolidation and improvement.

No one is perfect, everyone has room for improvement and the organisation has a moral responsibility to help every member of staff, where possible, reach their potential. To help achieve this, every member of staff should have a training and development plan. This may be an integral part of the appraisal process. The plan should include new challenges and also refresher sessions; it is always necessary to keep reminding us of good habits. It is also very easy over a period of time to pick up bad habits and short cuts. Refresher sessions help update staff and remind them of the 'perfect' procedure. For example, the guidelines on how to perform a pool test need to be followed closely in order to produce a valid result. If a pool attendant is repeatedly completing the tests it can be easy to forget the procedure and, for instance, not wait the exact period of time between stages and so on. The refresher course should help minimise these mistakes.

Training is needed if any new systems are introduced. It is imperative any new systems are fully introduced to anyone who may use them. For example, if a new telephone system is installed, all who use it must be clear on its operation. The consequence of this not being the case can be loss of business as customers may struggle to get through or are cut off. The same can be said of a new colour photocopier that is bought to reduce printing costs. If the member of staff does not know how to operate all the special features, any investment made on the initial purchase is lost.

Some procedures involve health and safety and may have legal implications. Staff need to be made aware of changes in a formal structured way, not by chance or a word in the corridor.

However the staff development and training is planned, it must be monitored and reviewed. Staff must be given deadlines and clear objectives to follow, and progress must be reviewed prior to the completion deadline. For example, Julie Wilmot must attend and complete her Institute of Sport and Recreation Management Operators Certificate before July 2001; this will be reviewed in September 2000 and February 2001.

Some organisations now dedicate a member of staff purely to staff development; most will identify a role with responsibility for this. If an organisation aims to remain competitive, it must constantly strive to update and move forward. Therefore it would appear that staff development and training is likely to become more important in the future and the number of jobs in this area is likely to grow. For example, at Adventure World theme park there is a permanent, full-time training manager who trains and develops up to 400 seasonal employees.

Appraisal interviewing

Appraisals are being used more and more frequently in the leisure and recreation industry. They allow both the employer and the employee to reflect on what has and has not been achieved over a period of time. The workplace is becoming busier and busier and often the time to step back and review progress is lost. The appraisal makes the time to do this and should allow both the employer and employee to be more effective. An appraisal can also be termed a performance review.

Aims

- ✪ **To improve performance of the employer and employee**
- ✪ **To allow the employer and employee to discuss, monitor and evaluate progress against previously set objectives**
- ✪ **To assess any salary or bonus payments**
- ✪ **To identify training and development needs**
- ✪ **To assess future career prospects or promotion**
- ✪ **To establish new objectives to be planned, monitored and reviewed within a specified time period**
- ✪ **To set an approximate date for the next appraisal**
- ✪ **To update any documentation, for example, the job description**

Reasons for the appraisal interview

As stated, it is not easy in the changing and busy environment of leisure and recreation to find time to reflect and monitor performance. Every member of staff needs to know how well they are performing, every member of staff needs direction and security and every employer needs to know how their team perceives their performance too.

The successful appraisal interview motivates staff. The aims and objectives agreed in an appraisal interview provide staff with a target to aim for and be measured against. It is human nature not to want to fail and so the appraisal is a useful motivational tool.

Generally, the more staff are motivated, the happier they are likely to be and the more productive they are. This increases job satisfaction for the member of staff and should increase profitability for the organisation. It is therefore desirable for everyone.

The considerations to be made before, during and after an appraisal interview are much the same as a recruitment interview; for example, a suitable room still needs to be booked and there should be no interruptions during the interview. However, there are additional considerations listed below.

Hints and tips

✪ **It is usually the line manager who will conduct the appraisal interview but sometimes the appraisee may prefer to be interviewed by someone else. This can arise if there is a personality clash or a disagreement between the two parties. Try to offer an alternative appraiser, usually the member of staff senior to the line manager. Remember the appraisal is a positive experience**

✪ **Ensure the appraiser is fully trained to carry out a successful appraisal. A poorly conducted appraisal can be disastrous**

✪ **During the appraisal interview, the appraiser and the appraisee are likely to know each other, probably well. This should not alter the level of planning and privacy during the interview. Ensure an appropriate venue is used with NO interruptions**

✪ **Aim to maintain a relaxed atmosphere**

✪ **Ensure both the appraiser and appraisee conduct the appraisal interview objectively. If you want a pay rise, give measurable reasons why you should be awarded one! If you are going to criticise, state the facts, give examples and provide some ideas for improvement**

✪ **Ensure the appraisal interview is planned with appropriate documentation. It is advisable that prepared questions and a set format are used**

✪ **To ensure equality of opportunity, all appraisals should follow the same format; as a consequence, many organisations have a set procedure**

✪ **Be positive but be honest**

✪ **If the appraisal becomes heated, all involved need to listen, remain calm, stick to the facts and refrain from shouting**

✪ **Always finish on a positive note; the appraiser should thank the appraisee and vice versa**

Activity 22.9

Some of the activities that you have completed have been with friends or as part of a group. Choose one activity and list some areas for discussion; they may include aspects such as attendance at group meetings or the ability to meet deadlines. Feed back your observations to the group, ensuring you have factual evidence to back up your statements.

How did it feel to praise someone you know?

How did it feel to criticise someone you know?

What was their reaction?

Activity 22.10

Team up with two other people. There are three roles to play:

1 You are the line manager, the appraiser
2 You are the appraisee
3 You are the observer

Pick one of the following (or all three if you are keen!):

★ A centre attendant in a large wet and dry side leisure centre has been reliable and trustworthy for the past five years. They have had 22 days off work this year but prior to this they had an average of less than a day a year. They are constantly late and their work is not up to your standard or their standard in the past. Every year they have received a generous bonus as a reward for excellent work BUT this year it is different. You have spoken to them but have no answers and this year their targets have not really been addressed.

★ A lively and very popular team leader at a theme park is due an appraisal. All targets have been achieved. The area concerned has won awards for superb customer awareness and has had a record number of letters of praise BUT the member of staff loves to talk and you have an hour to complete this appraisal.

★ An administrative assistant has had an awful year. Her husband has died, her own health has been poor and her job is changing quicker than she can cope. She needs support and training on the new systems BUT you haven't provided any. She has missed her targets but feels that this is not all due to her.

For each of these situations conduct an appraisal. Have a go at being the appraisee, the appraiser and the observer. Analyse how successful the appraisals were.

Equal opportunities

During the recruitment and selection process there are a number of pieces of legislation that must be noted and actioned.

These include:

- ⊙ **The Sex Discrimination Act 1975**
- ⊙ **The Equal Pay Act 1970 and a number of Employment Protection Acts**
- ⊙ **The Race Relations Act 1976**
- ⊙ **The Disability Discrimination Act 1996**

The implications of these are:

- ⊙ **Men and women must be paid the same amount for the same job**
- ⊙ **Both sexes should be treated equally**
- ⊙ **A candidate should not be treated unfairly because of their race or nationality**
- ⊙ **An organisation should make every practical effort to ensure that disabled candidates can be appropriately accommodated at work**

The organisation has a legal responsibility to ensure these are followed. It would be foolish to think these measures ensure that no one within these groups was ever discriminated against. Sometimes discrimination occurs through ignorance, for example fitting a public telephone in the reception of a leisure centre out of reach and view of a customer in a wheelchair. Education is the way to minimise any form of discrimination.

There can be instances where it is necessary to recruit a woman or a man or a black person. The law does allow for exclusions to be made, where there are genuine reasons. In leisure and recreation this will include employing a female leisure attendant to supervise the female changing areas.

One of the best ways to ensure discrimination is minimised is to study the organisational practices and ask the following questions:

- ⊙ **Would I ask this question of a man and a woman? If the answer is yes, generally go ahead and ask the question. If the answer is no, think first and consider what the reason for the question is in the first place. For example, 'Who looks after the children when you are sick?' The same principle can be applied to race and nationality**

✪ **Would a disabled person be able to function successfully in a particular role? Can the role be modified or the facilities be adapted to help in any way? The Disability Discrimination Act does not mean, for example, that a blind person could be a lifeguard at a swimming pool; this is clearly not safe or practical. It is aiming to provide opportunities for disabled people that able-bodied people enjoy as a matter of course**

In addition to legal responsibilities, an organisation also has some ethical or moral issues to consider. There are many groups in society that claim to be discriminated against. The laws already mentioned do not cover all of these. Such issues include sexual orientation, religious beliefs, trade union activity, political beliefs, social class and age. Most organisations do not want to discriminate on any grounds and so introduce a code of practice that is more comprehensive than the law. It is the best working practice to recruit and select candidates on their suitability for the job and no other reason. These additional considerations are ethical responsibilities, aspects that should be considered out of respect for others.

Many organisations produce a policy that states the commitment of the organisation to providing equal opportunities.

Activity 22.11

Request an equal opportunities policy from a leisure or recreation provider. Analyse it and comment on the following:

★ Is it easy to understand?

★ Does it cover the legal responsibilities?

★ Does it cover any ethical responsibilities?

★ How could you put the statement into action?

★ How easy is it to measure if the statement is useful or not?

Activity 22.12

You are recruiting a senior member of staff, an International Netball Games Co-ordinator, and have just interviewed six candidates for the position. One of the candidates is by far the best person for the role. She is in her late 20s, educated just as the person specification desired and has the right personality to fit into the existing team.

Our personal assistant is just processing the offer letter when she realises she knows the successful candidate; she tells you the young woman is in the early stages of pregnancy.

What do you do and why?

Activity 22.13

Newtown Leisure Centre interviews a man for a part-time receptionist's position and he is successful. In the initial discussions after the interview he is offered 12 hours a week. When the specific timetable is set up the man contacts you and states that at the times he is scheduled to work it is impossible for him to get a childminder for his two young children.

Again, what do you do and why?

Employment contracts

Once an employee has been offered a position within an organisation, a contract of employment should shortly follow, the sooner the better. Most people would prefer to see a contract that clearly states what is expected of them and identifies their working conditions, prior to starting a new position.

In 1993, a European directive stated that all employees working over eight hours a week must be issued with a contract of employment within two months of starting work. The following information must be provided in the contract:

✪ **Place of work**

✪ **Job title**

✪ **Rate of pay**

✪ **When pay day is**

✪ **Brief description of work**

✪ **Notice period**

✪ **Amount of paid leave**

✪ **Working hours**

✪ **Collective agreements, such as agreements made through a trade union on behalf of individual employees**

Hints and tips

✪ **Sometimes contracts of employment can be conditional, on a medical for example**

✪ **Contracts can change from time to time**

✪ **Contracts should be regularly updated so they are current at all times**

Other points to consider are described in more detail below.

Hours of work and annual leave

In October 1998, the European Working Hours directive was introduced. This states that:

✪ **Employees should work no more than 48 hours per week. If this is exceeded, a written and voluntary agreement should be secured between the employee and the employer**

✪ **Since October 1999, employees have had the right to four weeks' annual paid leave**

Standard working hours tend to be around 37 to 40 hours; this excludes a one-hour lunch break. Flexible working hours are becoming more and more popular. This scheme operates where employees work a set number of hours over a 4-week period but the daily hours can vary. Usually employees have to be at work during core hours, which tend to be the busiest periods of the day.

Most organisations have a process where staff apply for annual leave, if possible seven days in advance. The leave should always be confirmed before any specific arrangements are made.

It is essential that employers are flexible with their working arrangements. By operating a flexi scheme employees can choose some of their working hours without disrupting the business and so be far happier at work and therefore more easily motivated. On the other hand, the employees must realise the employers have a job to do. Sometimes a member of staff not being available can result in a service being withdrawn. For example, a pool cannot open without a lifeguard.

Notice periods

▼ ▼ ▼ ▼ ▼ ▼ ▼ ▼ ▼

Notice period
The time between resignation from a job and the employee leaving the job

▲ ▲ ▲ ▲ ▲ ▲ ▲ ▲ ▲

Generally, the more senior the job, the longer the notice period. Some senior roles, such as Director of Leisure in a local authority, will have a notice period of 3 months. Sometimes it is in the interest of both parties not to implement the notice period. For example, if an employee wants to leave and their job has finished, the organisation may be happy to reduce the notice period. In most instances the notice period is needed to allow the organisation to prepare for recruitment and selection.

Methods of employment

There are a variety of ways of employing a member of staff to do a job. The method chosen can depend on the organisation, their aims, the sector they operate in, the job and the candidate.

✪ *Full-time:* **The employee generally works over 37 hours per week**

✪ *Part-time:* **The employee generally works under 37 hours per week**

✪ *Contracted:* **The employee works under set conditions and over a set period, for example a 2-year contract at £18,000 per year and working 42 hours a week**

- ✪ *Permanent*: **The employee has a contract with no expiry date**
- ✪ *Casual*: **A member of staff who is employed only when needed**
- ✪ *Seasonal*: **Similar to a casual member of staff but employed at certain periods of the year when needed, such as working in a community centre during summer holidays or at Christmas in a themed restaurant**

In the leisure industry the methods of employment used vary. Most organisations will employ a core number of full-time staff, supported by a variety of staff employed either as part-time, casual, contracted or seasonal. In local authority provision, most positions are permanent and either on a full- or part-time basis. In the private sector there is also this combination but with a greater emphasis on casual staff. Both sectors use casual and seasonal staff, such as playscheme leaders during the summer. Positions that concentrate on a project are often contracted roles, such as a sports development officer employed to establish sporting links in a rural community. Funding of the position can also affect the method of employment; for example, an organisation receiving money from a governing body to look at drop out rates in a particular sport may offer a post that is contracted at a certain wage and for a certain period of time.

▼▼▼▼▼▼▼▼▼▼

Disciplinary procedure
A set process that allows the organisation to identify and resolve an issue concerning an employee

Grievance procedure
A set process that allows the employee to identify and resolve an issue concerning the employer

▲▲▲▲▲▲▲▲▲▲

Disciplinary and grievance procedures

These are two standard procedures that organisations should have in order to demonstrate sound management in the work place.

Unless these procedures are set and adhered to, the process will become invalid. The procedures will clearly explain what to do, whom to speak to, what will happen and when. All employees should be aware of these procedures. Their aim is to protect the organisation and the employee from unfair practices. Examples of this can include an employee who cannot do their job to the required standard or a member of staff who constantly swears. Most organisations will identify a set of rules and if these are broken a member of staff can be instantly dismissed. These can include theft, fraud, drunken behaviour and violence. These are termed gross misconduct.

You are the manager of Newtown Leisure Centre; this is a new wet and dry facility that is managed by the local authority. It is regarded as a fine example of how to maximise resources and provide excellent customer service.

Unfortunately, you have received an internal complaint. A female centre attendant who, as part of her role, controls stock in the bar is claiming she is being victimised by your assistant manager. She claims the barrels of beer now being ordered are too heavy for her to carry, that changes in shift patterns mean she is working more shifts at weekends and that the assistant manager is rude to her, particularly in front of customers.

You have never had any such claims before, relating either to victimisation or to the assistant manager, whom you professionally respect and enjoy socialising with.

You are part of a proactive and constructive local authority who do have a comprehensive set of procedures for disciplinary and grievance.

What do you do?

Consider the effects on your team.

Consider the procedures.

Sickness benefits

Many organisations operate a system where employees are paid when they are off work due to sickness; the method of calculating the rate of pay will depend on the organisation. This is called Occupational Sick Pay. Some organisations do not have such schemes and rely solely on Statutory Sick Pay (SSP). This sick pay is paid by the welfare state, which is funded by the government. Statutory sick pay is not automatically paid; eligibility can be affected by:

- ✪ *Age*: **SSP is not paid to anyone under 16 or over 60**
- ✪ *Earnings*: **There are different rates of sick pay depending on the level of earnings**
- ✪ *Contract*: **The length of time at work and the amount of work done can also affect the rate of pay**
- ✪ *Other benefits*: **If the employee is in receipt of other benefits, SSP may not be paid**

Maternity benefits

A similar system operates with maternity pay. Since 1998, all pregnant employees are entitled to 14 weeks statutory maternity leave, regardless of how long they have worked for an organisation. The 14-week period can be extended by up to 4 weeks if supported by a medical certificate. The maternity leave can start at any time after 11 weeks before the baby is due or as late as the day the baby is born. Two weeks' leave must be taken after the birth of the baby (this is extended to 4 weeks for factory work).

If a pregnant employee has worked for the same organisation for more than two years, the maternity leave is extended to 29 weeks at various rates of pay. Pregnant employees are allowed paid time off work to attend antenatal appointments.

Hints and tips

- **If an organisation employs fewer than 5 members of staff, they are exempt from this process**
- **It is the responsibility of the pregnant employee to complete the necessary documentation to claim maternity rights**
- **Statutory maternity pay is paid for 18 weeks**
- **Statutory maternity pay is not paid if the employee leaves the European Union**

Maternity pay and sick pay are complicated; advice should be taken from the personnel department or a suitably trained member of staff.

Paternity benefits

Paternity leave is time taken off work by the father when his baby is born. It is generally taken on a flexible basis, either immediately after the birth of the baby or when the mother comes out of hospital. Some organisations allow one week's paid leave, some make no provision at all. There is no statutory system for paternity benefits in the UK. However, following the introduction of European regulations in May 2000, fathers are entitled to up to three months' paternity leave upon the birth of a child or adoption. This is not paid leave.

Other benefits

- ***Compassionate leave*: Paid time taken off work due to exceptional circumstances, such as the death of a close relative or to attend a funeral**

- ⊙ *Emergency leave*: **Paid time taken off work for emergencies, such as a child being sick**
- ⊙ *Death benefit*: **A sum of money paid to the partner of an employee if they die whilst employed**

In January 1999 there was the introduction of the Fairness at Work Bill which looks to further extend maternity and paternity benefits. It also identifies that time is needed off work for emergencies and aims to incorporate this into a more comprehensive contract of employment.

In leisure and recreation there really are no hard and fast rules as to how these systems operate. All local authorities have agreed policies that are comprehensive. Some private companies are similar. The best advice is to check the benefits available to you in an organisation before starting work with them. If there are comprehensive systems in place, it can be generally assessed that the organisation is likely to care about their staff and should prove to be good employers.

Activity 22.15

Try to obtain a staff handbook from within the leisure and recreation industry. Look under the following headings:

★ Hours of work

★ Annual leave

★ Methods of employment

★ Methods of payment

★ Disciplinary procedures

★ Grievance procedures

★ Maternity, paternity and sickness benefits

Evaluate these benefits.

Put yourself in the position of an employee and ask yourself if they would be satisfactory to you.

Itemise 10 positive aspects and 10 negative aspects.

Compile a list of recommendations (be realistic).

Remuneration

There are different methods of calculating pay; the method used will depend on the job, the industry and to a certain degree, the organisation.

Methods of remuneration

✪ *Salary*: **Money received in a year, paid in twelve equal monthly instalments; for example, in a job advert it may say a tennis sports development officer at £14,000**

✪ *Wage*: **Weekly payments, for example £160 per week as a theme park rides assistant**

✪ *Piece rate*: **A rate of pay directly measured by units produced, for example £3.20 per 10 pizzas delivered**

✪ *Time rates*: **A rate of pay measured by the hours worked, for example £8.20 per hour as a fitness instructor**

✪ *Performance-related pay*: **Pay is calculated against the performance of the individual, for example £50 per sale of annual membership at a health club**

✪ *Profit-related pay*: **Pay is calculated against the performance of the organisation**

Many jobs are paid using a variety of methods of calculating pay; for example, a fitness instructor may be paid using time rates with an annual calculation of a profit-related bonus.

As well as the actual amount of money that is paid, there are other methods of rewarding staff. These include:

✪ *Company cars*: **It may be that a car is essential in order to complete a job successfully. A car may also be provided as a reward for loyalty and achievement; the better the performance, the better the car. However, this reward is taxed. The rate of tax depends on the value of the car and the miles driven for work per year. From April 2002, the tax will depend on the value of the car and the amount of carbon dioxide the car emits.**

✪ *Pension schemes*: **A non-contributory pension is where the organisation contributes to the pension fund of the employee and the employee does not. Most pensions provided by organisations (called occupational pension schemes) are contributory. Some contributions are made by the organisation and some by the individual. The rates of**

contribution differ. Some pay rises are awarded in greater pension contributions by the organisation

✪ *Health insurance*: **Private medical insurance can also be offered as a perk. The employee and often their family can enjoy free or subsidised cover**

✪ *Mobile telephones*: **These can be seen as a perk or they may be essential and awarded as a method of security, for example. Tax may be charged depending on the use of the phone**

✪ *Car parking facilities*: **In city centre locations, this will be attractive for employees as they may otherwise have to pay for public transport or parking fees**

✪ *Child care assistance*: **This can be a perk for parents returning to work, as fees for child care are often expensive and can often be a barrier to parents wish to work for your company**

Pay rises

Most people expect an annual pay rise that is linked to the general cost of living or inflation. Every year general living expenses rise, sometimes steeply (10 per cent) and sometimes gradually (3 per cent). The cost-of-living pay rise maintains the real wage or salary. For example, if an annual food bill for a family of four is £5,200 in 1998 and in 1999 the cost of living rises by 3 per cent, the food bill will increase by £156 to £5,356. If the family receives a pay rise of 3 per cent or below, then in real terms they are worse off. The British government is aiming for low inflation. We may even see a zero rate economy in the future.

Once this pay rise is awarded, an employee looks for further rises which reflect a job done well or targets that have been achieved. These pay awards can be decided in the annual appraisal or performance review. However, each job has a value and once this value is reached an employee needs to move into a higher valued job to receive a pay rise.

Income tax, National Insurance and personal allowances

The government needs to collect money in order to finance the business of the nation. One method of collecting this money is taxation. The tax taken directly from our salaries and wages is called income tax. The government also needs to fund the welfare state. This pays statutory sick and maternity pay, the state pension and other benefits. Here the money is collected as National Insurance contributions. You can calculate your tax and pay as follows:

Earnings	Rate of tax	
On the first £1,880	10%	The lower rate
On the next £27,520	22%	The basic rate
On any income over £29,400	40%	The higher rate

As the government set these, they may change

Table 22.2 *Tax rates for 2001–2*

The more you earn the more tax you pay

How to calculate your pay and tax

Therefore	Pay from employment per year	22,637.00	*Itemised on pay slip*
Minus	Tax-free amount	3,640.00	
		18,997.00	*From tax code*

On £18,997 tax payable is
Different rates of tax
lower rate 10% on £1,880 = 188.00
basic rate 22% on £17,117 = 3,765.74   *Amount over the year*
Annual Total tax = 3,953.74

Monthly pay would be £18,997 ÷ 12 = £1,583.08
Monthly tax bill would be £3,953.74 ÷ 12 = £329.48   *What is in your pocket!*
so each month net pay = 1,253.60

Calculating tax is hard! But we all need to know how to do it

A simple pay slip

Newtown Leisure Centre Jane Thomson 63 Law Avenue Chenly Surrey T314QL	• Don't forget in December, pay day is December 20th • Travel claims must be with personnel by the 5th for December payment		
		Tax code 350L.	
Call Payroll on 0645 321111 extension 264 staff no. 611321F			
611321F (£10,000 salary)	Payments		Deductions
	833.33	National insurance *10% of salary*	74.99
		Tax *At different rates of tax*	133.00
		Total payments	833.33
		Deductions	207.99
	833.33	Net pay	625.34

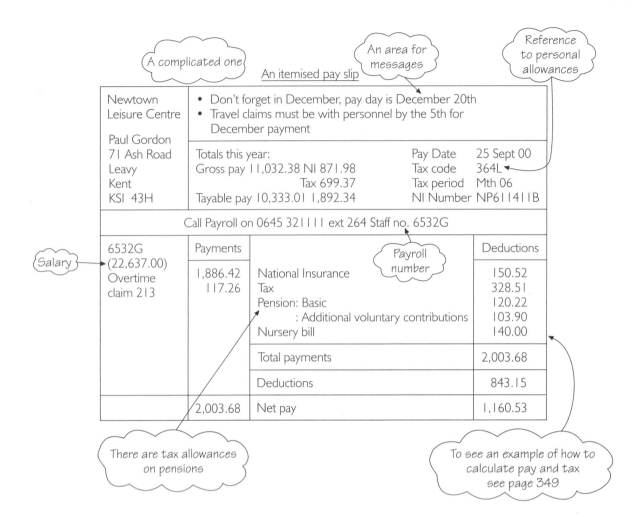

An itemised pay slip

A complicated one

An area for messages

Reference to personal allowances

Newtown Leisure Centre Paul Gordon 71 Ash Road Leavy Kent KSI 43H	• Don't forget in December, pay day is December 20th • Travel claims must be with personnel by the 5th for December payment		
	Totals this year: Gross pay 11,032.38 NI 871.98 Tax 699.37 Tayable pay 10,333.01 1,892.34	Pay Date 25 Sept 00 Tax code 364L Tax period Mth 06 NI Number NP611411B	

Call Payroll on 0645 321111 ext 264 Staff no. 6532G

Salary

Payroll number

6532G (22,637.00) Overtime claim 213	Payments		Deductions
	1,886.42 117.26	National Insurance Tax Pension: Basic : Additional voluntary contributions Nursery bill	150.52 328.51 120.22 103.90 140.00
		Total payments	2,003.68
		Deductions	843.15
	2,003.68	Net pay	1,160.53

There are tax allowances on pensions

To see an example of how to calculate pay and tax see page 349

The amount of income tax everyone pays will vary. It will be itemised on a pay slip (see above) and explained by the Inland Revenue, who collect tax on behalf of the government. Employees pay a certain percentage of their salary or wage as tax. There are three rates of income tax. For 2001–2 these are 10 per cent, 22 per cent and 40 per cent. The government sets these rates. Table 22.2 shows the different rates. Basically the more earned, the greater the amount of deductions made for tax. This system of taxation is called PAYE, which stands for pay as you earn.

Everyone is also allowed to earn a certain amount of money without paying tax. This is called a personal allowance. This allowance varies from person to person depending on circumstances such as whether you are married or not, whether you are a single parent or if you pay subscriptions to a professional organisation or not.

National Insurance contributions are also calculated as a percentage of the total salary; in 2001–2 it was 10 per cent. Your personal allowance is calculated as follows:

How to calculate your personal allowance

This is all calculated for you

The Inland Revenue send you a booklet explaining all of this

Tax allowances	£	Amounts taken away from your total allowances	£
Personal allowance	4,335	Car benefit	1,500
Married allowance	1,900	Other income	1,000
Professional membership	305		
	6,540		2,500

You need to tell the Inland Revenue if your circumstances change

Other aspects can be added here such as tax owed or a mobile phone

Then £6,540 − £2,500 = £4,040. This is the amount you can earn before paying tax. The tax code is 4040; take off the last digit and a letter is added as a code so 4040 add L therefore 404L

If you feel you are not being treated fairly there is a complaints procedure

The Inland Revenue decides this

Both National Insurance contributions and income tax are deducted from salaries and wages before we get them. This is called taxed at source. If an individual runs their own business and so is not taxed at source this is called being self-employed. Here a yearly tax return is completed and subsequently collected.

It is ILLEGAL to avoid paying tax.

Activity 22.16

Compare your response with that of your friends. Continuing your research into your 'perfect' job:

★ What is your expected rate of pay?

★ What is the method of payment?

★ Calculate the income tax and National Insurance contributions per year paid in this job

★ Calculate your personal allowance at current levels if you are single

★ Illustrate this on a pay slip

In the perfect world, which method of payment would you prefer and why?

Personal presentation

It is possible to tell a lot about a person from the way they look and the way they present themselves. Sometimes these assumptions are accurate; however, sometimes the opposite can also be claimed. All organisations aim to present a professional image and, as a representative of the organisation, all members of staff should aim to do the same.

First impressions are exceptionally important because they tend to last. The customer can also make assumptions from this first impression, for example 'he looks miserable, it can't be much fun here – I'll try somewhere else'. For these reasons, when seeking employment within the leisure and recreation industry or when at work, this first impression must create the desired impression. For example, a member of staff who has regular contact with the public should always be smart and clean; a candidate for interview should be the same. This does not mean that the only suitable dress for interview is a traditional suit. A smart tracksuit is more appropriate dress for a lifeguard. Taking this a step further, it is not essential that a sports coach is 6' 4" with a rippling tummy or lean and toned in designer sports gear.

There are codes of what is considered acceptable.

Appropriate dress

Clothes worn at work should be:

- ✪ *Functional*: **that is, appropriate for carrying out the demands of the job**
- ✪ *Clean*: **coffee stains do not look attractive**
- ✪ *Smart*: **a creased T-shirt looks unprofessional too**
- ✪ *Discreet*: **a thong leotard is fine in an aerobics session but not if the member of staff doubles up for reception duties**

Attitude to employment

Each member of staff is a paid representative of the organisation and should ALWAYS act in a professional manner.

Do:

- ✪ **Be loyal to the organisation**
- ✪ **Follow organisational procedures**
- ✪ **Respect the buildings and equipment where you work**

- **Be friendly and courteous with both colleagues and customers**
- **Separate private and professional life as far as possible**
- **Respect the views of others**
- **Treat both colleagues and customers as you would want to be treated yourself**
- **Be honest and constructive**
- **Ask if unsure**

Don't:

- **Criticise the organisation to or in front of the customer**
- **Discuss confidential details**
- **Argue or swear in front of the customers**
- **Lose your temper at work**
- **Consume alcohol at work**
- **Act in a way that can put ANYONE at risk**

All organisations will have certain expectations of an employee and for an employee to be successful these will need to be met or, where possible, bettered.

Activity 22.17

Visit four leisure and recreation venues. Whilst participating in an activity (so you don't look like you're staring!), note what your first impressions are of a member of staff. Consider their attitude and appearance and what you would do to be a better member of staff. Be constructive and remember: relevant comments only.

Personal and professional development

In today's changing environment, every organisation must constantly be looking to improve and update just to remain competitive. All organisations should aim to maximise the potential of each member of staff, just as each member of staff should aim to do the best they can. This development can be either through formal qualification and training or by informal development, over a period of time, of the individual's personal skills and qualities.

Methods of development

✪ *Off-the-job training*: **This is generally formal training that occurs away from the workplace and is often delivered by an external agency. For example, a day release college course or evening class. Another example can be attending a conference or training day put on by a professional body such as a Pool Plant operator's certificate put on by ILAM. Training tends to concentrate on the technical aspects of the job and product knowledge.**

✪ *On-the-job training*: **This training goes on in the workplace and concentrates more on developing personal skills and knowledge of the organisation as well as technical/product knowledge. For example, developing the self-confidence of a new employee to make presentations to other employees or developing the ability of an employee to make decisions (the right ones too). New employees are often allocated a mentor, who plays an advisory and supporting role in developing the employee. Qualifications can be taken on the job and include National Vocational Qualifications (NVQs). The number of employees receiving on-the-job training is rising. This is because the government supports the NVQ programme, it is cheaper to train a member of staff on the job as opposed to off the job and it is now more widely recognised that training is the way to improve.**

The aim of both methods of development is for the employee to be able to complete their job as effectively as possible.

Types of qualifications

✪ *Vocational qualifications*: **Vocational means workplace and these qualifications aim to prepare an individual for the workplace in** a given industry, for example an **A/VCE in Leisure and Recreation** aims to prepare you for employment in the leisure and recreation industry. These qualifications are often coursework based and aim to be as practical as possible. Other vocational qualifications are **NVQs** and various certificates specific to the workplace such as the **National Pool Lifeguard Award**

○ *Academic qualifications*: **Those that are not specifically related to the workplace. These tend to be more theoretical than practical and are often assessed by an exam. Examples include A level English or a BA in History**

There is some controversy about the comparative value of these two different types of qualifications. It is fair to say that they are different and both have strengths and weaknesses. It is hoped that in the future there will be less of a distinction between vocational and academic qualifications.

Activity 22.18

Visit your local careers office and ask them what qualifications are available to people wanting to work in the leisure and recreation industry.

Have a look at all levels, so GCSEs, Advanced level and above.

Ask your careers service what qualifications you would expect to take once in work.

List the vocational and academic qualifications, how are these split and give your comments.

How do you compare to this list and which qualifications would you like to take?

Activity 22.19

Thinking about what you would be doing at work, with a friend list your own and your friend's strengths and weaknesses. How do you think the strengths can be developed and the weaknesses minimised?

Motivation

People are naturally complex. Everyone is original and has opinions, feelings and beliefs that are unique. As a consequence, everyone has different reasons for choosing to do what they do. Both the employer and the employee need to understand these factors or motives when they affect the workplace. It has been widely documented that if an employee is motivated they are also more productive and so do a better job. The employer must strive to achieve a motivated workforce as the knock-on effect can lead to greater profits.

Many people working in the leisure and recreation industry choose to do so because they have a keen interest in sports. Most people go to work in the first place because they need to earn some money. Behaviour at work can depend very much on the aims of the individual; one person may put in extra hours as a lifeguard because they are saving up for their first car, and another may do so because they are keen to be viewed as the next duty officer. The difficult job is understanding all these individual factors and providing an environment where all can be stimulated as much as possible.

Various theorists have analysed motivation over the past century. Many theories show that motivation can be divided into two areas.

1   **Intrinsic motivators**

2   **Extrinsic motivators**

Intrinsic motivators are those factors that are 'internal' to the individual. Our feelings and emotions influence these factors, which give us internal satisfaction, a warm glow inside and a sense of emotional well-being. Examples may include being awarded greater responsibility, a line manager saying thank you for doing a job well and a respected colleague asking for help and advice.

Extrinsic motivators are those factors that are 'external' to the individual. In other words, things that can be altered or given to an employee. Examples include money and working conditions. Powerful motivators are the possibility of a financial bonus or perhaps a new office with new furniture and administrative assistance.

Both types of motivators are important and influential in producing an environment where employees can flourish and reach their potential. The power of these motivators depends on the individual. The motivators of the individual are also likely to change over time. John, an 18-year-old, was motivated to apply for professional footballer status by the prospect of a career in his favourite sport and at the club he supported so strongly. When John reaches 40 years old he may still be motivated by his love of football but may, for his career to progress, want to move to a different club. He may not do this because his children are settled in their school and his family

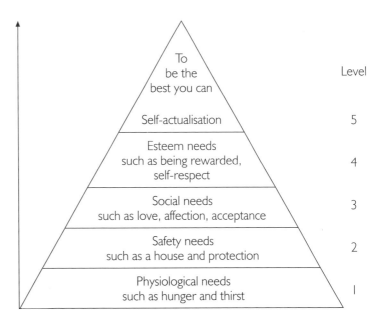

Figure 22.6 *Maslow's hierachy of needs*

is close by! Some individuals are motivated by money, money and money. These types of employees are difficult to motivate, as once they are given one pay rise they want another.

Motivation theory tends to show that, on the whole, intrinsic motivators are the key to attracting a member of staff and then keeping them. The theories show that these motivators are at a higher level. Money and bright new things are fine but they don't tend to give as much satisfaction, in the long term, as praise, trust and responsibility. It is unlikely that the real level of pay an employee receives, or working conditions, will go on improving significantly, year after year. For example, it is difficult to improve the working conditions of an employee once they are in a large new office with all the state-of-the-art equipment.

Abraham Maslow, in 1968, divided motivators into levels (see Figure 22.6) He felt that each level had to be satisfied before it was possible to move on to the next one. For example, no one was likely to think about satisfying a need for a house and security before they had satisfied their need for food and water. These levels can be applied to the workplace and help develop an understanding of why people act the way they do. Some examples include:

- **If a member of staff gets a telephone call to say that they have a burst water pipe at home, they revert from whatever level they are at to the need for security. The need for promotion suddenly seems insignificant to the fact that they may be without a bed for the night**

- **When we are ill everything else in our lives seems irrelevant; we just want to feel better and when we do we start to think**

about other levels of the hierarchy, such as sorting out a gas bill or booking some concert tickets and then going back to work. Our behaviour here is at the base level

✪ **If we have fallen out with a friend or argued with our parents, this can push a member of staff from seeking trust and authority at work to the desire to mend the personal rift**

All of these sorts of incidents happen every day and affect the working lives of millions. The successful employer will look to understand these incidents and work with them as opposed to ignoring them.

Hints and tips

✪ Communicate often and clearly. Offer praise where deserved, say thank you and well done and don't assume it is taken for granted

✪ Allow members of staff to make decisions, let them decide the best way to tackle a job, trust them to complete it successfully. Remember to monitor progress and offer advice (this doesn't mean say what needs to be done). If you give a challenge it is human nature not to want to fail. This is called **empowerment**. An example of this may be letting the centre attendants sort out their own rota. If they know everyone needs to work the same hours and that all opening hours need to be covered, they can sort it out the way that suits them best

✪ If there are a series of repetitive jobs to be completed, try to make sure that each member of staff has a variety of the jobs to do. This will help minimise boredom. For example, instead of the receptionist taking phone calls for 4 hours and the administrative assistant filing for the same period of time, let each do 2 hours on the telephone and 2 hours filing. This is called **job enlargement**

✪ If an employee carries out similar tasks repeatedly, the job can be redesigned to include other tasks of similar responsibility. This variety should help alleviate boredom and so motivate staff. For example, a lifeguard can also supervise a playscheme and supervise the sports hall. The role of the lifeguard can be redesigned so time is spent in all three areas. This is called **job rotation**

✪ Put members of staff into teams and give each team responsibilities. Empower each team to complete the tasks. Team members should develop a sense of loyalty to each other and a sense of belonging. At the end of the task they should enjoy a sense of satisfaction if the task is successful. Examples could include organising the staff Christmas party. This is called **team working**

✪ Study the number of days taken off sick as this can provide a useful measure of staff morale. If days sick are taken consistently in one- or two-day blocks, alarm bells should ring. If a workforce is motivated, on the days when they are tired and 'can't face it', the motivated member of staff will go to work out of loyalty and responsibility, whereas the demotivated and therefore underperforming member of staff will not

- ✪ Where possible, offer flexible working conditions so that the personal aspects of our lives can be accommodated. So if a member of staff needs to go to the dentist or pick up a child from school this can be worked into the schedule and an awkward atmosphere can be prevented

- ✪ Offer staff a telephone so they can make limited and important phone calls from work. In the future we may operate in a 24-hour society but that is not the case now. If a member of staff's hours of work clash with the banks, for example, and they need to make private calls, allow them to do so

- ✪ Acknowledge that we are all different; to some people there are more important things to life than work, and to others work is everything. Neither is right or wrong, just different. A successful employer or manager will be able to understand this

- ✪ Allow and encourage staff to be honest. Acknowledge that staff will be off work from time to time because their child is poorly, for example. Establish a procedure that copes with this so staff do not feel forced to lie and say they are poorly

- ✪ Be friendly; this is enough to help some people enjoy their job and try their best

Activity 22.20

We all do things for different reasons in both our private and working lives; at work two people can both be doing a great job for different reasons. Look at the four situations below and discuss what you think the motivators in each situation are.

1   John is 37. He lives in his own three-bedroomed house with a substantial mortgage. He is married with three young children and is hoping to move from middle to senior management in a large company that makes amusement machines. He is an independent worker who has earned respect. He is full of bright new ideas

2   Sarah is also married. She has a six-year-old daughter. Sarah has a recreation management degree and is working as an administrator at a local school. She is fun-loving and sporty

3   Peter is 62 years old and is considered wealthy. He is the Managing Director of a computer games company. He has no mortgage, runs two luxury cars and enjoys fine food, wine and holidays. He still continues to strive for more and works up to 65 hours per week on a regular basis

4   Jaqui is 18 and works behind the reception in a health club. She has no qualification or any interest in the leisure industry

Activity 22.21

In your class ask everyone to write down the reasons they are motivated to come to study. Then ask what the expected motives will be in their first job in leisure and then in 10 years and 35 years.

★   Compare the results

★   How do motives change?

★   Are there any common motives?

★   Ask your lecturer or teacher what their motives were at these stages and how they have changed

Quality assurance

Please refer to Unit 23 Business systems in the leisure and recreation industry to consider this subject in more detail.

▼ ▼ ▼ ▼ ▼ ▼ ▼ ▼ ▼

Quality assurance
Quality assurance is a series of practices that aim to ensure customer expectations are met

▲ ▲ ▲ ▲ ▲ ▲ ▲ ▲ ▲

Quality assurance became a buzz phrase in the 1990s; it has been increasingly recognised that in order to remain competitive, organisations need to improve customer service in all areas so that the needs of the customer are met and, where possible, exceeded.

In the UK, products have for many years been awarded the British Standards Institution 'kitemark'. This certifies the product has been produced to certain safety standards. This practice has been extended and certification can now be achieved to show an organisation operates with sound working practices. Many of these practices involve human resource management.

The awards available are:

✪ *Investors in People (IIP)*: **This is the most recent quality assurance certification. It is a QA certificate for people at work and is awarded by the Training and Enterprise Councils (TECs). To achieve accreditation an organisation must prove that staff are treated in a fair and positive manner and that appropriate working practices are in place and happening. The TEC, which is independent, usually visits the organisation on a number of occasions, interviewing staff and monitoring current practices in the workplace. When satisfied, the organisation is given accreditation and can use the IIP logo in their advertising and promotions. Standards are monitored and must remain at a satisfactory level to be maintained. Another increasingly popular quality assurance certificate in leisure and recreation is QUEST, which is particularly popular in leisure facilities but has recently been developed to include sports development**

✪ *BS 5750/ISO 9000*: **This is a QA process by which an organisation can show that it complies with quality standards as laid out in BS 5750/ISO 9000. It aims to assure quality for the customer. The organisation has to produce a quality manual listing working practices such as training documentation, the recruitment and selection procedure and after-sales care. Once practices are to the required standard the organisation has achieved 'kitemark status'**

✪ *Professional Body approval*: **These bodies award grades and certificates for meeting certain quality standards. For example, the Institute of Leisure and Amenity Management has a set code of practice that members will be asked to meet**

Activity 22.22

Have a look at the local paper on job night.

★ What percentage of adverts use the IIP symbol?

★ How many of these are in the leisure and recreation industry?

★ Request a recruitment pack from an organisation that has IIP status and one that hasn't. What are the differences between the packs in relation to quality?

Revision questions

1 Define human resources.

2 List three aspects to consider before recruiting a member of staff.

3 State six facts you would expect to see in a job description.

4 What is a person specification?

5 What is the difference between essential and desirable criteria in a person specification?

6 List ten methods of recruitment advertising.

7 How would you decide what method of advertising to use?

8 Where would you advertise for a Director of Leisure paid at £42,000?

9 How would you attract a trainee customer services manager to apply for a vacancy?

10 When you are shortlisting, name two pieces of recruitment documentation to which you need to refer.

11 State six aspects you would expect to be covered in a letter inviting candidates to interview.

12 What do you understand by the term equal opportunity?

13 What is an open question?

14 What is a closed question?

15 How long should an informal induction process last?

16 Why should an organisation be interested in developing staff?

17 Describe the following methods of employment:
- ✪ Full time
- ✪ Contracted
- ✪ Seasonal

18 Describe the following methods of payment:
- ✪ Piece rate
- ✪ Time rate
- ✪ Performance-related pay

19 Who collects income tax?

20 What do National Insurance contributions pay for?

21 What does IIP stand for?

22 What is quality assurance?

23 How often should an appraisal be conducted?

24 State two aims of an appraisal.

25 Give three examples of intrinsic motivators.

26 Give three examples of extrinsic motivators.

27 What methods can managers at a holiday camp use to increase motivation within the workforce?

28 Define the terms job enlargement and job enrichment.

Assessment activity

▶ **BACKGROUND**

Football is big business! Some football teams have floated on the stock exchange, some have links with other sporting and business interests, and some operate their own radio and television channels.

Your football team wants to be the best both on and off the pitch. In order to achieve this they are going to appoint a personnel manager to ensure the human resources of the football club are maximised.

You are that person and you have the ideal working conditions. You have been allocated a generous budget, plenty of administrative support and a fair deadline to complete your task.

▶ **TASKS**

1   Discuss the various organisational structures that can be applied to the football club. Choose the one that you feel suits best and give reasons for your choice

2   Establish a corporate recruitment process that reflects the image of market leaders

3   Your team needs staff development in order to interview and select the 'right candidate for the right job'. Prepare a staff training session which includes role-playing

4   Finally, produce a staff handbook that will help members of your team to understand the day-to-day operational aspects of the football club. Include such aspects as understanding your pay slip, time sheets, disciplinary procedures, and maternity, paternity and sick pay

Remember:

★   Be creative and professional, you need to create the right image

★   Some of the staff will be reading this and feel it is change just for the sake of it. Convince them it is not

Business systems in the leisure and recreation industry

23

Objectives

- **Learn about the business systems used in the leisure and recreation industry**
- **Understand how these systems work**
- **Investigate the evaluation of business systems and methods**
- **Learn how the quality of business systems is measured**

All leisure and recreation organisations, whether commercial or in the public or voluntary sector, rely on systems to operate their enterprises efficiently and effectively. With the rapid growth in new technologies, many business systems used in the leisure and recreation industry are now electronic or computer based, although paper-based systems still have an important role to play. This unit introduces you to the wide range of business systems available to organisations in leisure and recreation, including systems for customers, staff, financial accounting, and health, safety and security. Anybody hoping to work in the leisure and recreation industry needs to understand how these systems work, since they are likely to form a large part of a new entrant's day-to-day responsibilities. You will also investigate the evaluation of business systems and methods, as well as learning about how the quality of business systems is measured.

To get the full picture, read this unit alongside Unit 2 Safe working practices.

This unit is divided into eight main areas:

1 **Business systems**

2 **Evaluating suitable business systems and methods**

3 **How the quality of business systems is measured**

4 **Systems for customers**

5 **Systems for staff**

6 **Systems for financial accounting**

7 **Systems for health, safety and security**

8 **Methods used to operate business systems**

At the beginning of each of these sections you will see a list of key topics to help you fully understand what you need to learn.

Business systems

Key topics in this section

- **Introduction – what are business systems?**
- **Functions of business systems**

Introduction – what are business systems?

It is important for leisure and recreation organisations to have operating systems that are effective, reliable and efficient. Any system that supports an organisation in achieving its business objectives can be considered a 'business system', for example:

- **The procedures that are followed for handling customer complaints**
- **The process by which services are sold to customers**
- **The techniques that are used to monitor sales income and costs**
- **The procedure that is followed in a visitor attraction to ensure high standards of health, safety and security**
- **The processes that are followed in designing a new promotions brochure**

Since no two leisure and recreation organisations operate in exactly the same way, it follows that a business system will be unique to an individual organisation. There are, however, similarities in systems across organisations, e.g. two local authority leisure facilities may use the same accounting software to manage their finances, but the results will be specific to each individual business.

There is a wide range of business systems used in the leisure and recreation industry, which can be categorised as follows:

- *Administration systems*: **These are designed to ensure the smooth running of an organisation, e.g. payroll, payments to suppliers, ordering of supplies**
- *Communication systems*: **These are concerned with dealing with people inside and outside an organisation, e.g. handling customer complaints, inter-departmental meetings, telephone systems**

✪ *Information processing systems*: **These are designed to make sure that information is made available speedily and accurately, e.g. a customer database, spreadsheets showing sales and expenditure forecasts, an organisation's Internet site**

Functions of business systems

Leisure and recreation organisations use a number of business systems on a day-to-day basis. These systems have three basic functions:

1 **To conduct business on a regular basis, e.g. a booking system for an aerobics class**

2 **To manage information and maintain records, e.g. accounts or customer records**

3 **To support management decision taking, e.g. planning the future direction of a business or forecasting sales for future months and years**

Such systems influence all aspects of an organisation's operation, from legal requirements and financial planning, to customer service, sales and marketing. Above all, a business system will help an organisation achieve its objective, whether this is maximising profits or meeting wider social or community aims.

Activity 23.1

Working with a colleague, draw up a list of the business systems you would expect to see in a typical health and fitness club, under the following headings:

1 Administration systems

2 Communication systems

3 Information processing systems

Against each of your systems (e.g. taking payments, interviewing staff, producing accounts), write down any items of equipment associated with the system, e.g. computer, mobile telephone.

The concept of 'front office' and 'back office'

It is common for leisure and recreation organisations to divide their business functions into 'front office' and 'back office', developing systems in support of each. In simple terms, the 'front office' refers to the reception area of any leisure and recreation facility, the point at which the customer first makes contact with the organisation. The 'back office' refers to the organisation's functions that take place behind the scenes, for example accounting, maintenance and stock control, which the customer is unlikely to be aware of. There must always be a strong link between front and back offices for the organisation's business systems to be truly effective; for example, when a customer books an aerobics class (the 'front office'), information must be conveyed, possibly manually but more likely via a computer system, to the other functions and personnel that need to know, such as the instructor, accounts, memberships, marketing.

The concept of front and back office is widespread in the leisure and recreation industry. Leisure and sports centres operate on this basis, as do visitor attractions, transport companies, catering outlets, entertainment venues and tourist information centres. The division into front and back office allows management to focus resources on particular functions and train staff in these areas. The selection and training of staff to work in the 'front office' is particularly important, since it provides the visitor with his or her first impressions of the organisation. Staff with an understanding of customer needs and expectations and who are committed to providing excellence in customer service should be chosen to work in this high profile area. The environment in which the 'front office' is positioned also needs to be carefully planned, and should provide a clean, warm, efficient, welcoming and friendly atmosphere.

Activity 23.2

While on work experience, list the front office and back office functions that take place in the organisation. Explain the linkages between the two.

Evaluating suitable business systems and methods

Key topics in this section

● **Introduction**
● **Factors to be considered when evaluating business systems**

Introduction

In the leisure and recreation industry, nothing stays the same for long! Organisations, both large and small, constantly monitor their activities to make sure that their business systems remain effective. Evaluation of a business system will indicate any strengths and weaknesses; it is part of management's role in an organisation to reduce weaknesses to a minimum while at the same time building on the strengths of the business systems. Many organisations develop measures of effectiveness to help with the evaluation. Depending on the size of the leisure and recreation organisation, the measures may be carried out by staff from different departments. If this is the case, it is important that the evaluation of the business systems is coordinated throughout the organisation, ideally under one senior member of staff with responsibility for overall quality systems and standards.

Factors to be considered when evaluating business systems

Leisure and recreation organisations investigate a variety of factors when evaluating their business systems, including:

✪ *Value for money*: **All leisure and recreation organisations must strive to make the best use of their available financial resources by choosing business systems that offer the best value for money**

✪ *Fitness for purpose*: **This means choosing a business system that does what it is designed to do! All too often, particularly with computers, leisure and recreation organisations are persuaded to buy systems that are not always fit for purpose**

✪ *Accuracy*: **Systems must offer high levels of accuracy, especially when dealing with finances, e.g. payroll systems for staff salaries and wages, accounts software**

- ✪ *Efficiency*: **Any business system must be efficient, in terms of both the organisation's and its customers' needs, e.g. in the health and fitness industry, a central office that deals with customers' membership details must be able to liaise effectively with the host health and fitness club**

- ✪ *Ease of use*: **It is little use having a state-of-the-art business system if nobody knows how to use it! The skill in designing business systems, whether computer based, electronic or paper based, is to keep things simple**

- ✪ *Security*: **All business systems need to be secure, particularly those dealing with sensitive information, e.g. sales figures, personnel records, customer databases**

- ✪ *Legal requirements*: **Depending on the nature of the leisure and recreation organisation, business systems may have to comply with a variety of legal requirements, e.g. employment legislation, health and safety regulations, publication of accounts, the Data Protection Act (see page 382)**

How the quality of business systems is measured

- ● **Introduction – quality in business systems**
- ● **Quality systems concerned with the whole organisation**
- ● **Quality systems used in specific sectors of the leisure and recreation industry**

Introduction – quality in business systems

There is no doubt that 'quality' is one of the 'buzz words' in leisure and recreation in the new millennium. All sorts of leisure and recreation organisations, be they in the private, public or voluntary sectors, have pledged their commitment to introducing or enhancing the quality of the products, services and facilities they offer their customers. In an increasingly competitive environment, it makes good business sense to review an organisation's systems to see if any improvements can be made to the levels of customer service and quality of products on offer.

Some leisure and recreation organisations have sought external recognition of their activities, either by gaining certification under the British Standard (BS) 5750 (see page 375), now more generally referred to as ISO 9000 or BS EN ISO 9000, or by implementing the 'Investors in People' initiative (see page 374).

The largest Quality Assurance scheme used within the leisure and recreation industry is QUEST. This process uses extensive self-assessment, internal and external assessment against agreed industry benchmarks and criteria. Once achieved, mystery visits and further assessment and planning are required in order to maintain the QUEST status. A facility/unit may use the QUEST logo as a kitemark of quality. There are a number of areas of leisure and recreation where QUEST is useful. Sports development is a more recent area.

Others operate very well without the need to register formally for recognition, based on the fact that management has practised a customer-centred approach for many years. Whether or not external recognition is sought, the main purpose of implementing quality standards in leisure and recreation is just the same, namely to ensure that all business systems are fully documented and audited, so as to ensure high standards of quality at all times.

Carry out some research on local and national leisure and recreation organisations to find out what policies they have on quality in their organisations.

What do we mean by 'quality'?

In the leisure and recreation industry, quality is synonymous with satisfying customer needs; in other words, the introduction of any quality system or set of quality standards into an organisation must place the customer as the focus of all activity. This is borne out by the International Standards Organisation (ISO), which defines quality as:

The totality of features and characteristics of a product or service that bear on its ability to satisfy stated or implied needs.

Looking at this definition in a little more detail, it assumes that an organisation will have knowledge of the needs of its customers. You will have learned from units on your course that all leisure and recreation organisations have a wide range of customers, all with varying needs. Detailed market research is needed to identify customers and their needs, before the specific features and characteristics of products and services can be developed.

Quality systems concerned with the whole organisation

Quality systems concerned with the whole organisation include:

✪ **Quality control and quality management**
✪ **Total quality management (TQM)**
✪ **Investors in People (IIP)**
✪ **BS 5750/ISO 9000**

We will now look at each of these in greater detail.

Quality control and quality management

Quality control is concerned with monitoring product and service quality by identifying and addressing quality problems through checking and inspection. A health and fitness club will regularly invite feedback from customers on the quality of facilities, staff, coaching and activities, by carrying out questionnaire surveys and focus groups. Quality management, on the other hand, is a wider concept that attempts to make sure that standards of product and service quality are right first time every time.

Total quality management (TQM)

While quality control and quality management are important concepts, the development of total quality management (TQM) takes quality assurance one stage further by establishing a management philosophy and systems throughout an organisation, which recognise that customer needs and the achievement of organisational objectives are inseparable. The development of TQM in an organisation is a longer-term goal when compared to the introduction of a quality standards system such as BS EN ISO 9000 (see below); some would say that the implementation of BS EN ISO 9000 is merely a step (albeit a large step) along the road to total quality management.

Those who advocate a TQM approach consider that it has a number of benefits to any leisure and recreation organisation, including:

- ✪ **Increased profitability**
- ✪ **Increased competitiveness**
- ✪ **Closer relationships with customers**
- ✪ **Committed management and staff**
- ✪ **Closer relationships with suppliers and contractors**
- ✪ **Improved measurement of quality performance**
- ✪ **Improved decision making by management**

To be successful, the implementation of a TQM culture in an organisation will necessitate increased resources and prolonged staff training and management commitment.

Investors in People (IIP)

Investors in People is the national quality standard in the UK for effective investment in the training and development of people to achieve organisational objectives. Organisations, large and small, in all sectors of the economy, have achieved the standard or are working towards Investors in People. The standard provides a framework for improving business performance and competitiveness, through a planned approach to setting and communicating objectives and developing people to meet these goals. In other words, what people can do and are motivated to do in an organisation matches what the organisation needs them to do to be successful.

The Investors in People standard is a cyclical process based on four principles:

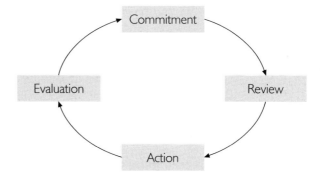

Figure 23.1   *The key principles of the Investors in People standard*

1   *Commitment*: **to develop all employees to achieve organisational goals and objectives**

2   *Review*: **of training and development needs regularly in the context of the organisation**

3   *Action*: **to meet identified training and development needs throughout people's employment**

4   *Evaluation*: **of the outcomes of training and development for individuals and the organisation, as a basis for continuous improvement**

These principles are summarised in the diagram shown in Figure 23.1.

The practical benefits of working towards and achieving a standard such as Investors in People include:

✪ **Reduced costs and wastage**

✪ **Improved productivity and profitability**

✪ **Enhanced product and service quality**

✪ **Improved staff motivation**

✪ **Enhanced customer satisfaction**

✪ **Public recognition**

✪ **Competitive advantage**

To become an Investor in People, everyone working for an organisation must be committed to achieving the standard; senior management, union representatives and all employee groups must play an active part in the process. The length of time needed to achieve the standard ranges between six and eighteen months, depending on the size of the task.

BS 5750/ISO 9000

This is a quality standard (also known as BS EN ISO 9000) that aims to ensure consistently high levels of product and service delivery in an organisation. Initially developed for manufacturing industry, this British Standard (BS) is now increasingly applied to service industries, including leisure and recreation.

The decision by an organisation to introduce a quality standard such as BS 5750/ISO 9000 should not be entered into lightly. It should be seen as a long-term initiative, rather than a process that will bring quick rewards. The comprehensive nature of such a standard will focus on:

✪ **Determining the needs of the customer**
✪ **Defining the quality of service required to meet these needs**
✪ **Planning how the level of service will be delivered**
✪ **Deciding who will deliver the agreed level of service and when**
✪ **Delivering the level of service to the customer**
✪ **Monitoring to ensure that the agreed level of service has been achieved**

The aim with a quality assurance system such as BS 5750/ISO 9000 is to ensure consistent levels of service delivery. Every employee, whether senior management, full-time or part-time staff, has a role to play in making sure that the service is delivered right first time every time. BS 5750/ISO 9000 requires the pulling together of the various strands of a leisure and recreation operation into one 'book of rules'. It will involve the re-examination of what is already written down and committing to paper that which is operated 'by custom and practice'. Figure 23.2 shows the five steps to implementing a quality standards system such as BS 5750/ISO 9000.

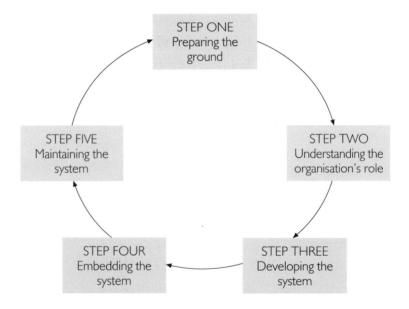

Figure 23.2 *The five steps in implementing a quality standards system*

Step one involves giving employees an understanding of the importance of quality and customer service, while at the same time undertaking market research to determine customer needs and requirements. Step two, understanding the organisation's role, tries to answer such questions as 'why is the job done?', 'where is the job done?', 'who does what and why?', and 'when is the job done?'. Once this understanding has been achieved, the job of documenting and developing the system can begin (step three). This may start with the preparation of straightforward operations manuals and ultimately develop into a full quality system for which external certification may be sought. Step four, embedding the system, will involve further training and clarification of roles, together with a clear explanation of the procedures and practices of all employees. Whether or not external certification is being sought, it is good practice to set up internal monitoring procedures to make sure that the system is maintained, updated and amended.

Quality systems used in specific sectors of the leisure and recreation industry

Specific sectors of the leisure and recreation industry have developed quality systems to meet their own specific circumstances. These include:

- ✪ *Charter Marks*: **The government introduced a series of Charter Marks in the 1990s for public sector organisations, including local authority leisure and recreation departments that provide excellent service to their customers**

- ✪ *Industry award schemes*: **Commercial organisations sometimes establish award schemes to reward their best employees or favourite companies, e.g. QUEST**

- ✪ *Customer charters*: **Organisations that are committed to giving their customers the best possible products and service sometimes produce a customer charter to demonstrate their commitment**

Systems for customers

key topics in this section

- **Introduction**
- **Customer records**
- **Booking/reservation systems**
- **Customer complaints and feedback**
- **Customer correspondence, communication and information**

Introduction

In the leisure and recreation industry customers are the most important part of any organisation. Put simply, without customers there would be no business! It follows, therefore, that all leisure and recreation organisations must have excellent business systems in place to be able to offer customers a high standard of service, in such areas as

- ✪ **Customer records**
- ✪ **Booking/reservation/membership systems**
- ✪ **Customer complaints and feedback**
- ✪ **Customer correspondence**

Each of these topics is covered in greater detail in the next sections of this unit.

Customer records

An effective leisure and recreation organisation must have detailed information about its customers in order to be able to provide them with the facilities and services they want, and to do so with attention to their desire for a good standard of customer service. A computerised business system is invaluable for providing such information on customers and can help highlight under-exploited opportunities or areas of an organisation that need more promotion. A theatre's database, for example, may indicate that residents of a particular area of a city do not visit the theatre in anything like the same proportions as those who live in other areas. The management may investigate why this is so, and may feel it worthwhile to mount a publicity campaign in the under-represented area in order to increase attendance.

Booking/reservation systems

Bookings and reservation systems used in leisure and recreation can be either manual or computerised. Many organisations that formerly used manual systems have transferred their data onto computers, because of the greater speed and storage capacity they offer. If we think of the example of a computerised booking system in a hotel's fitness suite, it will need to be able to handle a range of different types of bookings, including bookings from individuals and club bookings, which may be in advance or on a casual admission basis. Hire of equipment and bookings for particular facilities, e.g. pool and fitness equipment, will also be logged into the computer.

Smaller leisure and recreation operators may choose to adopt a manual system that meets their particular needs. Bookings for a variety of leisure and recreation products and services can now be made 'online' using the Internet.

Activity 23.4

While on work experience, carry out an in-depth investigation of the operation of your placement's booking/reservation system(s) and make suggestions for improvements.

Customer complaints and feedback

Even organisations with the highest standards of customer service will have to deal with customer complaints from time to time. Leisure and recreation organisations must have systems in place to handle complaints efficiently, with all members of staff fully trained to deal with difficult situations. You will remember that it is important to stay calm when handling a customer's complaint and to seek help if a situation begins to get out of hand.

Feedback from customers on their attitudes to a particular leisure and recreation organisation or product can be gathered either informally or formally. Informal feedback is often spontaneous, making it just as valuable as information that is given in a more formal manner. Indeed, many would say that a customer is more likely to reveal his or her true feelings and attitudes in an unprompted chat with a member of staff, than when that same member of staff is carrying out a questionnaire survey of users. Informal feedback can take many forms, including:

- ✪ **A remark to a member of staff about the poor standard of the food in a restaurant**
- ✪ **A member of staff overhearing customers praising the standard of service received at a coaching course**
- ✪ **A child heard complaining to his father about the length of time they are having to queue for a ride on a flume in a leisure pool**

It is important that management establish a system by which both formal and informal feedback is collected and monitored. Surveys, questionnaire interviews, observation and customer comment cards are just a few of the techniques that can be used. We are all well aware of the influence that unhappy customers can have on the image of an organisation and thereby its success. We all like to talk about our experiences, which, if negative, can spread very quickly by 'word of mouth'. This powerful mechanism can also be beneficial for those organisations that have provided an excellent standard of service.

Many leisure and recreation operators now have regular staff meetings at which employees are invited to share any informal feedback that they have picked up. They are also encouraged to record comments from customers on specially designed feedback forms, so that management can monitor the situation to see if corrective action is needed in any areas.

Customer correspondence, communication and information

When communicating with customers, it is important to have in place business systems that offer a speedy and reliable service. Whether communication is by letter, telephone, fax or e-mail, customers expect a response within a reasonable period of time. A key point is always to do what you have told a customer you will do! So if you have promised to return a telephone call or send a brochure, for example, you must make sure that it is done.

Systems for staff

Key topics in this section

- **Introduction**
- **Work records**
- **Recruitment and selection**
- **Personnel records**
- **Disciplinary and grievance**
- **Appraisal and staff development**
- **Induction and training**
- **Consultation and communication**
- **The Data Protection Act**

Introduction

In large leisure and recreation organisations, systems for dealing with staff matters are usually handled by the personnel or human resources (HR) department (Unit 22 Human resources in the leisure and recreation industry has more detail on HR systems and procedures). Regardless of the size of an organisation, it will need to carry out structured procedures for the appointment of staff, their training, appraisal and welfare while at work. These procedures will vary between organisations, but are likely to focus on:

- ✪ *Work records*: **e.g. job title, grade, holiday entitlement and salary/wages structure for staff in the organisation**
- ✪ *Recruitment and selection*: **e.g. interview guidelines, screening procedures**
- ✪ *Personnel records*: **e.g. accident and sickness records, references, personal details such as address, date of birth, bank account number**
- ✪ *Disciplinary and grievance*: **e.g. procedures for disciplining staff and records of staff interviews concerning grievances**
- ✪ *Appraisal and staff development*: **e.g. records of any staff appraisal interviews and action plans**
- ✪ *Induction and training*: **e.g. systems for inducting new staff and procedures for further staff training**

✪ *Consultation and communication*: **e.g. copies of all communication between members of staff and the organisation**

In smaller leisure and recreation organisations, information on employees may be stored and updated manually. If only a small number of staff are employed, this system will prove to be quite adequate. Larger organisations, however, are likely to use a computerised personnel records system, with the benefits of greater storage capacity, speed of use and accessibility to many staff at the same time. Information on employees that is held on computer, however, does fall within the scope of the Data Protection Act 1984 and 1998, which provides new rights for individuals and demands good practice from those who hold personal data on individuals. We look at the Act in more detail in the next section of this unit.

The Data Protection Act 1984 and 1998

Since 10 May 1986, all organisations that hold personal data about individuals on automated systems have been required to register with the Data Protection Registrar and to comply with the Data Protection Act (DPA). The exact definition of an 'automated system' is open to debate, but in general terms, information held on computer falls within the scope of the Act and, under the terms of the 1984 Act, that which is processed manually does not. Indeed, some organisations choose to store certain data on manual systems in order that it is not covered by the DPA. However, the 1998 Data Protection Act widens the scope of the 1984 Act by stating that a significant amount of data held manually is now covered within the legislation. The Act seeks to regulate the way in which data is gathered, stored and disclosed to third parties.

The 1984 Act established eight Data Protection Principles with which data users must comply (data users are defined as individuals, corporations or other agencies that control the automatic processing of data). The eight principles, which in reality are a set of points of good practice to which data users should aspire, are as follows:

1   **That the information held on computer shall be obtained and processed fairly and lawfully. Data would be said to have been obtained unfairly if the provider was deceived or misled about the purpose for which the information was being obtained**

2   **That personal data shall be held only for one or more specified and lawful purposes. A contravention of this particular principle would be, for example, when an**

organisation holds personal information for staff training purposes but chooses to use it for the selection of staff for redundancy

3   That data shall not be disclosed to persons other than those named in the registration document, nor for any other purpose than that registered under the Act. Health and fitness facilities, for example, which collect information on their customers to offer them discounted membership packages, cannot then sell the data to another company without contravening this principle

4   That personal data held for any purpose or purposes shall be adequate, relevant and not excessive in relation to the registered purpose. An organisation that holds data unrelated to the purpose for which it is registered or is clearly holding far more than is needed to satisfy the purpose, will be in breach of this principle

5   That personal data shall be accurate and updated as and when necessary. If an organisation, for example, holds a list of customers who have exceeded their annual credit limit, but the organisation makes no attempt to update the list when further payments are made, it is likely to be considered as having contravened this principle

6   That personal information held for any purpose or purposes shall not be kept for longer than is necessary. For example, a travel agency that holds a prize draw and uses a computer to store the names and addresses of those entering should destroy this data at the end of the promotion

7   That an individual shall be entitled, at reasonable intervals and without undue delay or expense, to know whether information is held on him or her and to have access to any data that does exist; also to have any data corrected or erased as appropriate

8   That the data user shall take reasonable security measures to guard against unauthorised access to, alteration, disclosure, accidental loss or destruction of the personal data

Under the Act, individuals who have data held on them have a range of rights in civil law, including:

✪ **Rights of access to the data**

✪ **Rights to compensation for inaccuracy of data**

✪ **Rights to compensation for loss, destruction or unauthorised disclosure of data**

✪ **Rights to apply to have any inaccuracies in the data rectified and, in certain circumstances, rights to have the information erased**

New Data Protection legislation came into force on 1 March 2000 with the implementation of the Data Protection Act 1998, which updates and reinforces the Data Protection Principles established in the 1984 Act.

Systems for financial accounting

Key topics in this section

- **Sales records**
- **Stock control and purchasing**
- **Staff payroll systems**
- **Customer accounts**
- **Customer payment**

Sales records

Accurate recording of sales volumes and sales revenue is an essential component of an effective financial system. As we saw in Unit 21 Financial planning and control, managing cash flow is vital to the success of many leisure and recreation organisations. Systems for recording sales can be manual but are increasingly computer-based nowadays.

Stock control and purchasing

Although leisure and recreation is a service industry, providing 'experiences' rather than 'products', there are a number of areas where it is necessary to undertake some form of stock control. These include:

- **Catering outlets**
- **Bars**
- **Retail units**

Leisure and recreation facilities often generate healthy extra revenue, sometimes known as 'secondary spend', from the sale of food, drinks, souvenirs, equipment and clothing, all of which will need careful control of stock. Stock control is a broad term, covering:

- **Storage**
- **Recording of stock levels**
- **Stocktaking**
- **Withdrawing stock**

Careful attention to stock control is particularly important in the case of food, which will deteriorate in quality if not stored in the right conditions. Holding too much stock of any sort is wasteful, since it ties up money unnecessarily and takes up valuable space. Records will be needed for all receipts of stock and stock issues.

Staff payroll systems

It is a fact of life that everybody expects and wants to be paid on time! Leisure and recreation organisations need to operate efficient payroll systems to keep their staff happy. It is more and more common for payroll to be a computer-based operation in the leisure and recreation industry, with software automatically calculating deductions for tax and National Insurance contributions.

Customer accounts

Accuracy is important when establishing a system for monitoring customer accounts. A computer-based system will automatically print invoices and payment reminder letters when a period of credit is exceeded.

Customer payment

Cash is the lifeblood of any leisure and recreation organisation. As such, it requires very strict control to record its movement through the organisation and to provide a check against negligence and fraud. It is essential that all members of staff are aware of the importance of cash, and that money, in its various forms, is credited to the organisation's bank account with safety and without any undue delay. A daily receipts summary will help keep track of cash takings.

The 'cash' received by the leisure centre will not consist only of coins and notes. Most leisure and recreation businesses will receive payment by one or more of the following methods:

- **Bank notes and coins**
- **Cheques and postal orders**
- **Credit cards, debit cards and charge cards**
- **Direct debits and standing orders**
- **Banker's drafts and certified cheques**

Although it is becoming a little unfashionable to carry coins and notes, there are still a lot of people who wouldn't think of using anything else. Cash is the main payment method in many leisure and recreation facilities, such as visitor attractions, leisure centres, catering outlets and sports venues. It is usual practice to issue a receipt immediately for cash transactions, which acts as proof of purchase. Cash paid into a bank account does not need 'clearing' and is immediately credited to the organisation's account.

Accepting cheques is a very common method of payment in many leisure and recreation organisations. Once paid into a bank account, it will take a minimum of three working days for the cheque to be processed, during which time it remains 'uncleared'; clearing is the process of passing the cheque to the customer's bank, debiting their account and crediting your own. Staff should always ask for a cheque guarantee card to be presented; most will honour cheques up to the value of £50, although it is becoming increasingly common to see £100 cheque guarantee cards in use. Cheques for values in excess of that quoted on the card should not normally be accepted; it is safer to ask the customer to provide another form of payment.

Credit cards are also widely used. The two most common cards in use in Britain are Mastercard and Visa, used on a whole range of credit cards offered by banks, building societies and even car manufacturers (Vauxhall and Ford have recently introduced credit cards). For the customer, credit cards are a very convenient way of making payment, since they can be used for postal, Internet and telephone bookings, as well as payment in person. They usually offer an interest-free period subject to certain conditions. Debit cards, such as Switch and Delta, should not be confused with credit cards, since they have a completely different function. A debit card is used in place of a cheque, with the holder's bank accounts being debited within three working days. Charge cards, such as American Express and Diners Club, unlike credit cards offer no extended credit facility. Their use in leisure and recreation facilities is mainly by business and corporate customers.

A banker's draft or certified cheque will be used when payment is required immediately and there is no time to go through the normal clearing process. Some people will pay a large amount by a certified cheque issued by their building society. Banker's drafts are an easy way of accepting payment in a foreign currency.

Travellers' cheques may be used for payment in leisure and recreation facilities by overseas visitors. Care should be taken to ensure that the cheques are not already countersigned before they are presented for payment.

Whichever method of payment is accepted, and depending on the policy of the individual organisation, the stages that the payment will go through are as follows:

1   **Payment received by the leisure facility**

2   **Receipt issued to customer**

3   Entry made on daily cash summary sheet

4   Receipts and summary sheets reconciled

5   Bank paying in slips completed

6   Monies paid into the bank account

7   Paying in slips stamped by bank

Systems for health, safety and security

Key topics in this section

- **Introduction**
- **Complying with relevant legislation**
- **Emergency procedures**
- **First aid provision**
- **Security of people and premises**
- **Reporting systems**

Introduction

A basic function of all organisations involved with the leisure and recreation industry is to provide a safe and secure environment for staff to work in, and for visitors to enjoy. The wide-ranging nature of leisure and recreation means that each industry sector has its own particular requirements in terms of systems for health, safety and security. For example:

- ✪ **Many indoor entertainment complexes are very large and often cater for the needs of hundreds, if not thousands, of people at any one time. Cinemas, theatres, sports stadia and indoor arenas must put health and safety at the top of their list of priorities**
- ✪ **The managers and staff of facilities have a number of health and safety concerns that must be addressed, e.g. the storage and handling of food, and ensuring safe means of escape in case of fire**
- ✪ **Visitor attractions, especially theme parks with complex 'rides', have to be aware of dangers to both staff and visitors from machinery and electrical installations**
- ✪ **Holiday centres will offer a range of sports activities that can, if not properly supervised, expose the participants and spectators to potential risks. Centres that offer swimming and other water-based attractions need to be especially aware of health and safety requirements**
- ✪ **Outdoor activity centres that cater for the needs of both young and old must ensure that staff are fully trained in**

supervising potentially dangerous activities, such as rock-climbing, watersports and fell-walking

Health and safety is not just the concern of the private sector in leisure and recreation; it is just as applicable to both the public and voluntary sectors, as this extract from the *National Trust Handbook* indicates:

> The Trust endeavours to provide a healthy and safe environment for visitors at its properties as far as is reasonably practicable, and to ensure that the activities of its staff and contractors working on Trust properties do not in any way jeopardise the health and safety of visitors. You can help the Trust by observing all notices and signs relating to this subject during your visit, by following any instructions given by Trust staff, by ensuring that children are properly supervised and by wearing appropriate clothing and footwear at outdoor properties.

Activity 23.5

While on work experience, carry out an investigation into the health, safety and security policies of your placement agency and list the ways in which the policies are put into practice.

Complying with relevant legislation

There is a variety of legislation that imposes certain duties on the management and staff of leisure facilities in relation to health and safety issues. For anybody considering working in, or already involved with, the leisure and recreation industry at whatever level, it is important to be aware of the ever-increasing impact of health and safety legislation.

To begin with, there is a common law duty of care, under which each citizen owes a duty to all others who may be affected by his or her activities. If a person takes insufficient care in relation to another citizen, and that person suffers damage as a result, the injured party may begin an action in the civil court to reclaim damages. However, this civil law only comes into action after damage has been suffered. Although the outcomes of civil cases have given the courts many opportunities to create precedents that guide the conduct of similar occurrences in the future, the civil law has always been considered an inappropriate instrument in the area of accident prevention. The advent of the Health and Safety at Work, etc. Act 1974 changed all this.

Health and Safety at Work, etc. Act 1974

The Health and Safety at Work, etc. Act (HSW Act) was introduced to provide the legislative framework to promote, stimulate and encourage high standards of health and safety at work.

Contents of the Act

The HSW Act is an enabling measure superimposed over existing health and safety legislation. In addition to placing duties of a general nature on employers, manufacturers, employees, the self-employed and others, the Act provides wide powers for the making of regulations. Part 1 of the Act, the part that concerns leisure and recreation organisations the most, aims to:

- **Secure the health, safety and welfare of people at work**
- **Protect other people against risks to health or safety arising from the activities of people at work**
- **Control the storage and use of dangerous substances, e.g. chemicals, and preventing their unlawful use**
- **Control the emission into the atmosphere of noxious or offensive substances from premises**

Scope of the Act

All 'persons at work', whether employees, employers or self-employed, are covered by the Act, with the exception of domestic servants in private households. About 8 million people who were not covered by previous health and safety legislation, such as the self-employed and those employed in education, health services, the leisure and recreation industries and in some parts of the transport industry, are now protected.

The HSW Act aims to gradually replace existing health and safety requirements by revised and updated provisions, which take the form of regulations and approved codes of practice prepared in consultation with industry. Regulations relating to health and safety matters are usually made by the appropriate government minister on the advice of the Health and Safety Commission. In reality, most regulations are made by the Secretary of State for Employment. Codes of practice have a special legal status. Although they are not statutory requirements, they may be used in criminal proceedings on health and safety issues, as evidence that the statutory requirements have been contravened.

Duties of employers

It is the duty of every employer to safeguard, so far as is reasonably practicable, the health, safety and welfare of all those in his or her employment. This duty is extended to others who may be affected by the operation of the facility, e.g. contractors, visitors and members of the general public. In practice the employer must have specific regard for the following:

1 **To provide plant and equipment that is not a risk to health**

2 **To ensure that work systems and practices are safe**

3 **To ensure that the work environment is regularly monitored in respect of health and safety requirements**

4 **To provide safe storage for substances that could pose a threat to safety and ensure their safe use**

5 **To provide a written statement of safety policy and bring it to the notice of employees (applies only to those employing five or more staff)**

6 **To provide adequate information and training for all staff in matters relating to health and safety**

Duties of employees

Employees have a duty under the HSW Act to:

✪ **Take reasonable care to avoid injury to themselves or to others by their work activities**

✪ **To cooperate with their employers and other agencies to ensure that the requirements of the Act are carried out**

✪ **Not to interfere with or misuse anything provided to protect their health, safety and welfare under the Act**

Enforcement of the HSW Act

The Act established the Health and Safety Commission (HSC) and the Health and Safety Executive (HSE) both to publicise the need for safety at work and to begin prosecutions for breaches of the act. The HSC is responsible to the Secretary of State for Employment for taking the necessary steps to secure the health, welfare and safety of people at work and also to protect the public against risks to health and safety arising out of a work situation. The HSE is the operating arm of the HSC and is responsible for enforcing the legislation under the HSW Act. HSE appoints and controls teams of inspectors who have wide powers to enter premises and examine records and staff to check that the Act is being complied with. Inspectors can also make enquiries into accidents that have occurred at places of employment. This covers accidents, not only to employees themselves, but also to visitors and would include, for example, people using sports centres and other leisure and tourism facilities.

If an inspector discovers a contravention of one of the provisions of the HSW Act or any of the earlier legislation that is still in force, he or she can take one of several courses of action:

1   The inspector can issue a prohibition notice if there is a high risk of serious personal injury. This effectively stops the activity in question until the specified action to remedy the situation has been completed. The notice can be served either on the person undertaking the activity or the person in control of it

2   An alternative course of action would be to issue an improvement notice if there is a contravention of any of the requirements of the Act. This notice gives a time limit for compliance with the relevant contravention

3   Over and above the issuing of either a prohibition notice, an improvement notice or both, any person found contravening the Act or any of its regulations may be prosecuted

4   The inspector has powers to seize, render harmless or destroy any substance or article considered to be the cause of imminent danger or serious personal injury

European Union (EU) directives on health and safety

Six new sets of health and safety at work regulations came into force at the beginning of 1993. They apply to almost all kinds of work activity, including leisure and recreation, and, like the health and safety laws we already have, they place duties on employers to protect:

✪ **Their employees**
✪ **Other people, including members of the public, who may be affected by the work being carried out**

These UK regulations are needed to implement six European Union (EU) directives on health and safety at work. They are also part of a continuing modernisation of existing UK law. The directives are part of the EU's programme of action on health and safety, which is an essential ingredient in the move towards a single European market. Most of the duties in the regulations are not completely new, but clarify what is already in current health and safety law. Any leisure and recreation organisation that is already complying with the HSW Act and the regulations linked with it should not find the new regulations at all daunting. A number of old and out-of-date laws have been repealed by the new regulations.

What do the regulations cover?

The new regulations cover:

✪ **Health and safety management**
✪ **Work equipment safety**

- ✪ **Manual handling of loads**
- ✪ **Workplace conditions**
- ✪ **Personal protective equipment**
- ✪ **Display screen equipment**

Health and safety management

The Management of Health and Safety at Work Regulations 1992 set out broad general duties that apply to almost all work activities in Great Britain and offshore. The regulations make more explicit what is already required of employers under the HSW Act and are principally aimed at encouraging them to take a more systematic approach to dealing with health and safety matters. In general terms, the regulations require employers to:

1 **Systematically assess the risks to the health and safety of employees and anyone else affected by the work activity, e.g. visitors, spectators and contractors. Employers with five or more employees will need to record their findings by drawing up a *risk assessment***

2 **Put into practice the measures outlined in the risk assessment. This will involve planning, organisation, control, monitoring and review; in other words, the management of health and safety**

3 **Appoint competent people to help devise and apply the measures**

4 **Set up emergency procedures**

5 **Provide employees with information about health and safety**

6 **Co-operate with other employers who may share the same work site**

7 **Provide adequate training for employees in health and safety**

8 **Provide temporary workers with particular health and safety information to meet their needs**

Work equipment safety

The Provision and Use of Work Equipment Regulations are designed to pull together and tidy up the laws governing equipment used at work. Instead of piecemeal legislation covering particular kinds of equipment in different industries, they:

- ✪ **Place general duties on employers**
- ✪ **List minimum requirements for work equipment to deal with selected hazards, whatever the industry**

'Work equipment' is broadly defined to include everything from a hand tool, through machines of all kinds, to a complete plant such as a leisure centre or indoor arena. The regulations include both general duties placed on employers and specific requirements to which they must adhere. General duties require employers to:

✪ **Make sure that equipment is suitable for its intended use**

✪ **Take into account the working conditions and hazards in the workplace when selecting equipment**

✪ **Ensure that equipment is adequately maintained**

✪ **Give adequate instruction, information and training**

✪ **Provide equipment that conforms with EU product safety directives**

The specific requirements of these regulations cover such items as the guarding of dangerous parts of machinery, stability of equipment, warnings and markings, to name but a few.

Manual handling of loads

The incorrect handling of loads causes large numbers of injuries and can result in pain, time off work and sometimes permanent disablement. The Manual Handling Operations Regulations came into force on 1 January 1993 and replace patchy, old-fashioned and largely ineffective laws with a modern, ergonomic approach to the problem.

They apply to any manual handling operations that may cause injury at work. Such operations should have been identified by the risk assessment carried out under the Management of Health and Safety at Work Regulations 1992.

Employers have to take three key steps:

1   **Avoid hazardous manual handling operations where reasonably practicable**

2   **Assess adequately any hazardous operations that cannot be avoided**

3   **Reduce the risk of injury as far as is reasonably practicable**

The regulations are backed up by general guidance that can help to identify the more serious risks within any work situation.

Workplace conditions

The Workplace (Health, Safety and Welfare) Regulations 1992 replace a total of 38 pieces of old law, making safety in the workplace a much easier topic to understand and making it clear what is expected of employers.

The regulations set general requirements in four broad areas.

1 *Working environment*

- ✪ **Temperature in indoor workplaces**
- ✪ **Ventilation**
- ✪ **Lighting**
- ✪ **Room dimensions and space**
- ✪ **Suitability of workstations and seating**

2 *Safety*

- ✪ **Safe passage of pedestrians and vehicles**
- ✪ **Safe opening, closing and cleaning of windows and skylights**
- ✪ **Use of safety materials in transparent doors and partitions**
- ✪ **Safety devices on doors, gates and escalators**
- ✪ **Construction and maintenance of floors**

3 *Facilities*

- ✪ **Toilets**
- ✪ **Washing, eating and changing facilities**
- ✪ **Clothing storage**
- ✪ **Drinking water**
- ✪ **Rest areas, including arrangements to protect people from the discomfort of tobacco smoke**
- ✪ **Rest facilities for pregnant women and nursing mothers**

4 *Housekeeping*

- ✪ **Maintenance of workplace, equipment and facilities**
- ✪ **Cleanliness**
- ✪ **Removal of waste materials**

Employers must ensure that any workplace within their control complies with the regulations.

Activity 23.6

While on work experience, carry out a simple audit of how well the facility meets the four general requirements of the Workplace (Health, Safety and Welfare) Regulations 1992.

Personal protective equipment (PPE)

The Personal Protective Equipment at Work (PPE) Regulations 1992 replace parts of over 20 old pieces of law. PPE includes most types of protective clothing, and equipment such as eye, foot and head protection, safety harnesses, life jackets and high visibility clothing. Employers must supply PPE free of charge to their employees, and have a duty to:

✪ **Make sure that the PPE issued is suitable for the risk involved**

✪ **Maintain, clean and replace PPE**

✪ **Provide storage for PPE when it is not being used**

✪ **Ensure that PPE is properly used**

✪ **Give training, instruction and information to staff on the use and care of PPE**

Display screen equipment

Unlike some of the other regulations described above, the Health and Safety (Display Screen Equipment) Regulations do not replace old legislation but cover a new area of work activity for the first time. Work with display screens is not generally high risk, but it can lead to muscular and other physical problems, eye fatigue and mental stress. Problems of this kind can be overcome by good ergonomic design of equipment, furniture, the working environment and tasks performed.

Under these regulations, employers have a duty to:

✪ **Assess display screen equipment workstations and reduce risks that are discovered**

✪ **Make sure that workstations satisfy minimum requirements**

✪ **Plan display screen equipment work so that there are breaks or changes of activity**

✪ **Provide information and training for display screen equipment users**

Display screen equipment users are also entitled to appropriate eye and eyesight tests by an optician or doctor, and to special spectacles if they are needed and normal ones cannot be used. It is the employer's responsibility to provide tests and special spectacles if needed.

Emergency procedures

All leisure and recreation organisations must ensure that they have adequate emergency procedures to follow in the event of an incident of any kind. Depending on the nature of the organisation, this could be an accident to staff or visitors, a fire, a bomb warning or a vehicle crash. Relevant staff must be fully trained in supervising the evacuation of people from buildings and vehicles.

First aid provision

First aid refers to treatment that can be carried out immediately at the scene of an accident, prior to the emergency services arriving. The Health and Safety at Work, etc. Act and its associated regulations, in particular the Health and Safety (First Aid Regulations) 1981, place a duty on employers to provide adequate first aid for both employees and non-employees, which in the case of leisure and recreation would include guests, visitors, spectators, customers and contractors. Every leisure and recreation organisation must have a sufficient number of first aiders, suitably qualified in first aid and able to decide if further professional help is required.

Security of people and premises

Customers who use leisure and recreation facilities, and the staff who serve them, have a right to feel confident that they and their possessions, together with the premises they are occupying, are safe and secure.

Security of people

When looking at the wide range of security concerns confronting the industry, the welfare of people must be the prime concern for all leisure and recreation organisations. 'People' will include:

✪ **Staff**

✪ **Visitors (invited or uninvited)**

✪ **Others (contractors, etc.)**

All employers have a legal duty under the Health and Safety at Work, etc. Act 1974 to ensure the health, safety and welfare at work of their staff (see page 391). There are many health and safety risks and hazards that may confront staff working in leisure and recreation, but providing a safe working environment that is free from any violence is becoming an increasingly important concern for employers. The Health and Safety Executive working definition of violence is:

> Any incident in which an employee is abused, threatened or assaulted by a member of the public in circumstances arising out of the course of his or her employment. (HSE 1992)

Being a service industry involving a high degree of contact between staff and customers, those working in leisure and recreation can expect to encounter uncomfortable and sometimes violent incidents during the course of their work. Verbal abuse and threatening behaviour are the most common types of incident. Physical attacks are comparatively rare.

Both employers and employees have an interest in reducing violence in the workplace. For employers, violence can lead to low morale and a poor image for the organisation, making it difficult to recruit and retain staff. It can also mean extra costs, with absenteeism, higher insurance premiums and possible compensation payments. For employees, violence can cause pain, suffering and even disability or death. Physical attacks are obviously dangerous but serious or persistent verbal abuse or threats can also damage employees' health through anxiety and stress.

The HSE recommends the following seven-point plan to tackle violence in the workplace:

✪ *Step one*: **Find out if there is a problem. It may seem obvious, but many employers are not aware of a problem until they ask staff directly**

✪ *Step two*: **Record all incidents. By using a simple report form, an organisation can begin to build up a picture of the problem**

✪ *Step three*: **Classify all incidents. Incidents that involve serious injury will be easy to classify, but those involving, for example, verbal abuse will need careful discussion with the staff involved**

✪ *Step four*: **Search for preventative measures. The way jobs are carried out can help reduce the risk of violence. For example, if a leisure and recreation organisation needs its staff to work late, it should either arrange for them to have a safe place to park their car or provide transport home. Changing from using cash to accepting cheques, credit cards or tokens can help reduce attempted thefts**

✪ *Step five*: **Decide what to do. A mixture of measures usually works best, and particularly if the employees are fully involved in deciding what needs to be done. It is often a question of striking a balance between the fears of the staff and the needs of the public. For example, many busy visitor attractions provide entertainment for customers who are forced to queue to get in. This helps to diffuse what can sometimes turn into a threatening situation for staff on duty**

✪ *Step six*: **Put measures into practice. Whatever measures are decided upon, the policy for dealing with violence should be included in the organisation's safety policy statement, so that all employees are aware of it**

- ✪ *Step seven:* **Check that the measures work. It is important to check how well the measures are working. If the problem persists, it may be necessary to go back and repeat steps two and three**

It may be that violence among customers is identified as a problem for an organisation. Similar steps to those above can be put in place to help deal with this situation.

Security of premises

Security of property in leisure and recreation involves:

- ✪ **The fabric of the building itself, including fitments**
- ✪ **The contents of the building**

Security of buildings

Buildings used for leisure and recreation purposes can be under many different types of threat. One of the most obvious and costly is robbery, but other threats include wanton damage, often carried out by youths, and daubing with graffiti. There are some fundamental rules for securing any type of property, including:

- ✪ **Fitting security locks to doors and windows, and window bars to high-risk areas such as equipment stores and bar areas**
- ✪ **Using closed circuit television (CCTV) or employing security personnel to monitor large areas, including car parks and staff and public entrances and exits**
- ✪ **Installing invisible beams and pressure pads in passageways and entrances to activate alarms**
- ✪ **Fitting intruder alarms which, for large organisations, should be capable of alerting a central monitoring station that operates 24 hours a day**
- ✪ **Introducing card access control using PIN systems to identify which parts of a building are for staff access only**
- ✪ **Installing security lighting, particularly in high-risk areas**

Security of the contents of the building

The contents of any leisure and recreation facility that are potentially at risk could be:

- ✪ **Equipment, e.g. computers, sports equipment, catering equipment, furniture**
- ✪ **Stock, e.g. wines, beers and spirits, food, sports clothing**

- **The personal possessions of the staff**
- **The personal possessions of the customers**
- **The personal possessions of any other people, such as contractors, who are on-site**

Most visitors will expect a facility to guard their possessions in exchange for a ticket, whether or not any payment is involved. This service is all part of making the visitor relaxed and in a better mood to enjoy their experience, whether it is a game of squash or a visit to an art gallery. Where visitors are not allowed to take possessions with them for security reasons, e.g. cameras are not allowed in certain museums and at certain events, secure storage must be provided by the leisure and recreation operator.

Some of the techniques mentioned under 'security of buildings' above will help protect equipment and possessions inside the building. Over and above these technical measures, all staff must be vigilant and alert at all times to suspicious characters and circumstances. As well as ensuring a pleasant experience for all visitors, it is the job of staff and management to safeguard visitors' possessions. In particular, staff should look out for people behaving in a suspicious manner, for example:

- **A customer who cannot provide proof of identity or who is hesitant when questioned in suspicious circumstances**
- **A customer who loiters for long periods of time or who seems unusually interested in what everyone else is doing**
- **Members of a group in a restaurant or other eating place leaving one by one, with the intention of not paying the bill**
- **People taking a particular interest in cars or other vehicles parked on-site**
- **Sudden disturbances between two or more customers, who may be trying to create a distraction to cover theft by an accomplice**

Activity 23.7

While on work experience, carry out an investigation to find out what measures are in place to deal with the security of staff and customers and their possessions.

Reporting systems

We saw earlier in this unit that the Management of Health and Safety at Work Regulations 1992 required employers with five or more employees to, amongst other things, systematically assess the risks to the health and safety of employees and anyone else affected by the work activity, e.g. visitors, spectators and contractors, by carrying out a risk assessment. The aim of the assessment is to identify potential risks and put measures in place to prevent them becoming incidents.

If an incident does occur in a leisure and recreation organisation, it is important that all details are logged in order to satisfy internal and external procedures, which could include the local authority, Health and Safety Executive (HSE), emergency services and insurance companies.

In order to minimise the likelihood of equipment failure leading to incidents, it is important for leisure and recreation organisations to have rigorous systems for the cleaning and maintenance of buildings and equipment. The importance of maintaining the fabric of a leisure and recreation facility goes well beyond the routine tasks associated with keeping the weather out. With visitors now demanding high quality standards, a facility that is poorly maintained or not cleaned on a regular basis will not be able to compete effectively with those organisations that give cleaning and maintenance a high priority. The image of a facility and its management is closely linked to its physical appearance. Add to this the fact that legislation demands a healthy and safe environment for both staff and visitors, plus the fact that a poorly maintained building will decrease in value, and it is not surprising that the cleaning and maintenance of leisure and recreation facilities has taken on greater importance of late.

The maintenance of facilities can be either routine or corrective. Work that is carried out as a matter of routine is often referred to as planned maintenance, while corrective maintenance involves tasks carried out in response to an emergency or failure of equipment or services. It is expected that by adopting a policy of planned maintenance, carried out at pre-determined intervals and according to prescribed criteria, an organisation will reduce the probability of the failure of systems or equipment and hence the need for corrective maintenance.

The normal cleaning routine of the facility should be part of the programme of planned preventative maintenance. Any minor defects should be reported to the appropriate authority and remedial action carried out. However, as well as this day-to-day activity, there also needs to be a systematic inspection of essential equipment and systems on a regular basis. Managers or supervisors should also implement frequent inspections of all parts of the facility, recording the findings on a report form.

It makes good sense to carry out a programme of planned inspection and maintenance of equipment and facilities, for a number of reasons, including:

- ✪ It is a cost-effective exercise, since preventative measures can save on costly major works in the future
- ✪ It will provide a healthy and safe environment for staff and customers
- ✪ It will ensure all areas are cleaned on a regular basis
- ✪ It will reduce the incidence of failure of equipment and systems

Methods used to operate business systems

Key topics in this section

- **Introduction**
- **Computer-based methods**
- **Electronic methods**
- **Paper-based methods**

Introduction

Leisure and recreation organisations use a wide range of methods to enable them to operate their business systems effectively. These include computer-based, electronic and paper-based methods. A number of factors, including the size of an enterprise, location, operating costs and levels of staff training, will influence the choice of method. In reality, most leisure and recreation organisations use a combination of all three methods.

Computer-based methods

The principal reason for installing a computer-based business system is that it can increase the efficiency and improve the effectiveness of the organisation in which it is operated. More specific reasons for choosing a computer system will vary between the different sectors of the leisure and recreation industry, but could include:

✪ *As a means of expanding the organisation*: **A small company may wish to expand its number of customers but realises that its manual system will not be able to cope with the extra information**

✪ *To make better use of staff resources*: **It is unlikely that a computerised business system will actually reduce the number of employees once it is introduced, but it will enable the same number of people to do much more, thus improving staff efficiency**

✪ *As a way of accessing a remote database*: **A leisure and recreation organisation may introduce a computer system so that it can gain access to data from other sources. A public** sector leisure centre may set up a direct link with its local authority mainframe computer in order to transfer and process data

✪ *In order to provide a better standard of service to its customers*: A computer system is likely to speed up the processing of such items as bookings, membership details, cash handling, credit transfers, invoicing, letters and mailing of publicity materials, as well as freeing staff to concentrate on delivering high standards of customer service

✪ *To provide information for management purposes*, which is regular, accurate, reliable and in a form which is easily understood

Personal and networked computers

Larger leisure and recreation organisations need the greater speed and capacity offered by mainframe computers and networked systems. In addition to these large-scale, integrated computer management information systems, which can handle complex data management functions, the use of microcomputers has grown rapidly in the leisure and recreation industries in recent years. It is becoming increasingly common to find these personal computers (PCs) not only on the desks of administrative staff but also on the desks of the managers themselves. Modern business computers, most of which conform to the standards established by the IBM personal computer, will run word processing, spreadsheets, database and DTP (desktop publishing) programs, depending on the type of software used. Smaller leisure and recreation organisations are able to provide acceptable levels of management information based solely on the use of PCs. Laptop PCs are particularly useful for staff whose job takes them away from their office. With the correct software, a laptop can carry out exactly the same functions as an office-based PC, with the added bonus of portability.

Word processing

This is the most common form of information processing found in today's leisure and recreation organisations. Computers loaded with word processing software, such as Microsoft Word or WordPerfect, have all but replaced typewriters in the production of textual information. Letters, reports, memoranda and other types of written communication can be quickly, accurately and professionally produced on a word processor. They can be stored in the machine's memory (on the 'hard disk') or on 'floppy disks', allowing amendments and deletions at a later date. Word processing software offers many features that can be used in the production of documents, including:

- **Tables, graphics and images can be incorporated into the text**
- **Text can be enhanced using such features as underlining, emboldening, varying font sizes and styles, italics**
- **Blocks of text can be moved within a document and between documents**
- **'Mailmerge' allows personalised letters to be produced quickly and accurately by combining a standard letter with a list of names and addresses**
- **Spelling and grammar can be checked with most word processing software**
- **Words and phrases can be searched for and either removed or replaced with an alternative**

Word processing software enables organisations of whatever size to produce high quality documents, particularly when using a laser or ink jet printer. Small leisure and recreation organisations often find that a standard word processing package is all they need to carry out a wide range of routine administrative tasks, from producing simple promotional materials to writing detailed reports and feasibility studies incorporating graphics and charts.

Databases

Databases are collections of files, data and records, stored on a computer-based system. The many sectors found within the leisure and recreation industry mean that databases are used extensively in many different situations, for example:

- **A health and fitness club will hold details of its members on a database, including names, addresses and telephone numbers**
- **The owner of a gift shop will have a database of all his suppliers**
- **A conference organiser will hold details of her clients on a database**

The main advantage of using a computerised database, such as Microsoft's Access, is that once data has been entered onto the system, it can be retrieved, amended or sorted much more quickly than using a manual database. Also, searches of the database can be made for specific purposes, for example the names of all those who participate in a particular sport.

In addition to offering a search facility, a computerised database can also:

- **Sort records numerically, alphabetically or in date order**
- **Carry out numerical calculations, e.g. total sales of a particular product in a specified month**

✪ **Export data, e.g. the names and addresses of clients could be transferred to a word processing file to use the mailmerge function**

It is important for leisure and recreation organisations to remember that information stored on computer falls within the scope and regulation of the Data Protection Act, giving rights to those whose details are held on the system (see page 382 for more detail on the Data Protection Act).

Activity 23.8

Research the leisure and recreation companies operating in your local area and put the information onto a database for future reference.

Spreadsheets

A spreadsheet is a very useful and powerful computer application that can be used to perform a range of numerical calculations. It can carry out simple arithmetical calculations, such as percentages and additions, and proceed to more complex automated calculations and analyses.

Spreadsheets are found in both large and small leisure and recreation organisations, and are used extensively for providing accounting information, such as cash flow forecasts, budget projections and tax returns. In its simplest form, a spreadsheet is little more than a grid consisting of a number of horizontal rows and vertical columns, into which data is written. Spreadsheets are particularly useful for a process known as 'sensitivity analysis', when the outcome of alterations to one or more elements of a spreadsheet will automatically be calculated by the programme. For example, a visitor attraction may have used a spreadsheet to calculate its total potential income for the forthcoming season, based on an admission price of £2.75 for adults. With a spreadsheet program, it is a simple matter to calculate the effect on total income of a reduction of 25p in the admission price.

Another very useful function of a database is that graphs and tables can be produced directly from information held on the database.

Desktop publishing

Desktop publishing, or DTP as it is sometimes known, is a sophisticated word processing system that is capable of producing very high quality documents from a standard PC. A desktop publishing system, such as Corel Draw or Aldus Pagemaker, provides its user with the means to produce a document with a number of features, including:

- **A range of typefaces and text styles**
- **Incorporation of pictures and other images by a process known as 'scanning'**
- **The ability to reduce and enlarge images and text**

DTP enables smaller leisure and recreation organisations to produce very professional documents at a reasonable price, including sales leaflets, information sheets, direct mail packages, posters and other point-of-sale materials.

Internet, intranet and extranet

The Internet is an interactive system of networked computer databases, which offers users a wealth of information via the World Wide Web (www). Leisure and recreation organisations can use the Internet to gather data, publicise their services and sell their products. Use of the Internet is revolutionising the distribution and sale of tickets and sports merchandise, for example. An intranet is a network of computer-based information whose use is restricted to selected individuals within an organisation, e.g. the staff in a season ticket booking office. An extranet is similar to an intranet, except that it can be accessed remotely by selected individuals, e.g. sales managers of a nationwide health and fitness company working away from their office base.

E-mail

E-mail (electronic mail) is revolutionising the leisure and recreation industry, from both the customers' and management's perspective. Customers can now e-mail their information and advice requests to a wide range of organisations in leisure and recreation, including:

- **Sport England's website, Sport Gateway**
- **Local authority sport and leisure departments**
- **Government sites such as the Department of Culture, Media and Sport**
- **National tourist boards**
- **Activity holiday companies**
- **Visitor attractions in the UK**
- **National governing bodies of sports**

E-mail is especially suitable for customers wanting information from facilities or events such as the Olympic Games since it offers a speedy service on a global scale.

From the business perspective, e-mail can increase staff efficiency and effectiveness, allowing virtually instant communication within a company or with colleagues working away from their normal base. Documents and images can be attached to e-mails and distributed to relevant colleagues. It is important for organisations to remember that customers generally expect a faster reply to their e-mail enquiries when compared with a more traditional postal or telephone enquiry. It is essential, therefore, that any leisure and recreation company offering an e-mail enquiry service is able to respond to enquiries within a reasonable time.

CD-ROM and DVD

Some of the information used by leisure and recreation companies is available on CD-ROM (compact disc read-only memory) and DVD (digital versatile disc), for example directories, atlases and events information.

Touch-screen technology

Electronic point-of-sale (EPOS) systems are being introduced in ever-increasing numbers to many leisure sector premises, especially pubs, clubs, bars and fast-food outlets. The only way the customer is likely to know that a facility has an EPOS system is when the staff use their 'touchpads' or 'scatterpads', the small touch-sensitive panels located behind the bar or counter, sometimes on the cash register itself. The benefits of EPOS to a leisure and recreation organisation are:

- ✪ **It gives the management control over cash transactions**
- ✪ **It improves stock control**
- ✪ **It frees staff to concentrate on improving customer care, rather than having to calculate prices and issue bills**

As well as performing all the normal functions of an electronic cash register, an EPOS system will log all transactions with time, date, items served, cost, method of payment and the member of staff who dealt with the customer. This not only reduces the possibility of fraud by staff, but also allows management to introduce incentives for staff who are meeting or exceeding their sales targets. The system will also mean that the busiest times can be better anticipated and allow better management of staff generally. The detailed management information given by EPOS will mean that stock levels can be monitored more closely, enabling the outlet to hold much smaller levels than would otherwise be the case, thus reducing overheads and improving cash flow.

Electronic methods

There have been huge advances in electronic communications systems in recent years in the leisure and tourism industries. Based on the premise that electronic systems will be faster and more efficient than paper-based alternatives, worldwide communications are now available to all organisations, regardless of their size of operation. The 'electronic office' is now a reality, with many organisations having introduced computer systems and electronic equipment to communicate internally and externally. Some of the most important electronic communication methods include:

- ✪ *Integrated services digital network (ISDN)*: **This is a sophisticated system developed by British Telecom that makes use of cable technology to transfer signals, allowing services such as video conferencing, desktop conferencing and data transfer to be offered**

- ✪ *Mobile telephones*: **The use of mobiles has grown dramatically in recent years, not least in all sectors of the leisure and recreation industry**

- ✪ *Fax transmissions*: **The number of fax (facsimile) transmissions has grown dramatically in the past five years. Like the photocopier before it, many leisure and recreation organisations can't think how they managed before the fax machine was invented! They combine the speed of the telephone with the accuracy of the printed word. Systems combining fax, telephone, copier and answering machine are now within the reach of large and small leisure and recreation organisations**

- ✪ *Paging systems*: **As with mobile telephones, pagers are used extensively in leisure and recreation, particularly in large facilities such as sports stadia and facilities**

- ✪ *Intercom*: **This is a useful way of communicating over relatively short distances**

- ✪ *Public address (PA)*: **This is useful at events when information needs to be transmitted to large numbers of people at the same time**

✪ *Video conferencing*: **This saves the time and expense of travelling for a meeting. Instead, the parties communicate with each other via a video link**

Paper-based methods

There are many different paper-based methods that a leisure and recreation organisation can use to liaise with people internally and externally. The principal advantage of written communication is that it provides a permanent record of what took place, which can be stored for future reference. Other advantages of paper-based methods are that:

✪ **They enable complex information to be sent, e.g. statistical data**

✪ **They can serve as a reminder to those in receipt of the communication**

✪ **The quality of presentation can be altered to appeal to different audiences, e.g. the quality of headed notepaper and use of colour**

✪ **They provide evidence of confirmation of a previous discussion, e.g. the list of names of participants attending a coaching course**

Some of the most common types of written communication methods used in leisure and recreation organisations include:

✪ **Letters**
✪ **Memoranda**
✪ **Promotional materials**
✪ **Reports**
✪ **Documentation for meetings**
✪ **Annual reports**
✪ **Advertisements**
✪ **Questionnaires**
✪ **Timetables**

Letters

The letter is the most commonly used type of external written communication. The reasons for sending a letter are many and varied, depending on the nature of the organisation. Typical situations when a letter may be sent include the following:

- ✪ **Letter to a job applicant to confirm interview details**
- ✪ **Letter to a customer thanking her for praising the standard of service received in a hotel**
- ✪ **Letter to a professional body confirming details of a forthcoming joint training seminar**
- ✪ **Letter of complaint to a supplier for non-delivery of goods**
- ✪ **Sales letter sent to all customers on an organisation's database**

With the advent of information processing technology, letters with a high standard of presentation can now be generated by most leisure and recreation organisations, whatever their size. The presentation and content of a letter is important, since it gives the receiver an impression of the quality of the organisation sending it; a letter with many spelling and grammatical mistakes, printed on poor quality paper with an old printer ribbon, does little to enhance the reputation of an organisation.

Activity 23.10

Draft a letter that could be used by the marketing department of a health and fitness club to send to its existing clients, informing them of the launch of a new membership package.

Memoranda

A memorandum (often shortened to memo) is commonly used within an organisation in place of a formal letter. It may be used for a number of reasons, including:

- ✪ **To confirm a verbal conversation**
- ✪ **To ask for information**
- ✪ **To remind a colleague of something**
- ✪ **To pass on instructions**

Promotional materials

Brochures, leaflets, posters and other promotional items have a vital role to play in all leisure and recreation organisations. Industries like leisure and recreation, mainly concerned with selling 'intangible' products and services, rely heavily on promotional materials to persuade customers to buy. Leisure centres print leaflets to attract customers to their facilities. Leaflets and other promotional items are often based on the AIDA principle, to attract *attention*, maintain *interest* create a *desire* and trigger *action* on the part of the customer.

Reports

Written reports are used extensively in leisure and recreation organisations for a number of reasons, including:

✪ **To present statistical information**

✪ **To investigate the feasibility of a new development, product or service**

✪ **To recommend changes to the management or staff structure**

✪ **To meet legal requirements, e.g. a limited company must publish an annual report and accounts**

✪ **To investigate a disciplinary matter involving staff**

A report should follow a logical sequence and structure, depending on its purpose. A typical structure is as follows:

1   *Terms of reference*: **This should state why the report was written, for whom it was undertaken, what it will aim to achieve and the date by which it is to be completed**

2   *Procedure*: **This part of the report should indicate how the information for the report was obtained, e.g. secondary research and/or primary research methods**

3   *Findings*: **This section is the largest in the report and will give the results of the investigations. It is likely that there will be a number of subdivisions within this section**

4   *Conclusions*: **This will be a summary of the main points found in the course of the investigation**

5   *Recommendations*: **This section will outline suggested courses of action, based on the findings and conclusion**

6   *Bibliography and sources of information*: **Although not always included, this section will indicate the main sources consulted during the investigation and may help to confirm the validity and credibility of the report**

Documentation for meetings

Part of the process of ensuring that meetings are effective and do not waste valuable management and staff time is a structured approach to their administration. Written communication in relation to a meeting should include:

- ✪ **Written notice of the meeting: This will be sent out in advance of the meeting, giving the date, time and venue. The notice may also include a closing date by which items for the agenda should be submitted**
- ✪ **Agenda: This is the list of items to be discussed at the meeting. It is helpful if it is distributed in advance of the meeting, but may be given out on the day**
- ✪ **Minutes: These are a written record of what was discussed at the meeting, usually compiled by the secretary and sent out to members who attended as well as those who were absent. At the next meeting, the minutes will be discussed and agreed as a true record of events**

Annual reports

It is a legal requirement for limited companies to publish an annual report and accounts for their shareholders. Large leisure and recreation companies, such as Whitbread and Virgin, produce glossy annual reports to contribute towards their image building. Public sector organisations, including the National Trust, Sport England and the Countryside Commission, also produce annual reports to give interested parties details of their activities and achievements. Many annual reports are made available in libraries for the public to consult.

Activity 23.11

Do some research in your own school or college library, as well as public libraries nearby, to find out which annual reports of leisure and recreation organisations are available.

Advertisements

Advertising plays an important role in the leisure and recreation industry. Written advertisements, in newspapers and magazines, inform people of services and products, with the aim of persuading them to buy. Leisure and recreation organisations may choose to design their own advertisements or buy in the services of an advertising agency.

Questionnaires

Questionnaires are usually made available in paper-based format, although e-mail questionnaires are beginning to be used by some leisure and recreation organisations.

Timetables

Leisure and tourism organisations involved with transportation need to inform their travellers of the times of travel. This is usually done by publishing a timetable, listing arrival and departure points and times. Leisure facilities that offer a program of different events and activities also need to publish timetables.

Index